Political Macroeconomics

POLITICAL MACROECONOMICS

Keizo Nagatani

CLARENDON PRESS · OXFORD
1989

Oxford University Press, Walton Street, Oxford OX2 6DP
Oxford New York Toronto
Delhi Bombay Calcutta Madras Karachi
Petaling Jaya Singapore Hong Kong Tokyo
Nairobi Dar es Salaam Cape Town
Melbourne Auckland
and associated companies in
Berlin Ibadan

Oxford is a trade mark of Oxford University Press

Published in the United States
by Oxford University Press, New York

British Library Cataloguing in Publication Data
Nagatani, Keizo
Political macroeconomics.
1. Macroeconomics
I. Title
339
ISBN 0–19–828642–2

Library of Congress Cataloging-in-Publication Data
Nagatani, Keizo.
Political macroeconomics/Keizo Nagatani.
Bibliography: p.   Includes index.
1. Macroeconomics.   2. Neoclassical school of economics.
3. Comparative economics.   I. Title.
HB172.5.N333   1989   339—dc20   89–34137
ISBN 0–19–828642–2

Typeset by Cotswold Typesetting Ltd, Gloucester
Printed and bound in
Great Britain by Biddles Ltd
Guildford & King's Lynn

Preface

The orthodox economic doctrine called neoclassical economics has a very simple structure. There are two building blocks: individual rationality and market equilibrium. Individual rationality stresses the importance of free choice (thanks to human intelligence) and the selection of the best alternatives by individuals; market equilibrium stresses the powerful role that markets play, through prices, in co-ordinating millions of individual plans into an orderly and consistent whole. And the market solution, economists are proud to demonstrate, leaves no room for improvement in terms of efficiency. This simplicity is both the strength and the weakness of neoclassical economics. Its strength is versatility: it offers an all-purpose software applicable to any problem involving free choice. Its weakness is in the price paid to achieve this versatility. The analytical structure of neoclassical economics is that of Newtonian physics. Individual rationality ensures that people behave like natural objects; the concept of market equilibrium is exactly the same as that of physical equilibrium, which is supposedly unique and impersonal. The price that economists paid for their versatile analytical framework was, in a word, the dehumanization of economics.

I was motivated to write this book by a desire to restore the human element in economics. I believe that economic activities are human affairs; that human rationality is much broader and livelier than the neoclassical rationality; that, when individuals with such active rationality interact with one another, the position of market equilibrium is not unique but multiple; and that there is no natural tendency for the market to converge to the best equilibrium.

The book has taken an embarrassingly long time to prepare. It has been a lonely voyage without a guide. Various chapters have been written between 1982 and 1987 in a random order. As a result, the chapters are not as closely linked to one another as I would have liked. Nor has my effort to speak the economists' language been very successful. Nevertheless, the primary objective has been simple and clear from the start: to write a humanized version of aggregate economic behaviour with special emphasis on the active rationality of individuals and on money as a means to power in today's political

Preface

economy. As for its macroeconomic content, the book is not intended as a substitute for standard macroeconomic textbooks, although most of the current issues in standard macroeconomics are covered; my hope is that it will serve as useful complementary reading in courses in macroeconomics, international relations, political science, and sociology. Game theorists may also find it of interest. But an author is not a good judge of his own book; I shall be most anxious to receive any comments and advice from readers.

Finally, my thanks go to the following scholars who read earlier versions of the manuscript and gave useful comments: Eric Davis of Carleton University, Erwin Diewert, George Feaver, and Anthony Scott of the University of British Columbia, Koichi Hamada of Yale University, Jean Waelbroeck of the Free University of Belgium, and the anonymous referees hired by Oxford University Press. Harri Singh gave editorial assistance which made the manuscript more readable. Last but not least, I am grateful to Andrew Schuller, Molly Scott, and Sue Hughes of OUP for their great generosity and patience.

K.N.

Vancouver
July 1988

Contents

Introduction

This book views the goal of macroeconomic policy as that of constantly monitoring the economy out of an unsatisfactory equilibrium and into a more satisfactory one. In order to achieve such a goal, there is a need for a much more comprehensive policy package than the conventional one. The problem of economic development and poverty is as serious today as it was forty years ago; the neoclassical theorems on free trade and specialization have proved ineffective to its solution. On the other hand, the Japanese economy, for all its peculiar and (neoclassically) irrational habits and strategies, has become the envy of the world. These facts suggest that there is room for an alternative, humanized, approach to macroeconomics, and the chapters that follow are an experiment in this unorthodox approach.

The organization of the book is as follows. Chapter 1 traces the history of neoclassical economics and considers the traits implied by that history; it expresses a dissatisfaction with the reductionist approach of neoclassical economics and offers instead a group approach to macroeconomic behaviour. Chapter 2 considers macroeconomics as a subject in political economy. It regards the neoclassical faith in efficient resource allocation through markets as inadequate, and views macroeconomic performance as the outcome of games played among the several major groups in the economy. It stresses the importance for macroeconomics of economic organizations and their 'internal markets'. These two chapters serve as an introduction to the rest of the book, which deals with specific organizations and problems.

Chapter 3 takes up bureaucracy as the most prominent organizations in today's political economy. Here the term 'bureaucracy' refers to its formal attributes as enumerated by Weber, and includes private corporations. The chapter stresses the fact that government and business bureaucracies today are, contrary to the popular Western view, very similar in their power, internal rules, and patterns of behaviour, and suggests that one of the reasons for the poor macroeconomic performances of many nations is the incompetence of business rather than of government or labour. In North America (and in the UK under Prime Minister Thatcher, I believe) the word 'bureaucracy' carries as bad a connotation as the word 'communism'. But the chapter suggests the alternative of relying on the wisdom of wise men and women in society is probably no better.

Chapter 4 deals with the central bank, the odd member in the governmental bureaucracy, with a varied reputation and dismal track record. Besides the well-known technical difficulties of monetary control, the chapter attributes the dismal record of the central bank to its lack of political power. Chapter 5 addresses itself to the apparent inconsistency between the central bank's professed goal of stabilizing the value of the currency and the chronic inflation that has characterized much of the twentieth century. The chapter seeks an answer to this phenomenon in the fact that the permeation of debt capitalism and democracy has shifted the equilibrium of the political economy from a frugal and conservative equilibrium to a more carefree and inflationary one.

Chapter 6 attempts to offer an explanation to the old but unsettled question of why money means power in today's political economy. More specifically, why is it that households, which are the dominant wealth-owners and creditors in the system, have no power, while the financial intermediaries, who are mere agents, have the upper hand over the consumers and producers of real goods and services? One of the most serious flaws of neoclassical economics is its static and real (i.e. non-monetary) character, which has made it incapable of dealing squarely with questions concerning money. This chapter makes a modest effort to correct the flaw.

Chapter 7 is concerned with the problems of labour management. With North American and Japanese management practices in mind, it explores ways of improving the performance of employment and productivity. The chapter concludes with an analysis of a co-operative firm which is capable of explaining the major features of Japanese wage profiles and labour productivity and, by implication, the North American counterparts. Chapter 8 looks at the alarming trend in Western societies whereby doctors, lawyers, and other 'professionals' and 'experts' intervene in people's economic transactions to claim the huge social surpluses floating in affluent societies. While this is an inevitable consequence of competitive individualism, it is feared that the resulting increase in transaction costs is reducing the economic efficiency of the system and the general welfare of the public.

Chapter 9 reflects on the contrasting styles of economic policy-making between Japan and Canada. This chapter is based on my own experience of living in these two economies and hence is rather personal in tone. I believe that democracy and aggregate economic efficiency tend to conflict with one another, and hence that each nation must devise its own style of policy-making. Chapter 10 concludes with some observations.

1

Macroeconomic Foundations of Macroeconomics

If all the seas were one sea,
What a great sea that would be!
If all the trees were one tree,
What a great tree that would be!
And if all the axes were one axe,
What a great axe that would be!
And if all the men were one man,
What a great man that would be!
And if the great man took the great axe,
And cut down the great tree,
And let it fall into the great sea,
What a splish-splash that would be!

Nursery rhyme[1]

1 INTRODUCTION

Neoclassical economics is based on two basic postulates, one at the individual level and the other at the aggregate level. First, individuals are well-informed and rational. Second, such individual rationality is carried over to the aggregate; that is, the aggregate behaviour never errs systematically. In other words, individuals are sages, and a million sages make a great sage. In contrast, the Keynesian counterparts of these postulates are, first, that individuals are not necessarily sages, and second that, even if they are, a million sages can make a great fool.

The difference is fundamental and profound. It is more a difference in *Weltanschauung* than a difference in assumption. Many of the debates that have taken place in economics concerning approach, modelling, and policy prescription ultimately can be reduced to a similar philosophical difference. But nowhere is this difference more

---

[1] Since I first used it in my brief essay (Nagatani 1983), the opening nursery rhyme has been popularized by T. C. Bergstron and R. C. Crones in connection with aggregation problems (*Econometrica*, 51: 1753). But the purport of the rhyme goes far beyond aggregation problems, in my opinion.

crucial than in macroeconomic theory. To neoclassicists following the 'reductionist' approach, aggregates are mere summations of individual quantities; therefore all the properties of aggregates derive from the individual data. In other words, there is no room for a macroeconomic theory separate from the theory of rational individual behaviour. To Keynesians—and here I am referring to 'fundamentalist' Keynesians—the aggregate behaviour is unique: its theory need not, and indeed cannot, be 'derived from' the theory of rational individual behaviour.

The purpose of this chapter is to identify, from the historical as well as the analytical standpoint, the source of this gap, and to suggest a possible direction for reconciliation. The chapter contends that the recent big splash—the so-called micro foundations literature—falls short of the goal, and that more genuine macro foundations are needed for macroeconomic theory. The chapter is organized as follows. Section 2 presents a brief survey of the general trend of scientific developments during the past two centuries, which, it is hoped, will help us better understand the origin and nature of both neoclassicism and Keynesianism. Section 3 summarizes past attempts at reconciling the above difference; it will be argued that these attempts have had too strong a Walrasian bias to achieve a useful synthesis of the two theories. Section 4 presents an outline of the theory of man's social behaviour in the hope that such a theory may be able to bring micro and macro theory closer together. Section 5 summarizes the macroeconomic implications of this approach.

2   HISTORICAL BACKGROUND

That neoclassical economics was founded in the decade of the 1870s had a significant influence on its general character. By the beginning of the nineteenth century, Newton's (1642–1727) theory of universal gravitation had been thoroughly established and elaborated in the fields of astronomy and mechanics. The new theory had passed various tests in these fields with flying colours. Newton's conviction that all inanimate phenomena could be embraced by a single set of general laws had been verified. The world view of causality and determinism implied in Newton's theory became the new philosophy. Darwin (1809–1882) applied it to biology. Comte (1798–1857) and

Mill (1806–1873) saw the possibility of applying the principle of causation and the methods of physical science to moral or 'social' sciences.[2]

Moreover, the Newtonian theory mothered a new and enhanced faith in human intelligence. Newton was led to science by a humble desire to understand God's design, and he remained a pious man all his life. A century later, however, Laplace (1748–1827) was able to remove God from his thinking. Laplace, having authored *Système du Monde* and *Mécanique Céleste*, was called the 'French Newton' by his fellow countrymen. Like Newton, he began his study in theology. Becoming impressed with the power of the Newtonian theory, he finally replaced the Super Being with 'Intelligence'. To Laplace, Intelligence—also known as Laplace's Demon—was a most perfect computer imaginable. It was not a transcendent figure but was more akin to the limit of the human intelligence (see Hahn 1967: esp. 18). In the meantime, the philosophical world was ruled by Hegel's (1770–1831) Rationalism. One may thus say that the mid-nineteenth century was, by and large, a period of complacency, filled with pride in man's accomplishments and a greater hope for the future.

It was in this intellectual atmosphere that the three founders of the neoclassical school—Carl Menger (1840–1921), Léon Walras (1834–1910), and W. Stanley Jevons (1835–1882)—spent their creative years. Each produced his *magnum opus* early in the 1870s. Not surprisingly, the central features of their new theory were the perfectly rational economic man and, as is seen most clearly in the work of Walras, a stable and harmonious view of the economy. The 'Marginal Revolution', by which their works are known, demonstrated that the results of optimization were expressible in terms of marginal quantities, and that prices bore direct relationships with these marginal quantities. It eventually produced a static equilibrium theory of price determination.

Although the three economists are often bundled together, there were as many dissimilarities as there were similarities among them. Focusing on the latter, one notes first that none of them had formal training in economics. Menger earned a doctoral degree in law, worked in the press section of the Austrian Cabinet, and wrote market columns. While writing these columns, he realized the inadequacy of the prevailing academic economics (which was

---

[2] The term 'social sciences' is said to have been coined by Comte.

predominantly historical and institutional). His effort to understand commodity prices led him to a new approach in his *Grundsätze der Volkswirtschaftslehre* (1871). The success of this book earned him the position of professor of political economy at the University of Vienna. Walras had the good fortune of having an economist father. Although he later benefited much from his father's work, his study of economics did not proceed smoothly. Having tried unsuccessfully to enter the École Polytechnique twice, he ended up in a mining school. Even though he had taught himself a sufficient amount of economics by his mid-thirties, his lack of a diploma prevented him from finding a professional position in France. He eventually settled in the Academy of Lausanne, Switerland. When he said 'I am not an economist. I am an architect. But I know economics better than economists do' (cited in Jaffé 1935: 187), he did so with a vengeance. In several places in the *Éléments d'économie politique pure ou théorie de la richesse sociale* (first edition 1874), Walras stressed his dissociation from the economists. Jevons's intellectual endeavours began in chemistry, botany, and astronomy, in that order. His passion for social reform later led him gradually into economics. If these were self-made economists, they were also self-taught mathematicians.

The second similarity is their solitary character. Menger's open defiance to historicism and his relentless pursuit of rational economics were certainly enough to make him an academic, if not a social, loner. His failure to publish many more works than his *Grundsätze*, and even to perfect it over the fifty years after its first publication, may be attributed to his habit of thinking too long and being too much alone. Walras was even more of a loner than Menger. Having had to leave the France he loved so much was bad enough. Even after the publication of the *Éléments*, its reception was far from enthusiastic (and remained so throughout his lifetime), and his efforts at gaining support from famous scholars such as Marshall and Edgeworth did not succeed. His *Correspondence* (Jaffé1965) amply shows Walras's constant insecurity and anxiety. He would console himself by reciting the following passage from Laplace's *Système*:[3]

About fifty years have passed since the discovery of the theory of gravitation, without any remarkable addition to it. All this time has been requisite for this great truth to be generally understood, . . . (Laplace 1809, vol. 2: 351)

Jevons described himself as a man of solitude, almost to a point of

[3] See also Walras (1954: 48).

being anti-social. His *Letters and Journals* (1886) reveals that his personal correspondence was almost exclusively with his family members. Although he disliked socializing, he was a man of lively mind and a prolific writer over an amazing range of scientific and social problems. His name was often in the news, such as on the occasion of the publication of *The Coal Question* (1866) and of 'Commercial Crises and Sunspots' (1879). One does not find in Jevons that academic fanaticism possessed by Menger and Walras, although Jevons was peculiar in his own way.

The third similarity is their bent for the natural sciences. Although trained primarily for the law, Menger took anatomy and physiology as model sciences for his new economics. He saw that a part of social phenomena exhibited a close analogy to natural organisms. He believed that 'natural organisms exhibit a really admirable functionality of all parts with respect to the whole, a functionality which is not, however, the result of human calculation, but of a natural process . . . unintended results of historical development' (Menger 1963: 130). To Menger, individuals were rationally calculating, but the behaviour of the system was something else. It was either 'organic' in the above sense or 'mechanic', that is, dictated explicitly by man-made laws and other social compacts.

Menger believed that one could apply the methods of natural sciences in studying the organic category of aggregate behaviour. Walras declared his mission to be to 'bring the theory of economic system closer to that of astronomy'.[4] Laplace was no doubt his mentor. One sees a close resemblance between Laplace's Demon and Walras's 'auctioneer', although Walras himself did not publicize the auctioneer's presence so much as have some of his recent followers. Like Menger, Walras was aware of the limited applicability of the methods of the natural sciences to economics. Lesson 2 of the *Elements* begins with a discussion on the distinction between science and art, in order to ascertain the extent of such applicability. Walras then contrasts *human* actions with those of *things* to show that only human actions are purposive. At this point the applicability of the methods of natural sciences to economics looked bleak, but Walras salvaged the situation. He argued that all phenomena manifesting human actions could be classified into two categories: those concerning human actions on things, and those concerning human

[4] Jaffe (1965, vol. II, Letter 834: 251). Countless similar statements appear throughout these volumes.

actions on other human beings. He called the former 'industry' and the latter 'institutions'. The study of industry constituted an applied science. The study of institutions, on the other hand, belonged properly to ethics.

Walras wanted to investigate the scientific part of the economic phenomena. More specifically, he set out to establish a theory of wealth: that is, a theory of exchange and of value in exchange and, somewhat tangentially, a theory of produciton of wealth. His theory of wealth, however, excluded the question of the distribution of wealth, for purely methodological reasons.[5] Jevons succinctly describes his work in the preface to *The Theory of Political Economy* (1871):

In this work I have attempted to treat Economy as a Calculus of Pleasure and Pain, and sketched out . . . the form which the science . . . must ultimately take. . . . I have endeavoured to arrive at accurate quantitative notion concerning Utility, Value, Labour, Capital, etc., and I have often been surprised to find how clearly some of the most difficult notions, especially that most puzzling of notions of *Value*, admits of mathematical analysis and expression. The Theory of Economy thus treated presents a close analogy to the science of Statistical Mechanics, and the Laws of Exchange are found to resemble the Law of Equilibrium of a lever as determined by the principle of virtual velocities. The nature of Wealth and Value is explained by the consideration of indefinitely small amounts of pleasure and pain, just as the Theory of Statistics is made to rest upon the equality of indefinitely small amounts of energy. But I believe that dynamic branches of the Science of Economy may remain to be developed, on the consideration of which I have not at all entered. (Jevons 1957: vi–vii)

Jeavons was particularly interested in statistical analysis. This interest began during the five-year period (1854–9) he spent in Australia as an assayer with the mint in Sydney in the area of meteorology. In later years he moved on to the statistical analysis of business cycles. He was an originator of the time-series analysis. He also did some pioneering works on the index number problem. In a word, he was the father of econometrics (Frisch 1956: 300).

Returning to the general trend of scientific developments since the mid-nineteenth century, we must note that the brief period of

---

[5] Walras, like Jevons, had a passion for social reform. Menger too is reported to have been a regular member of an élite discussion group on social issues. But they all sternly distinguished between the role of the theorist and the role of the social reformer, and never mixed the two.

complacency came to an end, as the Newtonian determinism and the inflated faith in human rationality came under attack on several different fronts. First, the quantum theory, focusing on the microscopic world of elementary particles, recognized an inherent and pervasive element of stochasticity in their behaviour, implying a certain degree of indeterminacy in physical motions. Second, the old issue of mechanism versus vitalism resurfaced: the issue was whether or not life could be eventually reduced to matter. Optimism in the physical or materialistic approach to the question of life gradually faded. Niels Bohr (1885–1962) and Erwin Schrödinger (1889–1961) both expressed the view that life was a unique phenomenon, incapable of reduction to physical matter. For social scientists, the issue may be rephrased as whether or not the behaviour of the living obeys the same laws as those that govern the behaviour of the inert. Henri Bergson (1859–1941), the French philosopher, dramatized the contrast between the two sorts of behaviour. In his *L'Évolution créative* (1907), Bergson attacks Darwin for his mechanical account of the process of evolution, and argues that the real facts of evolution are to be found in the creative surge of life, in an *élan vital*. He saw the essence of life in movement, change, growth, creation and freedom. He went so far as to suggest that, while the physical motions obey the law of increasing entropy, those of the living, and of human beings in particular, obey the law of decreasing entropy. Entropy is maximized in a state of equality (of heat, pressure, etc.) called 'equilibrium' in the physical sciences. The law of increasing entropy therefore means equilibrating movements. In contrast, the law of decreasing entropy describes a pattern of behaviour that defies and even destroys such a natural tendency towards equilibrium.[6] Note the similarity between Bergson's notion of creative evolution and Schumpeter's notion of creative destruction.

Third, a group of philosophers, later to become known as 'existentialists', challenged the Hegelian rationalism. As early as the 1840s, the Danish philosopher Søren Kierkegaard (1813–1855) called Hegelian rationalism an ivory tower invention and contended that

---

[6] Physical forces are two in kind. One is the force that operates between two masses at distance (such as the gravitational forces); the other is the force that operates between two masses in contact (such as friction and resistance). The so-called fundamental economic forces may be interpreted to correspond to the former, while the forces generated by the interactions among human beings correspond to the latter. The two forces work in conflict with each other.

the irrational was the true real. The titles of Kierkegaard's three books—*Fear and Trembling, The Concept of Dread*, and *Sickness unto Death*—indicate the essence of the new philosophy. To the existentialists, the individual is a haphazard existence. Thrown into this world by accident without a well defined goal, he lacks a sense of value and a direction in life. Yet he must choose his own destiny. He is filled with the fear of being free, the fear of having to make choices constantly without guidance and of having to take the consequences. Whereas Robinson Crusoe—that religious, knowledgeable, confident, and enterprising individual created by Daniel Defoe—was the model for the rational individual of the previous centuries, the stray individual depicted by the existentialists has shaped the model for the twentieth-century man in other branches of the social sciences.[7]

Although economists have been remarkably immune to this change, some have challenged the neoclassical model—built around the assumptions that the rational individual occupies the centre of the universe and that everything else revolves around him—in favour of a paradigm built around a more realistic model of man. Veblen expresses his frustrations as follows:

In all the received formulations of economic theory, . . . the human material with which inquiry is concerned is conceived in hedonistic terms; that is to say, in terms of a passive and substantially inert and immutably given human nature. The psychological and anthropological preconceptions of the economists have been those which were accepted by the psychological and social sciences some generations ago. The hedonistic conception of man is that of a lightening calculator of pleasures and pains, who oscillated like a homogenous globule of desire of happiness under the impulse of stimuli that shift him about the area, but leave him intact. He has neither antecedent nor consequent. He is an isolated, definitive human datum, in stable equilibrium except for the buffets of the impinging forces that displace him in one direction or another. Self-poised in elementary space, he spins symmetrically about his own spiritual axis until the parallelogram of forces bears down upon him, where upon he follows the line of the resultant. When the force of the impact is spent, he comes to rest, a self-contained globule of desire as before . . .

The later psychology, reinforced by modern anthropological research, gives a different conception of human nature. According to this conception, it

---

[7] At least in so far as the existentialists' criticism of the old rational man is concerned. On the other hand, its stress on the solitary and irrational nature of man leaves little room for theorizing. In particular, its neglect of the social nature of man is most serious.

is the characteristic of man to do something, not simply to suffer pleasures and pains through the impact of suitable forces. He is not simply a bundle of desires that are to be saturated by being placed in the path of the forces of the environment, but rather a coherent structure of propensities and habits which seeks realization and expression in an unfolding activity. According to this view, human activity, and economic activity among the rest, is not apprehended as something incidental to the process of saturating given desires. The activity is itself the substantial fact of the process, and the desires under whose guidance the action takes place are circumstances of temperament which determine the specific direction in which the activity will unfold itself in the given case. These circumstances of temperament are ultimate and definitive for the individual who acts under them . . . But, in view of the science, they are elements of the existing frame of mind of the agent, and are the outcome of his antecedents and his life up to the point at which he stands. (Veblen 1898: 389–90)

And, of course, there was Marx, writing of Bentham:

Bentham is a purely English phenomenon. . . . The principle of utility was no discovery of Bentham. He simply reproduced in his dull way what Helvetius and other Frenchmen had said with esprit in the 18th century. To know what is useful for a dog, one must study dog-nature. This nature itself is not to be deduced from the principle of utility. Applying this to man, he that would criticise all human acts, movements, relations, etc., by the principle of utility, must first deal with human nature in general, and then with human nature as modified in each historical epoch. Bentham makes short work of it. . . . Had I the courage of my friend Heinrich Heine, I should call Mr. Jeremy a genius in the way of bourgeois stupidity. (Marx 1906: 668, n. 2)

Marx believed that the 'human nature' was not a primitive datum in the economic system but rather a product of the 'mode of production' of the time. None the less, Veblen and Marx both raised a fundamental objection to the neoclassic reductionism.

Among the twentieth-century economists, Keynes offered a theory or a vision of human nature most in the spirit of the twentieth-century philosophy. Chapter 12 of his *General Theory* (Keynes 1936) describes the behaviour of the masses of individuals living in advanced capitalist economies who are richer and more calculating than ever before. Although they are overwhelmed by the complexities of the decision problems facing them, the masses tend to act in a peculiarly gregarious fashion.

One of the lasting contributions that Keynes made to economics has been his vivid description of the pattern of behaviour of the masses and the 'monetary economy' that nurtures it. By a monetary economy, Keynes meant much more than just an economy using money as a medium of exchange. A money-using economy can be as stable and predictable as the one depicted by the classical quantity theorists. According to them, the total expenditure of the economy was a constant multiple of the money stock, and that constant was as stable as some of the grand constants in physics. To Walrasian theorists, money is essentially a 'veil'. Keynes's monetary economy, in contrast, relies crucially on money for efficiency, but also suffers from sources of instability arising from the use of money. Its viability rests on the stability of asset prices and money wages, and yet its institutional setup is exactly such that asset prices tend to be precarious and the stickiness of money wages tends to cause and prolong unemployment. Discussing these matters (Keynes 1936: chs 12 and 17), he never refers to the kind of isolated individuals created by the neoclassicists. Rather, he refers always to the 'market', or the masses of individuals. The behavioural foundation of his theory is the masses of people, not the isolated individual.

Although Keynes emphasized the imitative character of individuals, he never explicitly denied the rationality of individuals. Walrasian students of Keynes such as Leijonhufvud (1968) declared consequently that the only difference between Keynes's theory and Walras's was that for Keynes individuals faced imperfect market information, whereas their Walrasian counterparts enjoyed perfect information. Although this verdict is not incorrect, it certainly is not sufficient. Uncertainty destroys the one-to-one correspondence between an action and its outcome. As long as individuals remained isolated and independent decision-makers, uncertainty could make little difference. Keynes, however, went farther and argued how, facing prospects of speculative gains and losses, presumably rational individuals tended to lose their cool and their independence and become rather mindless copiers, and how the institutional setup of a monetary economy tended to justify such a strategy. Keynes compared the game played among investors in the modern capital markets to such children's games as Snap, Old Maid, and Musical Chairs. Keynesian individuals may be as ruthless pursuers of self-interest as Walrasian ones, but when making decision, they are not the capable and self-assured actors in the Walrasian drama: they are a collection of rather stray individuals looking for models to copy.

3   WALRAS VERSUS KEYNES

The economic system that Walras constructed was in every way similar to the system of the physical world. It is a peculiarly orderly system. Walras did not, however, believe that all the economic phenomena could be explained within such a natural-scientific mould. Excluding that part of economic phenomena resulting from explicit interactions among humans, Walrus (and, indeed, Menger) carefully circumscribed the scope of economic phenomena that he considered to be quasi-scientific. More specifically, he singled out the price adjustment process in the market-place as the category of economic phenomena that resembled physical motions most closely. In addition to its limitation on scope, Walras's theory relied on a few highly restrictive assumptions to make the story run smoothly. One such assumption concerned the nature of the rational man. For his purpose, Walras wanted rational individuals to act like so many natural objects; he wanted the rational man's response to market parameters to be essentially the same as the response a balloon makes to changing outside pressure, and nothing more. It is a very constrained notion of rationality, which may be termed *passive* rationality. It may seem somewhat paradoxical that man, with free will and rational choice, should act like a physical object. But the paradox disappears when one realizes that Nature is an economizer. A balloon chooses a ball shape because that shape minimizes the strain on the surface; each planet has positioned itself in order to minimize the work needed to sustain its position, given the locations of the others; a rope hangs in the shape of a catenary 'because even a dumb rope knows that such a shape will minimize its centre of gravity' (Samuelson 1965: 486). Likewise, because of rational choice, a shopper facing two check-out lines will choose the shorter one, and a person who is tied to two different trees by his arms will hang in the shape of a catenary. Passive rationality ensures that human beings behave like natural objects, which is what Walrus wanted. As a result, economists have developed a theory of optimal behaviour so refined but so impersonal that a brilliant Martian could outperform all of us earthlings in the mastery of it. As a theory of human behaviour, however, it definitely lacks the imaginative and enterprising character of human beings.

The passive nature of individual rationality is also carried over to market or aggregate behaviour, through the assumption of static equilibrium. The dynamics of price adjustments or the equilibrating process is a purely mechanical process, especially in competitive markets. The state of general economic equilibrium is strongly physical-scientific in character. It is a state of maximum entropy, of sameness which, once reached, will sustain itself for ever. Physicists have called it the state of 'heat-death', a state that is lifeless and unbearably boring. The neoclassical notion of static competitive equilibrium is in fact nothing but a state of heat-death: all economic rents have been dissipated and everyone is making zero economic profits. Nothing is left to compete for. Walras describes an economy in such a state of equilibrium or in the process of getting there.

Given the immense creativity of human nature, the Walrasion theory is a very peculiar theory. Indeed, the accuracy of predictions based on it is suspect. One would expect human beings to do anything to avoid the heat-death. They would contrive and conspire constantly to recreate economic rents, because anything is more acceptable than perpetual boredom.[8] Even though human beings tend to react to simple stimuli with passive rationality, they actively exercise their free will and rational judgements to alter their environments to their advantage. This part of human rationality, corresponding roughly to what Walras called 'institutions', is completely missing in the neoclassical paradigm. Walras was aware of this problem, but thought the price was fair. The price, however, becomes unbearably high when one attempts to apply the paradigm to macroeconomics. Walras's *tâtonnement* game, for example, is not incentive-compatible; it usually pays some transactors to lie about their tastes and lead the auctioneer to some non-Walrasian prices. In such a circumstance it is only natural, therefore, for these individuals to gang up to manipulate the prices in their favour. Macroeconomic performance is influenced

[8] Boredom has long been a weighty subject in some other branches of social sciences. According to Robert Nisbet of Columbia University, 'Among the forces that have shaped human behaviour, boredom is one of the most insistent and universal. Although scarcely as measurable a factor in history as war, dsiease, economic depression, famine, and revolution, it is far from invisible in either the present or the past' (Nisbet 1982). In order to appreciate how unbearable a stationary state would be, consult the following hilariously wrong prediction made by Edward Bellamy, one of the leading political theorists of his time: 'If you could have devised an arrangement for providing everybody with music in their homes, perfect in quality, unlimited in quantity, suited to every mood, and beginning and ceasing at will, we should have considered the limit of human felicity already attained, and ceased to strive for further improvement' (Bellamy 1887: 84).

by such institutional factors as much as by physical and technological ones. Indeed, much of the so-called 'competition' is competition among human beings rather than competition against nature.

When the choice problem is simple, individuals do exercise their independent judgements and act like rocks or balloons. But when the problem becomes as complex as most economic decision problems are, the behavioural pattern of individuals undergoes a fundamental transformation. First, many individuals find the solving of these problems beyond their capabilities. Although problems can always be simplified enough for anyone to be able to solve them, the simplifying assumptions on which the solution hinges make the solution itself unreliable. Faced with such a situation, what is a rational individual supposed to do? The neoclassical reaction has been to stick to the reductionist approach: if uncertainty cannot be resolved, let individuals engage in stochastic optimization instead of deterministic optimization; and if the cost of gathering information about the 'true' distribution is prohibitively high, let individuals substitute their 'subjective' distribution for the true one and claim the job done. Apart from the extension to allow for uncertainty, the neoclassical approach has not changed: individuals retain the dignity and independence of the Walrasian scenario.

The neoclassical reaction suffers from a few serious oversights. First, uncertainty separates the intention behind an action and its consequence. A given action can produce a number of outcomes, and a given outcome could have been generated from a number of actions or intentions. Under such circumstances, the notion of individual rationality is reduced to a subjective rationality at most or a rationality by intent, which cannot, in general, be tested objectively in terms of the consequence of action. Even apart from uncertainty, the sheer complexity of many economic decision problems tends to force decision-makers to adopt short-cuts. As soon as the decision problems become complex, the power of the reductionist approach diminishes greatly. Simon (1972) and Radner (1975), for example, have stressed this last point, which has been termed 'bounded rationality'. These authors propose a theory of 'satisficing' behaviour in place of optimizing behaviour. Borrowing the psychologists' notion of 'aspiration levels', they assert that agents choose from among a limited set of alternatives those actions that meet the given aspiration levels. Although a formal distinction is difficult to draw, Simon stresses the difference between satisficing and optimizing:

The terms satisficing and optimizing are labels for two broad approaches to rational behavior in situations where complexity and uncertainty make global rationality impossible. In these situations, optimization becomes approximate optimization—the description of the real-world situation is radically simplified until reduced to a degree of complication that the decision-maker can handle. Satisficing approaches seek this simplification in a somewhat different direction, retaining more of the detail of the real-world situation, but settling for a satisfactory, rather than an approximate-best, decision. (Simon 1972: 170)

Second, when the problem is very complex, it may be rational for some individuals to purchase a solution from others rather than solve it themselves. Solving a complex problem requires high setup costs in the form of a good education in economics, subscription to a dozen major newspapers and magazines, a good computer facility, and access to inside information in both business and government. These costs are obviously beyond the capacity of ordinary citizens to bear. They may find it far more sensible to buy instructions or solutions from those who they consider have both the resources and the intellectual capabilities to arrive at 'rational' solutions. Theories of bounded rationality recognize the limited human capabilities in problem-solving and yet retain the reductionist philosophy: individuals know their limits and make compromises, but they are still their old, isolated, and independent selves. This is most puzzling. Rationality means that those individuals for whom the cost of problem-solving exceeds the benefit should stop doing it. Problem-solving activities have strong economies of scale and tend to generate specialized agents. The flourishing of economic consultants and advisers in modern times demonstrates that most people do not solve their economic problems in solitude, but rather buy the solutions in the market.

When put to a few economists, the hypothesis that a majority of ordinary people do not attempt to solve their own economic problems but copy someone else's solutions received an instant and strong rejection, because they thought that it would remove the entire concept of rationality from economics. They are, however, mistaken. Recognizing that people vary widely in problem-solving capabilities, and that people's costs of problem-solving also vary, I believe that it is *rational* for some to buy solutions from others rather than wasting time and money on trying to solve their own problems. This hypothesis involves an extension of the familiar notion of rationality to the activities of information-gathering and problem-solving. The existence of a large number of imitators in turn affects the behaviour of the independent minority. Forecasting the state of the mass psychology and manipulating it become more important goals of market analysis than just acquiring real knowledge about the economy and buisness. In Keynes's *General Theory*, individuals always appear in plural form and in the context of such market games:

A conventional valuation which is established as the outcome of the mass psychology of a large number of ignorant individuals is liable to change due to factors which do not really make much difference to the prospective yield; since there will be no strong roots of conviction to hold it steady. In abnormal times in partcular, when the hypothesis of an indefinite continuance of the existing state of affairs is less plausble than usual even though there are no express grounds to anticipate a definite change, the market will be subject to waves of optimistic and pessimistic sentiment, which are unreasoning and yet in a sense legitimate where no solid basis exists for a reasonable calculation . . . But there is one feature in particular which deserves our attention. It might have been supposed that competition between expert professionals, possessing judgement and knowledge beyond that of the average private investor, would correct the vagaries of the ignorant individual left to himself. It happens, however, that the energies and skill of the professional investor and speculator are mainly occupied otherwise. For most of these persons are, in fact, largely concerned , not with making superior long-term forcasts of the probable yield of an investment over its whole life, but with foreseeing changes in the conventional basis of evaluation a short time ahead of the general public. . . . The professional investor is forced to concern himself with the anticipation of impending changes, in the news or in the atmosphere, of the kind by which experience shows that the mass psychology of the market is most influenced. This is the inevitable result of investment markets organised with a view to so-called 'liquidity'. Of the maxims of orthodox finance, none, surely, is more anti-social than the fetish of liquidity, the doctrine that it is a positive virtue on the part of investment institutions to concentrate their resources upon the holding of 'liquid' securities. It forgets that there is no such thing as liquidity of investment for the community as a whole. (Keynes 1936: 154–5)

Here Keynes refers to modern asset markets. The same pattern of behaviour is observed on a much broader scale in democratic societies. Politics is a well-known example. Politicians are forced to cater to the whimsical demands of the masses. Their lofty personal beliefs and statesman-like aspirations count little towards their success. University teachers have succumbed to a similar pressure from students. As university enrolment has expanded rapidly, the aim of university teaching has changed from helping students learn how to learn to spoon-feeding knowledge at minimum pain to students. The leaders in a democratic setting are pressured to cater to what the masses want. This would not pose any problem if the masses comprised independent, rational persons. If they do not, there is little sense in attempting to build the theory of macro behaviour on the imaginary independent self. The proper foundation of macro behaviour should be the masses themselves. Indeed, economics needs a credible theory of mass behaviour.

Turning now to the past attempts by economists at interpreting Keynes's macro theory, we must note that the debates have been numerous and have touched on many different aspects of Keynes's theory. Two common features in these interpretative efforts exist among current economists. One is the conscious effort to reduce the differences between neoclassical theory and Keynes's theory to differences in pure logic, leaving aside the differences in premises and visions altogether. The other is a Walrasian bias which regards the Walrasian general equilibrium theory as the norm and tries to fit Keynes's theory into the former mould.

The first feature of these interpretative efforts is best exemplified by the famous controversy between Pigou and Keynes over the effects on employment of an across-the-board money-wage cut. According to price theory, Pigou argued, a fall in a factor price (normally) encourages production and leads to a decline in the product prices at given product demand schedules. But as prices fall, wealth-owners find the real values of their wealth increased as a result of the decline in product prices, which tends to stimulate the demand for their products. (If wages and prices keep falling, eventually a £1 note will be able to buy the entire annual GNP of the UK.) Thus, as wages and prices keep falling, a strong enough aggregate demand, which cannot fail to restore full employment, will emerge sooner or later.

In Keynes's opinion, Pigou's argument was based on an unwarranted assumption that the wage cut had no detrimental effect on the aggregate demand. But some obvious channels through which the aggregate demand would be affected existed: a redistribution of purchasing power from wage-earners to wealth-owners; a worsening of the terms of trade and the resulting fall in real income (although the trade balance would improve): wage cuts generating expectations of further cuts in future, aggravating the situation; a loosening of the money market and a decline in interest rates at a given money supply; and an increased real burden on the part of debtors (firms and governments). Many of these effects are negative, especially when general psychological effects are taken into account. As Keynes himself stressed, the trouble with Pigou's analysis was not that it had any logical flaws, but that it was based on certain unrealistic premises (including the social behaviour of man and the composition fallacy).

The second feature of the interpretative efforts, the Walrasian bias, has been notable ever since Klein (1947) laid down a research strategy which has been followed to date by the general equilibrium theorists. Klein, in his Preface, asked: 'What are the minimum assumptions that must be made in order to obtain the theoretical results usually claimed by the adherents of Keynesian economists?' The performance criterion is the *minimum deviation* from the neoclassical orthodoxy. In carrying out the task, theorists chopped Keynes's theory, which was composed of an indecomposable whole, into parts such as the theories of employment, interest, and money, for ease of comparison. Not surprisingly, the theory of employment became the central object of examination, partly because the chief novelty of Keynes's theory was the demonstration of underemployment equilibrium, and partly because it was a more familiar area of the neoclassical theory.[9] Once the focus was set on the labour market, the analysis became a matter of applying the familiar tools of the Marshallian demand–supply analysis. Although over the years many innovations have been brought into the picture (uncertainty and expectations, search, and even contractual arrangements), the results of these efforts to explain unemployment have been less than satisfactory. The worst aspect of this labour market approach to unemployment is its partial framework, which operates on the assumption that unemployment is a labour market problem and hence that it should be, and *could* be, solved within that market. If Pigou's argument was implausible because of his questionable *ceteris paribus* assumptions, the conclusions drawn from the labour market theory are even more vulnerable.

Indeed, this labour market approach is even a regression from the

---

[9] At least relative to the areas of money and interest, where neoclassical theory had never accomplished very much. It was Friedman and other monetarists who took up the task in these areas. The ingenuity Friedman has shown over the many years as a critic of Keynes is well known. However, his strongly natural-scientific approach to a monetary economy offers little guidance to the present line of thinking.

models of Barro and Grossman (1971) and Negishi (1979), because these models were at least adamant about the 'derived' nature of labour demand. In this context one is depressed to read R. J. Gordon, a leading macroeconomist of our time, summarizing his deep thought by stating that 'the phenomenon of gradual price adjustment is at the heart of fluctuations in output and employment' (Gordon 1981: 493). Once one accepts, as he does, the Walrasian paradigm, this is little more than a tautology. Judging from this quote, the majority opinion to this day appears to be that, if wages were very flexible, unemployment would disappear; if wages could be lowered sufficiently, firms would want to hire every able and willing worker in the system, irrespective of the general economic condition. Apart from a value in the game of logic, such a belief or assertion carries no significance. Furthermore, these economists are oblivious of the fact that their lives would be a hell if wages were indeed as flexible as they want or believe them to be. Someone might underbid Gordon, and the good professor might lose his job at the very moment he is writing to complain about inflexible wages. Knowing this, Gordon would have to maintain contingent contracts with ten universities to guard against such risks at all times. And if everyone else did the same, the whole system would be in chaos rather than enjoying full employment. To be fair to Gordon, one must stress that he does not advocate increased price flexibility, but merely reveals his conviction that prices are slow to adjust. Solow echoes Gordon by stating: 'I have long thought that this—I mean quick quantity adjustment and slow price adjustment—is the promising direction for macrotheory' (Solow 1981: 573).

Should we all thank these authors for their profound observations? I think not. First, the belief that flexible prices and wages guarantee an efficient, full-employment equilibrium is little more than tautology, an abstract statement relevant only to the stable, quasi-natural economic models of the theorists. Second, no one has ever precisely defined the very notion of price flexibility. Oskar Lange (1944) defined price flexibility as the reciprocal of price elasticity, that is as the ratio of the percentage change in the price of a good to the percentage change in the excess demand for the good. This reads well, but as soon as one starts thinking about how to measure the excess demand, one's mind begins to boggle. Economists generally tend to interpret excess demand as a deviation from the assumed stationary Walrasian equilibrium point. They are mistaken. The dual decision theory of constrained choices can be invoked to question its validity. Furthermore, once one recognizes the dynamic stock adjustment process, which the dual decision theory and even Keynes himself tended to overlook, one realizes that the demand-for-labour function depends not only on wages and labour's marginal products, but also on the magnitude of the error to be corrected (which is measured by the gap between the actual stock or employment and the desired stock of employment relative to the prevailing state of expectations). When this gap is positive and large, firms are anxious to curtail their employment stocks. Three measures of this demand-for-labour exist: the Walrasian demand at the going real-wage rate (i.e. the stock of employment at which its marginal product is equal to the going real wage); the actual volume of employment; and the desired demand at the going wage rate (but allowing for the error), in descending order.

A similar ambiguity exists concerning the measures of labour supply, e.g. the notional and effective supplies. Depending on which measure one uses for excess demand, the wage flexibility will differ drastically in value. In particular, even if wages were flexible enough relative to the 'effective' measure of excess demand, it would not be strong enough to put a stop to the falling trend in employment, let alone to reverse it. This is one reason why the Gordon–Solow type of rhetoric cannot be taken seriously. The chief reason for deprecating such a rhetoric is the existence of errors registered in the form of wrong levels of stocks. Neoclassical economics traditionally ignores stocks and works with 'hydraulic'[10] models connecting flow variables. This strategy in effect precludes errors and assigns unreserved and undeserved importance to price variables. But in a realistic adjustment process induced by errors carried over from the past, price variables naturally have a very limited power. To believe otherwise, one commits the most elementary mistake in economics of forgetting the severe limitations imposed by the host of *ceteris paribus* assumptions.

Returning to the Walrasian bias in the micro foundations literature, Negishi (1979) has relentlessly pursued 'the minimum assumptions' needed to produce Keynesian underemployment equilibrium. He sets out by closing many easier avenues: he rules out wrong expectations; assumes away heterogeneity of labour; assumes the economy to be competitive, with perfectly flexible prices and

---

[10] This expression is due to Coddington (1976).

wages; precludes all types of unemployment other than involuntary unemployment arising from deficient demand; and rejects the dynamic disequilibrium interpretation of unemployment. On the other hand, he makes two non-Walrasian assumptions: (1) all exchanges are monetary, and (2) agents form plans on the basis of their subjective or perceived demand curves for their goods or services. The assumption of monetary exchanges means that an agent's spending plan is dependent on the success of his selling activities. The assumption of perceived demand curves reflects the agents' concern over the difficulties that arise in their selling activities, making these curves downward-sloping and likely kinked at the prevailing level of sales, despite their otherwise competitive environments. The weaker the firm's perceived demand for its products, the lower will be its demand for labour; and the weaker the household's perceived demand for its labour services, the lower its demand for products. When the demand forthcoming from one party coincides with the demand perceived by the other party, in both the product and the labour markets, the economy is in (short-run) equilibrium. Its location is generally different from the Walrasian full-employment equilibrium. The model thus admits the existence of Keynesian underemployment equilibrium without assuming rigid prices and wages.

Negishi's masterly analysis, along with his thorough survey of the micro foundations literature up to the late 1970s, brings out some important new implications of his model which make the conventional Walrasian general equilibrium theory look like a very special case. First, his model admits a variety of equilibria, depending on the agents' subjective assessments of the economy. In this sense, he develops a theory of conjectural equilibria of which the Walrasian equilibrium is a special case. Second, the price variables no longer assume the mystical omnipotent role of guiding the quantities. A one-to-one correspondence no longer exists between them: underemployment equilibrium can occur at the Walrasian equilibrium prices. Altering prices may not affect quantities, and changing quantities do not imply a set pattern of price changes. Third, indeterminacy of the price variables implies the need for a new—and in Negishi's own words 'sociological'—theory of price determination, including inflation.

These results are quite remarkable, for they differ greatly from those of the neoclassical orthodoxy—even with a minimum change in assumptions. Keynes would certainly be pleased to see them, because Negishi has proved the existence of underemployment equilibrium within an almost purely neoclassical framework, which was Keynes's primary goal. But in the *General Theory* Keynes aimed at something more than playing this kind of logic game. He appears to have tried to present a *modus operandi* pertinent to an advanced capitalist economy on the basis of a socio-psychological theory of man's behaviour. For this purpose he brought a substantial amount of historical and institutional data into macroeconomics. This feature separates Keynes's macro theory from the rest.[11] However, it also makes a reduction of his theory to neoclassical formalism biased and generally ineffective.

Keynes made many interesting observations. He stressed certain externalities inherent in the behaviour of individuals living in advanced economies, such as the paradox of thrift, people's liquidity preference and myopia, and the generally imitative and sometimes mobbish pattern of behaviour of the masses. These features, though alien to the neoclassical theory, were considered essential to macroeconomics. Keynes has sometimes been criticized for being a poor price theorist (see, e.g., Leijonhufvud 1968: 32), but this kind of criticism is entirely beside the point. On the other hand, Keynes himself was not completely sure of what to do with the neoclassical orthodoxy. He kept the neoclassical theory of the firm basically intact, even though this is at odds with his acute socio-psychological analysis of the masses and is deplorably naive compared with Schumpeter's (1950) analysis of modern corporations. Keynes even went so far as to say that, once the aggregate demand was adequately controlled, the neoclassical price theory would apply in full force. His judgement was again too naive and optimistic because it was oblivious of the fact that government-supported full employment was not the same as full employment without government support. As economic protection of the citizenry became the professed responsibility of the government, its intervention soon became institutionalized and, by the very nature of fiscal policy, became group-specific, industry-specific, and in some cases even firm-specific. To many

---

[11] This difference may be best illustrated in his notion of the 'long run'. To Keynes, the long run was an historical date, say 50 or 100 years from the time of his writing. It was the likely future state of the British economy taking all its institutional features into account. This usage is in sharp contrast to the neoclassical usage, in which the long run refers to the stationary state built into an abstract dynamic model.

business firms as well as households, this meant a change in the incentive structure, which in turn encouraged them to learn to prey on the public purse. In order to understand the working of today's highly politicized economy, one must take its institutional details into account, for people's behaviour and policy effects are heavily dependent on them.

4 MACROECONOMIC FOUNDATIONS

This section attempts to sketch a sensible direction in which a proper macroeconomic foundation is to be sought.[12] By way of summing up the above discussions, I shall enumerate a set of postulates.

1 All individuals are selfish maximizers within their own perceptions and abilities ('selfishness').
2 The capacity of the human mind for formulating and solving complex problems is very small compared with the size of most economic problems whose solution is required for objectively rational behaviour in the real world ('bounded rationality').
3 Individuals in a given society differ widely in problem-solving abilities, and the mean value of the distribution is quite low ('diversity of abilities').
4 Individuals care not only about their own personal gains but also about what others think of their actions ('society-consciousness').

The first postulate of selfishness is no different in spirit from that of the orthodox economic theory. The only proviso is that the perception and the ability of the individual concerned determine the degree of rationality of the solution and, what is more important, the degree of self-confidence in the solution itself. Neither is the second postulate of bounded rationality novel. These two postulates together imply that individuals are not sages, and that the response an individual makes to a given stimulus is not likely to be firm and predictable. They contain nothing essentially macro.

The third and fourth postulates, in contrast, *are* essentially macro, for they relate to the group characteristics of individuals. The third postulate of diversity of abilities stresses differentials in the abilities of individuals within a group. This *relative* lack of abilities, rather than

---

[12] A brief discussion of this matter is found in my essay (Nagatani 1983) under the same title.

the *absolute* lack of abilities stressed by the second postulate, seems crucial to the imitative pattern of behaviour by the majority of individuals as well as the predatory behaviour by those who are capable and enterprising. For one thing, it implies different costs of decision-making and different degrees of self-confidence for different individuals. For another, it creates a belief in the minds of many individuals that there are other more capable individuals whose judgements they trust more than their own. This sets in operation the law of comparative advantage. Individuals with relatively low abilities would rather imitate others than make genuine personal decisions of their own. The assumed low mean value of people's abilities implies that a majority tends to act as imitators.

By 'ability' I mean something like IQ. For any large random sample of people, the IQ is distributed approximately normally around a mean of 100. An IQ of 100 guarantees at most a fair performance in secondary schools. Although it is hard to pin down what the ability relevant to economic success is, such abilities, I suspect, are distributed much like the IQ. Another point that needs clarification is whom to copy once an individual has decided to copy. Again, it is impossible to provide a general answer. Most people copy just about anything and anybody: they copy other people's orders in restaurants; if a long queue is formed around a particular shop, many just join it. Economic decisions are made in much the same way. Given that most people are imitators, a potential market is thus created, with a rent to be reaped. So-called 'professionals' and 'experts' have then emerged to claim the rent.

The fourth postulate of society-consciousness states that individuals' egos are modified by their desire to be similar to others. Every human society has developed a set of moral codes to govern its members' behaviour. Where no explicit code of conduct exists, some sort of convention is usually employed. The chief benefit of these social rules is that they spare people the trouble of making decisions. (It is indeed surprising how many people hate making decisions!) In economics, in contrast, no such rules or 'superegos' exist. Orthodox economic theory gives the individual's ego supreme authority. But whether this freedom of choice is genuinely and fully exercised by individuals is a moot point. I have already alluded to their limited capabilities. If limited abilities were the only barrier to rational decision-making, the proportion of imitators would have to be considerably lower than it actually is; for winning a market game typically requires an individual to act ahead of the crowd, or to adopt a stance in opposition to the crowd, and everyone knows that. Many individuals do not take such winning (but risky) strategies, not only because they lack confidence in their own judgement, but, more importantly, because they are afraid of becoming outliers. Even when the outcome is favourable, the outlier pays a substantial price for being different from others. A lone winner in a game of chance is branded a 'gambler'. He faces the likely consequences of a lowering of his social status, and a loss of friends.[13] A lone loser is simply a failure as a human being. On the other hand, an investor, say a corporate portfolio manager, who has sunk with the crowd walks away unscathed. Faced with the combination of an almost total lack of criteria by which to judge the rationality of the behaviour of the crowd around him and the severe penalty that society imposes on outliers, an individual is strongly motivated to follow the crowd. This motivation will be stronger, the greater the risk involved; weaker, the greater an individual's self-confidence.

These postulates lead to a *model* of man that is quite different from that of the traditional economic man. His tastes and technology are no longer the 'isolated, definitive human datum', but can be influenced by others. The following simple discussion illustrates the difference between the orthodox economic model and my own. Let a number of individuals (e.g. buyers in a given market or workers at a given work-place) be indexed by i. Let $U_i(x_i)$ be the genuinely personal part of the benefit function of the ith indiviual and x_i be his decision variable affecting such benefits. This U function represents the conventional performance criterion of the economic man. The last two postulates imply, however, that the individual has a desire to imitate or conform to others. Such a taste can be expressed by another function: $v_i(x_i, \bar{x}_i)$, where $\bar{x}$ stands for some average quantity of the other participants. The ith individual's preferences may then be expressed as the sum of the two functions u_i and v. For concreteness, let

$$u_i(x_i) = a_i x_i - \frac{b_i}{2} x_i^2$$

and

$$v_i(x_i, \bar{x}_i) = -\frac{c_i}{2}(x_i - \bar{x}_i)^2,$$

where a_i, b_i, and c_i are all positive constants. First, the optimal

---

[13] 'The fear of success' is the term psychologists use to describe the psychic cost of succeeding.

solution in the conventional model is the value of x_i, $x_i^* = a_i/b_i$. Second, when the imitation effect is present, the optimal solution changes to

$$x_i^{**} = \frac{a_i + c_i \bar{x}_i}{b_i + c_i},$$

a typical Cournot solution. In particular, when the number of participants is two, $\bar{x}_1$ may be set equal to x_2 and $\bar{x}_2$ to x_1. The Cournot solution becomes the pair

$$x_1^{**} = \frac{a_1(b_2 + c_2) + c_1 a_2}{(b_1 + b_2)(c_1 + c_2) - c_1 c_2}$$

and

$$x_2^{**} = \frac{a_2(b_1 + c_1) + c_2 a_1}{(b_1 + b_2)(c_1 + c_2) - c_1 c_2}.$$

Comparing this pair with that bearing single asterisks, we notice the following. First, the total 'output', i.e. the sum of the two x's, may be greater or smaller in the latter case than in the former. Second, the difference in individual outputs is smaller in the latter case than in the former; i.e.,

$$\left| x_1^{**} - x_2^{**} \right| < \left| x_1^* - x_2^* \right|.$$

Third, this reduction in the difference in individual outputs has been produced by both individuals moving towards the mean, i.e. with the individual who had a larger x^* reducing his output and the individual who had a smaller x^* increasing his output. Thus, while the imitative behaviour definitely reduced individual differences, it has an ambiguous effect on the total output. When x is interpreted as effort input by workers, the model becomes one of labour management (see Jones 1984). A labour union applies a strong conformist pressure on its members. Depending on how the 'norm' is set, such a conformist group behaviour may raise or lower the productivity of the workers as a group. When x is interpreted as sepculative demand, the model can explain the kind of mass infatuations observed in history from time to time. For this purpose, write $u_i(x_i)$ as $Eu_i\{(q_i - p)x_i\}$, the expected capital gain. Using the same quadratic approximation, the individual solution becomes

$$x_i^{**} = \frac{a_i(\bar{q}_i - p) + c_i \bar{x}_i}{b_i\{\text{var } q_i + (\bar{q}_i - p)^2\} + c_i}$$

where q_i is a random variable representing the subjective distribution of tomorrow's price, $\bar{q}_i$ is the mean of this distribution, and p is the current price. The current price depends on the strength of the current market demand. It may be expressed approximately as $p = k(n-1)\bar{x}_i$, for some positive coefficient k. In the absence of the imitation factor, a strong market demand and hence a high p discourages the ith individual's demand. But if his desire to imitate is sufficiently strong, the second term in the numerator may more than offset this dampening effect through p. If so, we have the case of a speculative mania that has characterized modern asset markets. This destabilizing influence of the gregarious behaviour of the masses constitutes a fourth property of the model based on our four postulates.

5   SUMMARY

Let us now summarize the implications of the above discussion for macroeconomics.

First, and most importantly, the individual is not at the centre of the universe; he is not the isolated, definitive human datum from which macro behaviour can be derived by aggregation. While he still pursues self-interest, mental pressure, both internal and external, tends to make him act as an imitator/conformist. This capability of being influenced by others separates human beings from physical objects. By confining its scope to the relation between man and nature and adhering to the natural-scientific methods, neoclassical economics has succeeded in exalting economics to an exact science. The result has been a total dehumanization of economics. Macroeconomics must break from this tradition and be built on more plausible macroeconomic foundations.

Second, once individual tastes and technology cease to be definitive data, a variety of aggregative outcomes become compatible with given micro data. When individuals are imitative, the aggregate performance generated by a given population can vary drastically, depending on the manner in which the population is organized and on the prevailing psychology in society. It is said, for example, that the average productivity of Japanese auto workers is several times as high as that of their British counterparts. Trying to attribute such a large difference in productivity to the differences in individual workers' qualifications or capital equipment would be senseless. The difference is more likely to have come from factors that have traditionally escaped the attention of economic theory, that is from a variety of organizational/institutional differences affecting the workers' morale. As another example, consumption expenditures fell drastically during the Great Depression, and again after the oil shock of 1973, far more than the income and wealth variables could account for; the difference may be attributed to the panic psychology that swept the consumers. These examples show what the interactive forces among human beings can do to macro behaviour.[14]

Third, as has been remarked in connection with the illustrative model, the effect of imitative or conformist behaviour on aggregate performance is generally ambiguous. But in view of its ubiquity and strength, one must recognize its presence and, whenever possible, learn to exploit it to national advantage, as Japanese leaders have done so successfully. Americans and Britons who have long taken great pride in their individualism may not be receptive to such an idea. But of Americans, Keynes said:

[E]ven outside the field of finance, Americans are apt to be unduly interested in discovering what average opinion believes average opinion to be; and this national weakness finds its nemesis in the stock market. (Keynes 1936: 159)

One should, however, note that Britons have to their credit a spectacular case of mass infatuation known as the South Sea Bubble, which involved the Minister of the Exchequer and the honourable directors of the Bank of England. It seems fair to say that people generally are gregarious creatures. One group often looks more individualistic and heterogeneous than another, not because its members are more independent, but because it is subject to more divisive social rules. Physical setting are also important in conditioning individual behaviour. Any Westerner who has spent one week in Tokyo would agree that the Tokyoites are more rule-observant, and do things in a much more orderly fashion, than many others. This is, in my opinion, not because the Tokyoites are less individualistic than

---

[14] Similarly, the effects of a given policy can vary from one occasion to another. The US tax cut in 1964 had a strong expansionary effect, but a similar tax cut in 1981 did not. Granted that the former was consumption-oriented while the latter was investment-oriented, the contrast between the two cases points to the importance of the 'state of mind' of the public. Although economists have not generally been keen to collect psychological data, their potential significance is very high and their use should be encouraged.

others, but because that is the only way for the dense population to survive.

A gregarious nature of people implies certain patterns of macro behaviour characteristic of human societies. Myopia and intertemporal inconsistency constitute one such pattern and were Keynes's major concern. More generally, the aggregative consequences of action by millions of stray individuals are likely to be volatile and inefficient. These observations lead to policy implications quite different from those of neoclassical theory. Neoclassical theory views an economic system as a quasi-natural system which tends of itself to an efficient competitive equilibrium. It denies, in principle, the need for active policy intervention, except to advocate competitive individualism as the guiding philosophy for society. Its emphasis on the passive rationality of individuals and the orderly interactions among them leads to a conservative ideology. In contrast, the present approach, based on only imperfectly rational and gregarious population, points to the need for leadership in general, and for policy guidance for the economy in particular. Imitators need a model to follow, and this inherent demand by the citizenry for leadership creates a huge potential economic rent to be reaped by the persons or groups that win it. Whether a national leadership role is assumed by bureaucracy or by business, there will be one; otherwise society would be in chaos. The oft-advocated notion of *laissez-faire* is not a plea for a leaderless society: rather, it is nothing more than the voice of business in quest of the national leadership.

In addition to political leadership, a number of professional groups have successfully established themselves into institutions fulfilling similar leadership roles in their respective fields; lawyers, accountants, and economists are but a few obvious examples. Because their opinions and advice are in great demand, these goups enjoy handsome rents. These phenomena would be hard to explain if individuals were the self-assured and independent likes of Robinson Crusoe instead of their insecure and imitative selves. Institutionalizations, on the other hand, tend to impose pressure on their members to conform to the values these institutions stand for.

All in all, it seems more accurate, and more fruitful, to describe today's macroeconomy—its basic behavioural pattern and policy responses to changes in environments—as being governed by the startegic games played by a number of dominant institutions than as a quasi-natural phenomenon shaped by millions of isolated, passively rational, individuals. Such a system possesses no unique equilibrium of a natural system, but multiple equilibria. Moreover, policy responses tend to be strongly coloured by the tenet held by the group in power and by its self-interest. In situations like this, the allocation of value ceases to be mechanical and becomes 'political' in the sense defined in the next chapter. Competitive indivualism alone cannot guarantee a high performance of such a system. The manner in which individuals are organized and the rules governing the conduct of individuals and groups, including the political leaders themselves, become equally important.

Fourth, as a general principle of policy guidance in the type of society described above, the most important question is how to build into the myopic aggregative behaviour a long enough time horizon. Again, to quote Keynes,

Investment based on genuine long-term expectation is so difficult to-day as to be scarcely practicable. He who attempts it must surely lead much more laborious days and run greater risks than he who tries to guess better than the crowd how the crowd will behave, and, given equal intelligence, he may make more disastrous mistakes. There is no clear evidence from experience that the investment policy which is socially advantageous coincides with that which is most profitable. It needs *more* intelligence to defeat the forces of time and our ignorance of the future than to beat the gun. (Keynes 1936: 157)

But who should be given the task? Traditionally, business has claimed its suitability for the job, but its overriding concern with quick profits makes it a questionable candidate. Moreover, it has become increasingly dependent on the public purse. I personally would rather vote for the bureaucracy, its widely held negative image notwithstanding. For this choice to work, however, it is essential that the *quality* of the bureaucrats be high—high enough to command the respect of the rest of society. This would require the establishment of a nationwide system through which suitable young candidates were selected and trained as public administrators. Such a programme would cost very little but should yield great benefits. In many countries, including Canada, the recruitment of civil servants is conducted too casually, resulting in a high turnover and less-than-desirable quality of employee. And this, in turn, results in an ineffective execution of policy measures. It is strange that our society should have failed, in this era of professionalism and increasing politicization, to build special training institutions for civil servants (and politicians!) comparable to business schools for businessmen.

Broadly speaking, macroeconomic policy is becoming ever more sophisticated and complex, and increasingly is aimed at short-term stabilization. With improvements in data compilation and computer facilities, it is hard to do otherwise. But the overall efficacy of short-term stabilization policies has always been questioned. Given the wide margin of uncertainty surrounding policy actions in the short run, I believe it useful to shift the focus from short-term stabilization policies to the more fundamental, long-term matters such as improving the quality of labour and management, searching for better industrial relations, planning for future industrial structure, and establishing steady trade relations with others; for as history shows, if the economy is healthy and strong in the long run, lesser short-run problems will tend to take care of themselves.

Fifth and finally, how can this alternative view of human beings be developed into a macro theory useful for purposes of diagnosis, prediction, and prescription? I suggest studying the historical and institutional characteristics of major groups of the economy (such as political parties, bureaucracy, central bank, business, labour, and consumers), extracting from this study their tastes or behavioural patterns, and then performing hypothetical comparative-statistics exercises to determine how these groups are likely to respond to a given exogenous shock, and how the interactions among them are likely to shape the course of the economy. Policy decisions are endogenized in this exercise, for they themselves are the results of the interactions among these groups. In this respect I differ from Keynes, who had great faith in the judgement and leadership of the few super-intellectuals in society. Only the ideal monocratic bureaucracy of Max Weber could fill such a role. In this context, we may note that the above approach is equally applicable to the international economy, which today is more susceptible to foreign shocks than ever before. As a result of such susceptibility, economic problems are increasingly becoming global problems. This implies that more and more economic problems will be dealt with by international bodies in the future, which in turn implies that the future course of national economies will become increasingly dependent on the outcomes of the world economic games played by coalitions of nations.

Many of the economic problems of our time, such as inflation, unemployment, productivity, world trade, and international monetary order, are human in character. Take inflation for example. Establishing a money–inflation causality, even if possible, would not carry us very far towards understanding inflation. Inflation is not a natural phenomenon: it is man-made. In order to understand inflation fully, we must therefore know who causes it and why. Or take the productivity question. What factors determine the productivity of a group of workers? How should the wide disparity in labour productivity observed across different industrialized economies be explained? Gven the similar technological and material opportunity sets available to advanced economies, the productivity differences among them are likely to be caused not by wrong factor mixes, but by the human elements affecting morale in the work-place. If so, searching for ways to improve labour–management relations and other conditions in the work-place is just as important as searching for better methods of production.

It is hoped that a more humanized approach as suggested in this chapter will prove useful for a better understanding of these macroeconomic problems.

2

Macroeconomics as Political Economy

Political economy, considered as a branch of the science of a statesman or legislator, proposes two distinct objects: first, to provide a plentiful revenue or subsistence for the people, or more properly to enable them to provide such a revenue or subsistence for themselves; and secondly, to supply the state or commonwealth with a revenue sufficient for the public services. It proposes to enrich both the people and the sovereign.

Adam Smith, *The Wealth of Nations*, vol. I, p. 375

1 INTRODUCTION

Modern economics began as political economy. The barest form of political economy is found in the mercantilism that dominated the era of absolute monarchs. Adam Smith's *laissez-faire* doctrine was no less concerned with political economy. *The Wealth of Nations* was primarily a reaction to the mercantilist habit of regarding commerce as the source of prosperity and equating gold and silver with national wealth. This tradition of political economy continued throughout the classical era.

But when the founders of the neoclassical school began to theorize economics in a natural-scientific mode, the political economy of Adam Smith was reduced to a mundane affair of little theoretical significance. Referring to Smith's passage just quoted, Walras contended:

But it seems to me that this is not, strictly speaking, the object of a science. Indeed, the distinguishing characteristic of a science is the complete indifference to consequences, good or bad, with which it carries on the pursuit of pure truth. (Walras 1954: 52)

Jevons's letter to his sister Henrietta, dated 28 February 1858, also reveals his low opinion of Smith:

I am glad you find political economy tolerable. *The Wealth of Nations* is perhaps one of the driest on the subject ... (Jevons 1886: 101)

To the founders of neoclassical economics, economics ought to be a science as objective, exact, and detached from human elements as any branch of the natural sciences. They were after 'pure truth', and chose the price formation process in competitive markets as an object specially fit for such attempts. When Walras, who aimed at 'bringing economics closer to astronomy', found a precise mathematical expression for his vision of an orderly state of general economic equilibrium, it consisted of a collection of systematic relationships among the prices of various products and factors. Walras described these relationships as the natural limits to which the prices tend. Because such prices included those of the factors of produciton, the theory 'explained' income distribution of the agents in the system, and its naturalistic flavour gave Walras's account a degree of holiness. Later, when the efficiency property of a competitive equilibrium was proved, neoclassical general equilibrium theory started to loom even larger than a statement of pure truth; it became a bible, fostering the view that economic phenomena were impersonal, quasi-natural, and even divine. It is this pretence to objectivity more than anything else that has enabled neoclassical economics to fend off its critics successfully and to reign as orthodoxy for more than a century. But it has also dehumanized economics to such an extent that no dialogue is possible between economists and other social scientists.

The fact remains, however, that economic affairs are human affairs, and that humans are different from natural objects. Humans do not possess the degree of 'passive rationality' possessed by inert objects because fo their passions, impulses, and enterprise. On the other hand, humans possess a great deal of 'active rationality' which inert objects do not. In economic activities, humans may not always choose the optimal quantities in response to given market parameters. Indeed, they are not content to choose quantities passively in response to market parameters, but will attempt to alter the parameters themselves (including rules of the market game) in their favour by using other humans as means to their own ends. But once one allows for this type of activity, price formation ceases to be an impersonal process: the allocation of value becomes a human affair. One is in the realm of political economy.

This chapter proposes to view macroeconomics as a topic in political economy, where politics is defined as 'the authoritative allocation of value', after the concise definition given by the political scientist Easton (1953). Nothing new in this view exists, but it needs to be expressed, given the way macroeconomics is currently practised.

Today's macroeconomics suffers from a few categorical defects. First, it is devoid of human elements; it does not have so much as an elementary theory of human behaviour in its social setting; it still strives to get closer to astronomy. Its reductionist approach fails to recognize the central concept in political economy, namely power. Second, it is devoid of the twentieth-century features of the advanced capitalist economies it avers to be studying; it has made little effort to deal squarely with such countries' huge financial accumulations and their effects on the working of these economies; it has been blind to the transformation from family capitalism to corporate capitalism and the massive growth of governmental and business bureaucracies and the global principal–agency problem that this transformation has brought with it.

Third, it operates on the belief that there are universal truths in macroeconomics independent of time and place, and it seeks such truths; it refuses to recognize the fact that what constitutes an optimal policy (in the sense of enriching the people and the sovereign) depends on the particular historical setting in which the economy is situated. Fourth, it cannot 'endogenize' policies themselves; it is forever studying the effects of various policies, but not why particular policies are adopted in particular circumstances. In reality, policy formation is part of the political-economic process and should be the object of macroeconomic investigations. Politicians are the most gregarious species in our society, and as a result economic policies tend to reflect the fashion of the time.

Today's fiscal conservatism is a prime example of such fashions; and it is not so much a solid scientific verdict as bare politics that has brought this about. It is a by-product of a decade-long hardship. The 'economy of government', readers may recall, headed the list of public issues in popularity in the USA in the depths of the Great Depression; today, the world is going through the same phase. No policy is all good or all bad. Deficit finance and the accumulation of public debt are not all bad, either. For economists to take a religious stand on issues like this is undesirable. To put the matter in historical perspective, we have only to remember that the fastest growth in public debt in modern history was recorded by Britain during the eighteenth and nineteenth centuries. If one believes historians' words, the Million Loan of 1693 was the first English national (funded) debt. Adam Smith (1776, V, III) gives the British public debt outstanding at £21,515,742 in 1697, £78,293,313 in 1748, and £129,146,322 in 1775, a year when the regular annual revenue base of the British government was only £10 million. And the worst was yet to come with the rise of Napoleon. Smith called the practice of funding government debt and its rapid growth 'ruinous'. But did this phenomenal growth of public debt really weaken, let alone ruin, the British Empire? If one answers this question in the negative but is also critical of today's deficit finance and growing public debt, one must be making an historical judgement which is necessarily particular to time and place. All the policy issues are of this nature, and there is nothing wrong with them. The current macroeconomics unfortunately seeks definitive abstract answers to these issues. As a result, there is much ado about nothing: namely, too many doctrinal debates which cannot be settled by scientific means.

2   INDIVIDUAL RATIONALITY AND SYSTEM'S EFFICIENCY

Adam Smith is widely regarded as the discoverer and proponent of the principle of *laissez-faire* and the theorem of the invisible hand. True, one finds in *The Wealth of Nations* a clear statement of the principle, if not the theorem:

As every individual, therefore, endeavours as much as he can both to employ his capital in the support of domestic industry, and so to direct that industry that its produce may be of the greatest value; every individual necessarily labours to render the annual revenue of the society as great as he can. He generally, indeed, neither intends to promote the public interest, nor knows how much he is promoting it. By preferring the support of domestic to that of foreign industry, he intends only his own security; and by directing that industry in such a manner as its produce may be of the greatest value, he intends only his own gain, and he is in this, as in many other cases, led by an invisible hand to promote an end which was not part of his intention. (Smith 1776, I: 400)

As is well known, this idea was later to be examined in the formal general equilibrium model of Walras, and to be confirmed in the form of an optimality theorem of competitive equilibrium.

But whether a group of individuals or a community can achieve an orderly social life founded solely on the norm of individual rationality is one of the oldest and most unsettled issues in the social sciences, and economists are undoubtedly in the minority as to their views. Hobbes

(1588–1669) answered this question negatively. He argued that, if individuals' choices were founded only on the rational calcualtion of utility, nothing would prevent some of them from using others as means to their own ends, and that in such a state life would be 'nasty, mean, solitary, brutish, and short'. A majority of today's sociologists would side with Hobbes on this issue. What about Smith himself? True, Smith saw a great potential in a market economy organized on the principle of *laissez-faire*. But he was too keen an observer of human nature to equate the vague potential with feasibility—to believe the principle to become the economic norm of itself. One could indeed regard *The Wealth of Nations* as a testimony to the perverse human nature which tends to work against the theorem of the invisible hand. Nations' self-interest tends to move in the direction of beggaring all their neighbours (I: 436); businessmen's interests are focused on how to restrain competition from outside (I: 107–9); governments tend to forget their fiscal responsibilities and indulge in deficit finance (II: 389–430), to cite a few examples. Smith even offers a penetrating remark on the incentives of hired workers; how the industry of a journeyman tends to be lower then that of a self-employed worker, and that of a worker hired on time rate even lower than that of the journeyman who works by the piece (I: 275). In modern language, Smith seems to be saying that free will and the ingenuity of individuals tend to be applied towards rent-seeking activities, and the growth of economic organizations tends to aggravate the situation—the problem known now as the principal–agency problem. Smith could not have believed that the mere education of the public would bring a system of *laissez-faire* in reality. It is even doubtful if he himself had a clear idea as to how to implement the principle into a viable institution.

The fundamental inconsistency between individual rationality and efficient social outcome can be brought out more formally using the tools of modern economic theory. Consider the problem of maximizing social benefits subject to a set of aggregate resource constraints. This problem has, as its 'dual', the problem of *minimizing the resource rents* subject to non-positive profit constraints. The two problems are mathematically equivalent and so, therefore, are the solutions.[1] Now think in terms of the dual problem. What it takes to minimize the

---

[1] In linear models, the duality is perfect: if one problem has a solution, so does the other; and the values of the objective functions are the same. In nonlinear models, certain regularity conditions are needed to ensure duality.

resource rents, among others, is to put all the resources into a common societal pool and let the potential employers bid competitively for their use. That this procedure is in direct conflict with the private ownership of resources should be obvious, because a rational resource-owner naturally seeks the highest possible prices for the resources he owns, by haggling, lobbying, and other means.

Technically speaking, this kind of rent-seeking behaviour makes little sense in a world of perfect information. But that is not much of a consolation. One thing the real world guarantees is imperfect and asymmetric information. In such circumstances, free interaction of individuals in the market-place does not, as a rule, lead to an efficient social outcome; in extreme cases, markets may collapse altogether. For some time economists have been aware of this problem but have tended to play it down. They have regarded the variety of externalities generated in the economy as largely unintended outcomes of individual actions rather than as the consequences of purposefully exploitative or predatory actions of individuals against one another. Coase (1960) expresses an optimistic view that, as property rights become more fully established, the damaging effects of externalities on resource allocation will disappear. Groves and others (1973, 1977) suggest that an incentive mechanism exists which would turn a non-cooperative Nash solution Pareto-efficient.

Given the active rationality of individuals and the imperfect environment in which they operate, however, one cannot expect these suggestions to be of great practical value. Laws and rules can never be fine and tight enough to eliminate deviant behaviour. Besides, although these suggestions are directed to the efficiency question, the distribution question is something else. A market economy can function only on the basis of a multitude of rules. Governments' fiscal activities involve the choice of taxation schemes and spending priorities. They have direct distributive effects. Even those policies aimed at efficiency, such as free trade, have a grave distributive effect. Monetary policies, which are usually regarded as more distributionally neutral than fiscal policies, nevertheless have substantial distributive effects. Controlling interest rates and exchange rates, not to mention altering banking regulations, clearly favours some and hurts others. Democratic governments typically arrive at such a choice on the basis of the estimated impact of proposed actions on the public's support of them. This means that governments' decisions, and hence the distribution of value, are susceptible to the pressures put up by various coalitions of individuals and institutions. Actively rational individuals therefore would not be content with choosing optimum quantities under given rules. They would seek changes of rules in their favour through overt and covert political campaigns. Thus, when the active rationality of individuals is taken into account, economic activities become inherently political in nature. The very rules on which the economy operates become endogenized. The making of prices ceases to be the impersonal process of the conventional economic theory and becomes part of the political–economic game. The aggregate performance index of an economy, such as GNP, is naturally influenced by the rules it chooses. In short, macroeconomics becomes a subject as much of politics as of economics.

3   A POLITICAL–ECONOMIC FRAMEWORK FOR MACROANALYSIS

In a political economy, a given aggregate endowment of resources does not automatically yield a given level of GNP. Aside from the usual sources of allocative inefficiencies known to economists, many motivational and organizational sources of inefficiencies exist, as noted by Leibenstein (1966) and others. Organization theorists such as McGregor, Maslow, and Herzberg offer diagnoses of human motivation in general terms. Economists working in the area of industrial relations stress the damaging effect of workers' absenteeism, tardiness, carelessness, slowdowns, and sabotages on labour productivity, and the need for devising rules to reduce it. Still others offer models of political coalitions and their implications for the aggregate economic performance.

While this is unquestionably the right direction for future economics to take, economists conducting research in this pioneering area appear to be operating with great restraint, which arises from a sense of fear—fear of renouncing the neoclassical orthodoxy; fear of alienating themselves from the professional mainstream; at a deeper level, fear of revolting against the sacred belief in individual freedom and democracy. To professional economists this fear is very real, and it is hard to blame them for it. History shows that all revellions against neoclassical orthodoxy, including those led by Marx, Schumpeter, Veblen, and Galbraith, have lost the challenge match and remained heresies. The only exception, if any, has been the revolution by Keynes. But the secret of Keynes's success has never lain in the anti-neoclassical ideas he propounded but in the amenability of his theory, at least at a formal level, to the neoclassical orthodoxy. It is the *IS–LM* model part of Keynes's theory that has been widely accepted, because it could be worked into the neoclassical general equilibrium model; everything else that Keynes wrote has met the same fate as the other rebellions.

In other words, Keynes's theory owes its success to the support of the Walrasian students of Keynes, from Hicks down to Hahn, Clower, and Leijonhufvud. In such an environment, the safe strategy is to ignore all the non-neoclassical elements (which unfortunately include the all-important human element in economic activities), as the majority of economists do. When economists recognize 'market failures' caused by the deviant behaviour of actively rational individuals, their first reaction is to assert either that the magical force of competition will correct such failures, or that the government will readily take care of them. Neither assertion has much credibility. Rules aimed at restricting competition abound; governments do not possess the ability to monitor the behaviour of individuals and keep such rules from emerging. The sweeping assertions of economists, though utterly unscientfic, serve only one purpose: that of defending the neoclassical orthodoxy.

This chapter proposes a paradigm that goes beyond these traditional bounds in order to capture the central feature of today's economies, namely, the political game played among the several powerful groups of agents. The new political economy paradigm is built on a few basic premises. First and foremost, it replaces the axiom of passive rationality with that of active rationality. Economic agents do everything within their power to enrich themselves and constantly seek ways to increase their power; they are not content with reacting passively to market signals but will attempt to alter the market rules in their favour, often by forming political coalitions. Just as nature dislikes a vacuum, so human societies dislike the absence of such coalitions. Economic equilibrium of atomistic competition is an extremely unnatural state, a state that is incompatible with man's active rationality.

Second, twentieth-century societies are managed by professional agents. Politicians, governmental bureaucrats, corporate managers, union leaders, and hired workers are all agents in the sense that they do not own the means of production or administration but are hired to do specific tasks for the principals. Because agents are also actively rational individuals, their duties and their self-interests more or less conflict with each other. Although capable execution of the tasks for which they are hired is an important principle guiding their behaviour, it is not the only one, or not even necessarily the dominant one. Serving the principals well is, in theory, the guiding principle for agents, but it may become merely a side-constraint, subject to which they pursue maximum benefits for themselves either as individuals or as a group. Political leaders may use their power to enrich themselves subject to the constraints vaguely defined by the existing body of laws and the mandate given to them; business managers may seek personal gains subject to the constraint that the company maintain an acceptable rate of dividend payments to the owners; union leaders may be bribed subject to certain minimum lines set by their unions; and hired workers may shirk responsibilities subject to some minimum work norms set by their contract.

This type of behaviour is often described as 'deviant'. It is undesirable from the societal standpoint, but eccentric or exceptional it is not. It is perfectly normal behaviour for agents with active rationality. If the alternative is the naive assumption that politicians work selflessly for the people, or that business managers always seek maximum profits for the owners, or that hired workers always operate at maximum efficiency, historical evidence seems to be decidedly in favour of this less pleasant but more sensible hypothesis about human behaviour. The principals, namely the millions of ordinary citizens, are in a much more vulnerable position today than in the past in this regard. It is true that they enjoy expanded legal rights and better information than ever before. But they have also become more dependent on the services of professional agents. They cannot even manage their own health and wealth for themselves. Agents, in the meantime, have organized themselves into powerful institutions to promote their collective benefits. When public policy choices are made through the political dynamics among such major institutions or groups, they generally have ambiguous effects on the well-being of the principals as a whole.

Third, the masses fail to organize themselves into an effective political group to counteract the predatory behaviour of the powerful coalitions. The reason for their failure is multiple. One is the low average 'ability' of the masses, which prevents them from assessing their own situation correctly and working out an effective strategy. Another is the large size and the great heterogeneity of tastes and interests of the individuals. The large size reduces the prospective rate of return on political activities (see e.g. Riker 1963 and Olson 1982). The heterogeneity makes it difficult to agree on any concerted action. Becker (1983) argues, in the usual Chicago style, that each person has an equal ability to form a coalition of his liking, and that the competition among coalitions tends to remove the inefficiencies of rent-seeking activities. This argument is difficult to swallow. The fact is that some 90 per cent of the population in any society is an unorganizable mass of individuals, and that they consequently remain prey to the other 10 per cent of smarter and more aggressive members of society. But for this large and inane mass of individuals, political activities would surely be far less profitable, and therefore far less popular, than they are.

To sum up, a political economy is an economy in which actively rational individuals engage in political activities. Political activities in this context include not only formal political campaigns and lobbies aimed at changing rules and regulations in the activists' favour, but also more covert types of 'deviant' activities to evade unfavourable rules and regulations. Political activities use up real resources; as a result, the performance of a political economy is categorically poorer than that of a neoclassical economy in which people are only passively rational. But a neoclassical economy is so unnatural, in the light of basic human nature, that it is irrelevant even as a reference model. Given that actively rational individuals are rent-seekers, and that today's economies are run by professional agents, the political elements are significant determinants of the performance of a national economy.

This political-economic approach has the following implications for macroeconomic management. The conventional welfare maximization as a guide for policy choice must be rejected as naive and impractical. Given the diversity of the population and the self-interest of the policy-makers, the notion of welfare maximization is obscure and unverifiable at best and open to abuse at worst. Any policy can be justified as welfare-enhancing, as is always done; any policy has some redistributive effects. Giving policy-makers too much room for choice not only does not lead to a better social choice, but also encourages their self-serving activities.

Second, it is not advisable to give too much power to a single group, whether it be a group of politicians, bureaucrats, businessmen, or labourers, because the group in power would be certain to use such power to enrich themselves. It is imperative for a civil society to keep the variety of groups in mutual check and balance and to match the power with social responsibilities. For example, one of the universal problems in advanced economies is that the business sector has so much political-economic power and yet assumes no responsibilities for the economic ills of its own making.

Third, each society must strive to create and maintain a political climate conducive to lesser conflict and better co-operation among the various groups. In some countries the intergroup conflicts are so intense that their economic ills are endemic. The Polish economy is an example of one in which a large part of the people's energies is consumed in political struggles, leaving little for productive economic activities. The economy of Brazil, which was once regarded by many as the future giant of the world because of its enormous potential, has also suffered from perennial political instability. Here, one notes the generally poor political climate among developing economies. These economies typically live off the proceeds from the sale of one or two traditional raw materials, while relying almost totally on imports for industrial as well as consumer goods. The political climate in such mono-culture economies tends to be unstable for two reasons. First, these economies become specific role-players in a large economic bloc and lack the degree of integrity necessary for national economic autonomy. They cannot even choose their own destiny. The resulting frustration finds its outlet in often violent nationalistic movements. Second, mono-culture economies do not rely on domestic consumption for livelihood. Domestic consumption is not only unimportant for domestic producers, but is even considered an evil. In such circumstances, the consuming masses have no value to the capitalists except as a source of cheap labour. As a result, the relation between capital and labour becomes strained, leading to a polarization of politics. A significant part of the so-called development problem lies in these political difficulties, which economic theory has largely ignored.

4 THE WORKING OF A POLITICAL ECONOMY: AN ILLUSTRATION

Consider an economy consisting of two groups of individuals. Group 1 owns a given total amount $\bar{X}$ of resource X which may be used for either economic or 'political' activities. Similarly, group 2 owns an amount $\bar{Y}$ of resource Y which can be allocated from the same two types of activities. The model assumes that 'X-inefficiencies' arise from the diverting of economic resources for political activities. The goal of political activities is to increase one's relative share of society's total economic output.

Let the amounts of the two resources allocated for economic activities be (x_e, y_e), and let $E(x_e, y_e)$ be the total output of society. Here the relation between the two factors is one of collaboration. As for political activities, let $P_1(x_p, y_p)$ be the fraction of the total output accruing to group 1 and $P_2(x_p, y_p) \equiv 1 - P_1$ be the similar share for group 2, where (x_p, y_p) denote the political inputs of the resources. P_1 is assumed to be increasing in x_p but decreasing in y_p. In the political arena the relation between the two factors is one of competition. Next, each group's utility is assumed to depend on its own share of the output ($U_1 = P_1 E$ and $U_2 = P_2 E$), and the economic welfare of society is assumed to be the sum of the group utilities: $W = U_1 + U_2 = E$. Finally, P_1 and E functions take the following specific forms for ease of illustration:

$$P_1 = \frac{x_p^a}{x_p^a + y_p^a}, \quad 0 < a \leqslant 1 \tag{1}$$

$$E = b x_e^c y_e^{1-c}, \quad 0 < b, 0 < c < 1. \tag{2}$$

Both functions are concave in their two arguments.[2]

Now let group 1 choose an allocation of its resource $\bar{X}$ between x_p and x_e for a given allocation of group 2's resource so as to maximize U_1. The result is group 1's reaction function of the form

$$y_p^a = \frac{bc x_p^{1+a}}{a\bar{X} - (bc + a)x_p}. \tag{3}$$

A similar operation for group 2 yields its reaction function:

$$x_p^a = \frac{b(1-c)y_p^{1+a}}{a\bar{Y} - \{b(1-c) + a\}y_p}. \tag{4}$$

The intersection of these two equations determines the non-cooperative game solution known as the Nash or Cournot solution.

---

[2] The function P_1 becomes meaningless when $x_p = y_p = 0$. This difficulty can be averted by putting underpads beneath these variables. Assume this is done. Formulating political games as zero-sum games seems to be popular among political scientists; see e.g. Riker (1963).

In Figure 2.1, the reaction functions of group 1 and group 2 are labelled R_1 and R_2, respectively, and the Cournot solution is shown by point C. The curve I_cI_c is both the output isoquant and the social indifference curve associated with the Cournot solution.

This Cournot solution has a few important features. First, it is the only 'stable' equilibrium in the present non-cooperative game, in the sense that the sequence of alternate moves by the two groups, each according to its reaction function, moves the system towards it. The Pareto-efficient equilibrium is clearly at point O but is unstable in the same sense. Second, a worsening of the economic environment (a decline in the parameter b) shifts the Cournot point closer to O' by inducing both groups to shift their resources away from economic activities and into politics, the consequence of which is an aggrava-tion of the economic sufferings of society. Conversely, an improved economic environment tends to reduce political conflicts and enhance society's economic welfare. In this sense, a political economy has an inherent element of instability. Third, an increase in the value of parameter a also shifts the Cournot point towards O'. This parameter may be interpreted as the 'political climate' of society; its increase means an increased confrontation between the two groups and a greater diversion of resources for political activities.

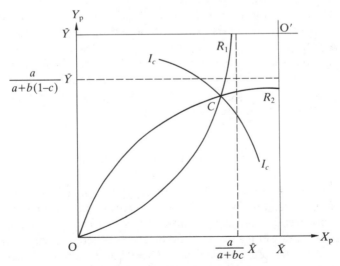

Fig. 2.1   Political equilibrium.

Of particular importance are the effects of economic policies on such a parameter. Because every conceivable economic policy has some differential effects on the economic welfare of different (groups of) citizens, and because the citizens in politicized economies are accustomed to assessing each policy mainly in terms of its *relative* benefits to them, even a well-meaning effort on the part of the government to increase a reasonable index of the nation's economic welfare such as GNP can have undesirable side-effects on the political climate. Let E be the level of the national economic welfare and G be the government's effort level (of a given policy mix) aimed at enhancing E. The non-cooperative solution in the above illustration may be written symbolically as $E\{G, a(G)\}$, where $a(G)$ measures the effect of G on parameter a. The G that appears first measures the direct effect of G on E, which is generally positive. The second G, operating through a, measures the indirect effect of G on E, which may be positive, zero, or negative. A partisan policy may well have a negative indirect effect. A monomaniac policy, such as fighting inflation before everything else and balancing the budget at all costs, also tends to have a negative indirect effect. In cases where the indirect effect is negative and large, the economy may be trapped in a suboptimal position in which a greater effort by the government yields no result. Clearly, a change in the policy mix is called for in such a situation. But what constitutes a desirable policy mix depends on the historical, cultural, *and* economic characteristics of each national economy: some economies are youthful and have a high potential, while others are aged and stagnant; some peoples are economically more group-rational than others; in general, different economies face different constraints. The task of macroeconomics is to achieve and sustain an adequate aggregate performance for such a complex and, in some fundamental sense, deviant economy.

5   A DEMOCRATIC TRAP

The previous section has described a typical prisoners' dilemma situation in which the waste of real resources in intergroup conflicts constitutes a source of macroeconomic inefficiencies. There is another covert but important source of inefficiencies inherent in democratic societies. In such democracies many social and economic rules are determined by voting. The outcome of such voting, though clearly a reflection of people's preferences, is not necessarily conducive to economic efficiency. Consider, for example, a group of workers or students with varying innate abilities. Assume that the 'performance' of an individual, measured by output or academic achievement, depends on the individual's innate ability and effort level. Assume further that the 'utility' of an individual depends positively on the 'reward' he receives and negatively on effort exertion. Now suppose that the choice of the reward formula is up to the workers or students. The choice ranges from a share-alike rule, under which every member receives the same group average, to a competitive rule, under which each individual receives his output or achievement. One can even think of a super-competitive rule, under which high achievers receive transfers from low achievers in addition to their own rewards. But let us assume, for simplicity, that the choice is between the share-alike rule and the competitive rule. It should be intuitively obvious that each individual, talented or untalented, will exert more effort and will achieve more under the competitive rule than under the share-alike rule. But whether a voting will select the competitive rule is another matter, because a higher achievement does not necessarily imply a higher utility. There is a tendency for untalented members to prefer the share-alike rule to the competitive rule. Depending on the distribution of abilities among members, the group may opt for the share-alike rule despite its negative implications for the aggregate performance.

It is interesting to note in this context that, if the members' abilities were uniform, they would all choose the competitive rule over the share-alike rule. Herein lies the fundamental dilemma of democracy. The theory of democracy accepts the fact that different people have different tastes, different religious faiths and political beliefs—different everything except abilities; it breaks down once it admits that some individuals are inferior to others. No political theorists or leaders in North America, right-wing or left-wing, will admit this. The consequence is that all men and women are created equal in ability, at least in theory. But once this premiss is accepted, the competitive rule should be the right rule, and achievers should attribute their accomplishments entirely to their greater effort of exertion as a matter of personal choice. In short, everything the right-wing ideology stands for flows naturally out of it. Leftists' theory, in contrast, should really start with the denial of the premiss of equal abilities and make it its goal to improve the lot of the less gifted. But no left-wing leader would dare to call his supporters incompetents in need of help, because doing so would most certainly antagonize the supporters; he too must proceed on the premiss that all individuals are equally gifted. As a result, his logic becomes strained, and his policy package (especially economic policy package) tends to consist of vague statements of ideals or a collection of small complaints. This is one of the reasons why the rightists fare better in public elections than the leftists. Right-wing rules produce a large number of dissenters, however. Any political leader in power must recognize this and make an effort to motivate them. Without such efforts, a democratic ship will experience rough sailing.

6   CONCLUSION

A majority of economists today still believe that a macroeconomy is a quasi-natural system, that they can eventually discover its objective laws of motion by continued applications of the Popperian test procedure, and that managing an economy is a matter of maximizing an identifiable and agreeable aggregate welfare index subject to the laws of motion of some abstract model economy.

This chapter proposes a political-economic approach to macroeconomics. It accepts Adam Smith's definition of political economy and adapts it to fit today's complex societies. This approach holds that economic activities are human affairs; that humans are actively rational self-servers, eager to gain power in society by forming coalitions and other means; and that the actual policy decisions reached largely reflect the interest of the group in power. Because 90 per cent of the population in any society is unorganized and unorganizable, they provide a permanent source of profits for the interest groups. The masses rely on their constitutional rights and on other institutionalized welfare policies such as public education, health care, minimum wage laws, and unemployment insurance for the protection of their economic benefits. Subject to these constraints, however, the policy-makers in democratic societies continue to pursue their personal and group benefits. The essence of a political economy is conflicts. The name of the game is power.

The key to a successful operation of a macroeconomy, in contrast, is a collaboration among members of society. Economists traditionally have belittled this fundamental contradiction by appealing to the theorem of the invisible hand. From the present political-economic standpoint, however, a state of competitive equilibrium is a state of vacuum, a state of unclaimed economic rents which would be destroyed instantly by a shrewd rent-seeker. The political-economic approach accepts rent-seeking activities as normal; it regards policy-making itself as a rent-seeeking activity.[3] In such an economy, it is not useful to view these groups categorically as evils, as Olson does; nor is it realistic to believe, as Becker does, that the forces of competition will turn them into saints. The inclination to form coalitions is such an integral part of rational human beings that an important aspect of economic management is to accept these groups as they are but to strive to keep the various interest groups in relative peace. The political climate depends on many factors. Some of these factors are historical data; but others are controllable, being mostly a matter of rule-making and institutional reform. In a nutshell, the idea is (1) to synchronize group interests as much as possible (so that all benefit or suffer from a good or bad performance of the economy); (2) to properly delimit the room for discretion of those who are in power (so that their self-serving activities may be kept under control); and (3) to match power with social responsibility as closely as possible.

At any rate, the object of the political economy approach is first to better understand the policy choices made in the real world, and then to search for ways to improve policy choices in the future. The chapters that follow may be viewed as examples of applications of this approach.

[3] This is not to deny the possibility that great statesmen may appear from time to time, just as the human race has produced exceptional talents like Einstein and Segovia. But it would be wrong to model man after these exceptional members.

3

Bureaucracy

The development of the modern form of the organization of corporate groups in all fields is nothing less than identical with the development and continual spread of bureaucratic administration . . . and however much people may complain about the 'evils of bureaucracy', it would be sheer illusion to think for a moment that continuous administrative work can be carried out in any field except by means of officials working in offices. For bureaucratic administration is, other things being equal, from a formal, technical point of view, the most rational type. For the needs of mass administration today, it is completely indispensable. The choice is only that between bureaucracy and diletantism in the field of administration.

Max Weber, *The Theory of Social and Economic Organizations*, p. 337

1 INTRODUCTION

Man's ability to associate with others voluntarily and purposively not only separates him from inert objects but also generates rich social behaviour. Such human interaction has led to the emergence and growth of organizations in every aspect of our social life. Today's societies are dominated and controlled by organizations, both politically and economically. Especially powerful are those large organizations run by bureaucracies.

Every organization is formed initially by a group of individuals with a common goal in order to facilitate the attainment of that goal. In the beginning the organization is merely an agent serving the interests of the members. Such organizations come and go as the common interests of members wax and wane. And many organizations, such as private clubs, never grow out of a primitive co-op stage. Some, however, over the years, grow to such an extent that they acquire great political and economic power. Instead of humbly serving their members, they turn around to make their members serve them.

A common feature of all large and influential organizations, including governments, business corporations, labour unions, churches, universities, and the Salvation Army, is their bureaucratic structure. This develops out of the need for mass administration. The power these organizations acquire maybe nothing more than a by-product of growth. Whether or not the power is sought as a goal, size none the less becomes a source of power. Once an organization reaches a certain critical size, it begins to represent something bigger than what its founders envisioned. It begins to assume its own personality or character, built around its professed goal but formalized by its own constitution and fortified by a variety of rituals; and eventually it begins to impose its will on its members. The weight of history adds to its authority. The organization in turn provides its members with an umbrella under which the members enjoy security, prestige, and power. The leaders of large organizations today command far greater respect and power than self-made millionaires. Young talents are increasingly drawn into large organizations, thereby strengthening bureaucracies in both the public and private sectors. One notable consequence of such bureaucratization is that, whether one likes it or not, important social choices are made increasingly through the political games played by powerful bureaucracies.

In relation to the actual pace of bureaucratization in the past century or two, people's perceptions of the reality have lagged far behind. One reason is that the permeation of bureaucracies is a relatively recent phenomenon, belonging largely to this century, so far as large *economic* organizations are concerned. Even the very word 'bureaucracy' is of recent origin, having been derived from the cloth covering the desks of French government officials in the eighteenth century. Another and stronger reason for the lag is the persistence of the myth of individual capitalism which took firm root in many western societies so long ago. The fact that the modern social sciences were founded in the mid-nineteenth century, just before the process of massive bureaucratization, has contributed to the persistence of the myth. In economics, in particular, theorizing has been aimed exclusively at modelling the behaviour of Economic Man and proving the efficiency of a *laissez-faire* economy built on the classical notion of competitive individualism. Anything that is not individual has been made a suspect at best and an evil at its worst.

Of the two categories of bureaucracies, governmental and private/corporate, the latter has largely escaped attack by success-fully personifying itself. (Corporations call themselves legal *persons*.)

Governmental bureaucracy has consequently come to bear the brunt of criticism, hatred, and ridicule. Having been deprived of 'efficiency', governmental bureaucracy has had to find its *raison d'être* in a much more nebulous area of 'equity', thereby making its tasks difficult in several respects. First, whatever it does, it cannot win the unanimous support of the people; in this sense it can never succeed. Second, whatever it does, it cannot, almost by definition, be efficient, that is profitable; any activity whose efficiency can be measured in dollars or pounds will have been undertaken by the private sector. Third, pursuing the equity goal, that is providing for the economic protection of the people, inevitably expands in scope and volume with the permeation of democracy. Personal income taxes have been increasing rapidly world-wide, primarily in order to assist the less fortunate members of societies through recent economic hardships; for example, in 1985 Canada's personal sector paid $75 billion to various levels of governments in the form of direct taxes but managed to get back $60 billion of it in the form of governmental transfers. This type of activity is bound to increase the size of the budget and, in hard times, budgetary deficits.

Fourth, the *impersonal* character of the government makes it an unlikely folk hero. People in general, and those in individualistic societies in particular, take a dim view of faceless and emotionless artificial 'persons'. Knowing this, private business organizations make every effort to be personal and personable: customer services departments are staffed by agreeable personnel; the business sections of newspapers carry photographs of newly appointed executives. The same thing cannot be said of government. Governments have a major disadvantage over private businesses in that their products are 'public goods' which are inherently impersonal. A government's benevolence fails to have the same impact on the beneficiary as that by a private citizen or corporation, precisely for this reason. Of the large number of individuals who owe their survival to government assistance, few have any sense of appreciation towards that government.[1] The government must consequently fight a losing battle against business; while business is judged by success, government is judged by failure.

Today's large business organizations are as bureaucratic as governments, in the technical sense of the term. Both have the same formal hierarchical structure; both recruit their cadres from the same

---

[1] 'Signor, the *Camorra* takes ten lire a month from me, but guarantees me security. The state might take ten times ten, but would guarantee me nothing', according to a Neapolitan manufacturer. Quoted in Weber (1947: 311).

pool of university graduates on the basis of academic merit; in both institutions these cadres hold the power of decision-making subject only to a broad mandate given by their constitutions. On the surface, therefore, there is no reason to believe that one class of organization should be superior to the other. There is of course the matter of profits. Business organizations seek profits, which forces them to be efficient, and in turn implies diligence, imagination, innovation, and other virtues of a free enterprise system. Governmental organizations, in contrast, are not after profits and therefore cannot claim these virtues—or so goes the folklore of capitalism (see Arnold 1937). But in today's politicized economy, dominated by large business organizations, this myth carries little credibility, for the following reasons.

First, profits are not an accurate measure of efficiency; they come not only from genuine entrepreneurial skills and luck, but also from monopoly and other economic rents (many of which are created by governments), and even from tax avoidance and evasion. In the terminology of Buchanan *et al.* (1980), profits result as much from 'rent-seeking' as from 'profit-seeking'. Second, and more importantly, the pursuit of profits by businesses, large and small, has a tendency to produce certain undesirable consequences for the economy. Defective and unsafe products are frequent and numerous, indicating that business suffers from the same type of weakness usually attributed to governmental bureaucracy. Even more serious, from the standpoint of macroeconomic management, is the erratic pattern of business investment. Investment typically comes in waves. When it is strong, it tends to be carried out to excess. This is then followed by a period of 'correction'.

Clearly, there are certain human elements in such business behaviour that have evaded the conventional neoclassical theory. Investment not merely closes the gap between the marginal efficiency of capital and the cost of capital, but also introduces new technology and new products. Investment, in other words, has some element of 'creative destruction'. Investment decisions are influenced by more than the kind of rational calculation that economic theory preaches— something like 'animal spirits'. Investment booms, which often lead to excess capacity, can be understood only in context of such spirits, of the urge to be ahead of rivals.

In addition to the competitive spirit, some economists, notably Schumpeter, have drawn attention to the imitative tastes of entrepreneurs. As an English banker put it, in the context of the alarmingly large loans made by the major banks around the world to some proven high-risk countries, 'There's a comfort in being one of the herd. There's always a temptation to hold on too long—you don't want to bow out, in case you were wrong' (quoted in Sampson 1981: 296). One can rationalize this type of gregarious behaviour. According to Parsons's influential sociological theory, for example, individual personalities are shaped though the internalization of systems of social norms or values. Individuals are thus much more homogeneous than depicted by economists. Homogeneous individuals tend to think and act alike. Gregarious behaviour is also capable of an economic explanation. When the decision involves assessing an uncertain environment, those who are relatively incapable or poorly informed find it rational to purchase the assessment of the environment by a more capable or better informed person than themselves and act on it, or, put more simply, to copy his behaviour. In any event, such imitative behaviour produces potentially avoidable ups and downs of the economy and accompanying welfare losses.

Can a bureaucratized economy cope with this problem better than an individualistic economy? One is tempted to answer this question in the affirmative because of the highly rational structure of today's governmental and business bureaucracies. But if the behaviour of the major banks cited above is any indication, the answer is not obvious. There are indeed reasons to believe that bureaucratization may even encourage imitative patterns of behaviour. In bureaucracies, the concept of rationality as guiding principle is an objectified, 'procedural rationality'. A corporate portfolio manager is not judged by how much profit he has made but by how well he did his homework in making his decisions. Conscious of such a rule, he would devote much of his time and effort to seeking the opinion of others and watching how others behave, instead of pursuing his own beliefs. As the executive offices of business bureaucracies are filled more and more by advanced degree-holders, as in North America, there is a good chance that collective business behaviour will exhibit more rather than less gregarious behaviour.

2   THE PURE THEORY OF BUREAUCRACY

In his *Wirtschaft und Gesellschaft* (1922/*The Theory of Social and Economic Organizations*, 1947), Max Weber (1864–1920), one of the last great and versatile social scientists, presents a pure theory of bureaucracy. Weber's approach to the social sciences is essentially historical. He denies the applicability of the methodological canons of the natural sciences to social–cultural problems. But at the same time, he insists that general theoretical categories are as essential to the proof of causal relationships in the human and cultural field as they are in the natural sciences. To him, all empirical knowledge is in the nature of the case abstract; and although scientific conceptualization never fully exhausts reality, it is indispensable to a deep understanding of social events. More specifically, Weber's theoretical framework centres on his 'rational ideal types'. Accordingly, in the following discussion, the term 'bureaucracy' should be interpreted in this sense.

Any large organization requires certain degrees of 'imperative co-ordination'; that is, commands from a given source within the organization must be obeyed by its members. The effectiveness of a system of imperative co-ordination depends on the willingness of the organization's members to obey the commands, which in turn depends on the legitimacy of the authority assumed by the commander. 'Legitimate authority', according to Weber, is based on three principal grounds:

1 rational—resting on a belief in the legitimacy of patterns of normative rules and the right of those elevated to authority under such rules to issue commands ('legal authority');
2 traditional—resting on an established belief in the sanctity of immemorial traditions and the legitimacy of the status of those exercising authority under them ('traditional authority').
3 charismatic—resting on devotion to the specific and exceptional sanctity, heroism, or exemplary character of an individual person and of the normative patterns or order revealed or ordained by him ('charismatic authority').

Legal authority is not only the most advanced type of legitimate authority, but also the most relevant to modern bureaucracy.

The effectiveness of legal authority, Weber continues, rests on the acceptance by members of an organization of the validity of the following mutually interdependent ideas.

1 Any legal norm or rule may be established on grounds of expediency or rational values or both, with a claim to obedience at least on the part of members of the corporate group.
2 Every body of law consists essentially of a consistent system of

abstract rules, and administration of law is held to consist of the application of these rules to particular cases.

3 The typical person in authority occupies an 'office'. In the action associated with his status, including the commands he issues to others, he is subject to an impersonal order to which his actions are oriented.

4 The person who obeys authority does so only in his capacity as a 'member' of the corporate group, and what he obeys is only 'the law'.

5 Members of the corporate group owe this obedience not to the person in authority as an individual, but to the impersonal order. Therefore an obligation to obedience exists only within the sphere of rationally delimited authority.

Weber goes on to enumerate the fundamental features of 'rational legal authority' as follows.

1 There is a continuous organization of official functions bound by rules.

2 There is a specified sphere of competence by such devices as a systematic division of labour, the provision of the incumbent with the necessary authority to carry out his specified functions, clearly defined means of compulsion, and definite conditions under which the means of compulsion may be put to use.

3 The organization of offices follows the principle of hierarchy.

4 The rules regulating the conduct of an office tend to be technical, and their rational application requires specialized training. As a result, the administrative staff of a rational corporate group typically consists of 'officials' with proper qualifications.

5 As a matter of principle, members of the administrative staff should be completely separated from ownership of the means of production or administration.

6 Administrative acts, decisions, and rules are formulated and recorded in writing.

7 Legal authority is exercised by a bureaucratic administrative staff.

Finally, the individual officials in the bureaucratic administrative staff function according to the following criteria.

1 They are personally free and are subject to authority only with respect to their impersonal official obligations.

2 They are organized in a clearly defined hierarchy of offices.

3 Each office has a clearly defined sphere of competence in the legal sense.
4 The office is filled by a free contractual relationship.
5 Candidates are selected on the basis of technical qualifications. In the most rational case, their qualification would be tested by examination or guaranteed by diplomas certifying technical training, or both. They are appointed, not elected.
6 They are remunerated by fixed salaries in money, for the most part with a right to pensions.
7 The office is treated as the sole, or at least the primary, occupation of the incumbent.
8 The office constitutes a career. There is a system of 'promotion' according to seniority or achievement, or both. Promotion is dependent on the judgement of superiors.
9 The official works entirely separated from ownership of the means of administration and without the appropriation of his position.
10 He is subject to strict and systematic discipline and control in the conduct of his office.

As for the elected members who normally head governmental bureaucracies, Weber regards them as officials only in a formal sense; ministers and presidents are essentially 'amateurs'.

This essentially exhausts what Weber says about the ideal type of bureaucracy. Today's bureaucrats in both public and private sectors indeed function according to the criteria listed above. In other words, society has achieved the most rational form of bureaucracy, which, by virtue of its knowledge and skills, is capable of efficient mass administration. Weber should be congratulated for correctly predicting the historical pattern of bureaucratic developments. More remarkable, however, is the gap between the apparently ideal bureaucracies that exist and the widely held negative image of them, especially of governmental bureaucracy.

In my opinion, three major factors that Weber overlooks contribute to this gap. First, the fact that modern business corporations are themselves bureaucracies has been largely ignored, in favour of the afore-mentioned myth of indvidual capitalism. According to the myth, the basic impetus of economic progress is the free will of individuals, and the individuals include legal persons set up for business purposes. This personification has absolved business from the 'evils' of bureaucracy. Weber notes that 'the capitalist entrepreneur is, in our society, the only type who has been able to maintain at least relative immunity from subjection to the control of rational bureaucratic knowledge (Weber 1947: 339). This is simply not true any more. While it is still possible to find examples of successful small business operators (such as the Lebanese immigrant family, movingly described by George Gilder (1981), who have turned their small savings into a prosperous grocery store in Boston), it would be anachronistic to expect these small independent operators to shoulder the future of our economy.

Second, Weber overlooks the extensive political intervention into governmental bureaucracy. In Weber's view, politicians are basically amateurs and therefore are expected to be mere figureheads in the hierarchy of governmental organizations. What ideas they may have must be evaluated scientifically and translated into concrete policy formulas by professional bureaucrats. Because the bureaucrats are recruited and promoted on the basis of knowledge and skill (and independently of their political tenets), they can maintain job security and neutrality from possible political interference. This neutrality in turn enables them to supply the effective task of check, counsel, and planning. But reality has never been so simple. Politicians have learned an easy and effective method of breaking the seemingly solid bureaucratic system. They have increasingly taken over the power of appointing senior officials in the hierarchy, by picking those civil servants whose political tenets agree with theirs and by drafting their favourite lawyers, businessmen, and other talents from outside the bureaucracy. Once personnel matters are in the hands of the politicians, the bureaucrats' job security and neutrality are virtually lost. Moreover, in countries where the majority of the highest administrative positions are occupied by casual outsiders, as in North America, the prospect of devoting one's life to public service cannot be very exciting, except for those individuals who intend to use their bureaucratic career as a stepping-stone to a political one. Such political intervention makes the recruitment of civil servants more difficult; it also lowers the morale of civil servants, resulting in a lower quality of bureaucrats.

Last but not the least, Weber fails to bring out fully the nature of rationality in bureaucratic organizations. He naively equates rationality with efficiency. True, modern bureaucracy is undoubtedly more efficient in broad historical comparison with those organizations functioning under patrimony and nepotism. Trevelyan describes the English bureaucracy in the early nineteenth century thus:

During the first half of the [nineteenth] century, the permanent Civil Service had been jobbed. The offices at Whitehall had been the happy hunting-ground of Taper and Tadpole. Whig and Tory Ministers looked on all such patronage as the recognised means of keeping political supporters in good humour. The public services were filled with the nominees of peers and commoners who had votes in Parliament or weight in the constituencies. Since the privileged families were specially anxious to provide maintenance at the public expense for those of their members who were least likely to make their own way in life, the reputation of Whitehall for laziness and incompetence was proverbial. Heavy swells with long whiskers lounged in late and left early. It was only possible to carry on administration with any degree of efficiency by supplying the departments with able chiefs brought in from outside. (Trevelyan 1937: 356–7)

The issue, however, is not whether today' bureaucracy is better than older forms, but whether the rationality of today's bureaucracy is conducive to effective mass administration. To answer this question, one must study the meaning of rationality in the bureaucratic environment. Readers may feel that, because rationality has long been a central concept in economics, it needs no explanation. That is not the case, however. First, the concept of rationality in economics is strictly personal in character. Second, rationality is judged by the results of an action, and not by the procedure of decision-making. Third, although this concept of individual rationality has been applied to groups of individuals in the theory of teams and coalitions and has led to the concept of 'group rationality', this latter concept is still based ultimately on the individual rationality of the members. Similarly, even when economics deals explicitly with large groups such as business firms, governments, and nations, it customarily treats them as individuals. Such an individualistic concept of rationality is not applicable to organizations. An organization is not merely a place in which the individual members pursue their own goals: it is a unit with an explicit goal of its own. How its members perform is assessed not by the individuals themselves, as implied in economic theory, but by the other members. The rationality of an individual's behaviour must now be objectified; he must rationalize his action to others by reference to the rules, precedents, data, and the opinions of outside experts. Only those actions that can be so rationalized may be called rational.

But the new rationality is no longer goal-oriented: it is a *procedural rationality*. It is synonymous with accountability. Here the term 'procedural rationality' is related to that of Simon (1978), but is more socially oriented. Simon uses the term to describe the scientific content of the individual's decision-making process. The use of a computer algorithm, for example, augments man's limited ability to solve economic problems. His bounded rationality becomes less bounded. In this sense, the use of a computer is part of procedural rationality. Simon's concept, however, is still a strictly personal concept. In contrast, this chapter emphasizes the social character of rationality in a bureaucratic environment in which decision-making is a multi-stage process. Each individual involved in it knows this. Furthermore, each has a specific person to whom he answers. The role of the person in the middle of this multi-stage process is to critically examine the work and opinion that have come up from below, to improve upon them with his own knowledge, skill, and experience, and to pass them on to his supervisor. He is specifically aware of two things: first, his personal opinion as a middle-man is not going to be final; second, he is judged by his superiors by the objective quality of his work. For him, Simon's procedural rationality is of course important. But his perception of the problem and incentive to work are controlled by his *accountability* to his supervisor. His attention to procedural details is motivated not by a desire to reap the benefits of a good decision for himself, as in Simon's theory, but by a desire to do a good job *in the eyes of his supervisor*. The difference is subtle but fundamental. In bureaucracies, everyone is a role player within a limited sphere. A multi-stage setup for decision-making does more to narrow the sphere of the individuals involved than to improve the quality of the final decision to be reached. It can even induce them to act irresponsibly. This is one important reason why the apparently rational bureaucracies regularly exhibit less than satisfactory performances.

This objectification of rationality, and the consequent change in the nature of the concept of rationality, appears to hold the key to the udnerstanding of the different patterns of behaviour of individuals both in isolation and in organizations. Objectified rationality differs from subjective rationality, and the former tends to dominate the latter in a social setting. In the case of a small organization, the conflict between individuals fortunately disappears with time as each member learns more about the others, and the house rules, if any, will be minimal in the long run. But in larger organizations the rules are many and complex, and the need for a rationalization of one's behaviour does not diminish with the passage of time. It is often said that the key to success in bureaucracy lies not so much in how innovative one is as in how well one avoids violating the code of rational conduct. Governmental bureaucracies are blamed for putting too much stress on procedural rationality. Excessive attention to such rationality does tend to create more formalities and slow down work; this tendency is undeniable. But to argue that the sacrosanct profit goal prevents business organizations from slipping into these problems is an overstatement. True, the profit motive sometimes forces businesses to make choices with little regard for administrative procedures. But these are exceptions; even in emergency cases, decisions are usually made by a team of executive officers in full recognition of seniority and jurisdictions. Moreover, faced with emergencies, governmental officials behave in a similar manner.

When both governmental and private business bureaucracies act according to the principle of procedural rationality, the mythical contrast between the public and private sectors largely disappears and certain basic similarities become pronounced. In terms of the type of recruits they draft, their hierarchical structure, and incentive mechanisms, the two bureaucracies are very similar indeed. It is absurd to believe that the performance of one is far superior to that of the other. Yet such a belief has permeated our society. Thus, society (and most notably our mass media) unquestioningly puts the entire blame for all economic ills on the government, while treating business as the innocent victim. In this context it is useful to remember that, as a rule, the governmental departments in charge of specific industries are the spokesmen of the interests of the industries they represent. It is impossible therefore that the government would keep messing up the good work of business, as is generally believed.

A major problem in our economic management is the lack of a sensible allocation of responsibilities between the two bureaucracies. By 'sensible allocation of responsibilities' is meant an allocation that reflects the economic powers of the two. As things stand, the allocation of responsibilities is extremely uneven. Roughly speaking, business and government sectors share the production of goods and services, employment, and the public's savings in a ratio of 3 to 1, whereas the responsibilities of national economic management are placed entirely in the government. In Canada, as in many other countries, there is not a single conceivable circumstance in which one could blame business for its incompetence. Thanks to the myth of individual capitalism, business has largely escaped the public responsibilities of economic management. Taking advantage of the commercial code and company laws written for Lilliputians, business firms, Gullivers included, have acted as a collection of independent profit- and rent-seekers and predators of the public purse, while saving big speeches about their social responsibilities for friendly chamber of commerce gatherings. This leaves all the important tasks of economic management to the governmental bureaucracy, the foremost of which is to map the future industrial structure and carry out the requisite co-ordination for it. Clearly, without the full co-operation of the business world, this would be too heavy a task for even the most competent bureaucracy imaginable. The end result of this uneven allocation of responsibilities is a massive expansion of the governmental bureaucracy and rising costs of running it, without commensurate achievements. It is an irony that in the meantime businesses have had remarkable success in reducing their tax obligations. If corporate taxes in Canada had kept pace with personal income taxes since the 1950s, current government spending would not be in deficit.

3   HOW TO MAKE THE MOST OF THE TWO BUREAUCRACIES

Given the existence of the two dominant bureaucracies and the code of procedurally rational conduct governing the behaviour of people in these bureaucracies, an important key to the successful economic management of a nation must be the effective combining of resources of the two bureaucracies to improve the nation's economic lot. The question is how to accomplish an optimal degree of co-operation between them.

In my opinion there are two major issues to be considered. One is the question of a sensible allocation of responsibilities between the two bureaucracies; the other is the question of running the bureaucratic machines efficiently, namely, of managing the bureaucrats themselves. These two issues are examined below.

Of the two, the allocation of responsibilities is the more urgent. In many countries, and notably in North America, the existing allocation is almost one-sidedly in favour of the governmental bureaucracy; in these countries the civil services are burdened with responsibilities far in excess of their capabilities. Quite predictably, the result is a mushrooming of rules and regulations lacking coherence and effectiveness. The frustrated public keeps urging the government to do more, and the government responds to the pressure by increasing the size of its bureaucracy. Politicians, sensing the public's discontent, try to get things done quickly by bypassing the bureaucracy altogether; but being amateurs themselves, most of their 'ideas' fail to be implemented into effective policies. New ideas make frequent headlines, but commensurate efforts at their implementation are typically absent. In Canada, even the most important and controversial policies such as a new tax are often announced by politicians at their idea level, are then tried out on the public on a tentative basis, and are withdrawn if they prove unpopular. It is extremely difficult to expect policies lacking the conviction of the framers themselves to earn the public's support. All in all, government bureaucrats are overburdened with responsibilities and tasks and at the same time are underused in their capacities to act as counsellors and planners.

Business bureaucracies, in the meantime, have chosen the lucrative and carefree position of being private 'persons' engaging in continuously lobbying the government. Lobbying is a well-established means of communication from the ruled to the rulers in democratic societies. These societies have as many lobbying groups and organizations as there are justifiable causes. I do not intend to denounce the lobbying activities of business categorically as acts of greed and rent-seeking. I do, however, object to their *manner* of lobbying. The difference between businesses and other lobbying organizations such as an anti-poverty group lies in the resources they command. Collectively, business monopolizes the production and distribution of goods, and its financial branch is the custodian of the savings of the public. Moreover, the largest firms today are larger than many of the small *nations* in the world in their scale of economic activity. Yet, despite their immense economic power, business firms, large and small, adopt an individualistic strategy in lobbying the government. The government thus faces numerous individual lobbies which are industry-specific, area-specific, and in many cases firm-specific. And most unfortunately, these lobbies are *ad hoc*, and civil servants do not possess the knowledge or authority to be able to deal properly with them. Experience shows that random individualistic lobbying is the best strategy by which to prey on the public purse. For society, however, this is a major moral problem. Governments today, in effect, run a free, no-fault insurance against business casualties in various guises: tax laws allow extensive carry-overs and carry-backs of losses in addition to the many special tax credits and deferrals for business investment and R & D expenditures; unemployment insurance and other welfare programmes support the workers whom business releases as it sees fit; central banks stand by to grant emergency loans for major casualties.

The availability of such an insurance affects business behaviour in a generally negative way. It tends to reduce the precautionary effort exerted on the part of the insured by favouring, in effect, high-risk activities over carefully thought-out, sound activities. That the major US banks have lent over twice their capital to the proven high-risk countries can be understood only in the light of a belief that the US government stands behind the huge risks involved. As is generally the case with all types of insurance, the basic problem here is one of asymmetric information. The insurer cannot assess the effort levels or competence of the insured; conseqeuntly he is forced to treat all casualties as victims of unfavourable circumstances and to award indemnities accordingly. But from the macroeconomic standpoint, if an economy does poorly it is because the nation's business sector is not doing its job well relative to its foreign rivals. And there can be no shifting of this responsibility to other groups in society. Consequently, I find it outrageous that business, after its decade-long dismal performance, points its finger at government and labour for *their* incompetence, when the real incompetence originates in business.

Today this tragi-comedy is proceeding at full steam. Conservative governments all over the world are eager to squeeze a little more money from the already hard-hit masses, all in the name of rebuilding the economy. Personal and sales taxes are up, social services are down, and corporate taxes are on the verge of extinction. Consumers are asked to pay for the incompetence of business. While it is perfectly reasonable to argue that everyone should sacrifice a little in hard times, the worst part of such 'restraint' policies is that they lack fairness and that they have not got to the root of the problem, which is to make business accountable for its own incompetence and thereby to make it act responsibly. In a resource-based economy such as Canada's, the conflict between capital and labour tends to intensify in hard times. Squeezing the household sector depresses consumption and savings. But to the hewers of trees and the diggers of ores, a reduction in domestic spending is of little concern; moreover, an easy access to the world capital market protects these actors from the rising cost of capital that results from reduced domestic savings. It is not a mere coincidence that the conflict in Canada is most overt in the two western provinces that are most heavily dependent on natural resources.

One practical way to ensure that big business behaves responsibly is to force it to centralize its lobbying activities by establishing a central lobbying organ of its own, with firms across industries as members. This organ would be responsible for appraising and co-ordinating the individual lobbying appeals. It would be forced to develop a broader and longer-term outlook over the nation's industrial structure and the pattern of its future developments. Needless to say, the same task could be carried out by government, as is done in many Western countries; but the significant merit of this proposal lies in its ability to place responsibilities where they belong and to enforce the plans with minimum political interference.

The other issue of importance is to upgrade the quality of governmental bureaucracies. Once the anti-government prejudice is removed, and once the overburdening that is caused by the cloth of business is corrected, we can expect a substantial improvement in the performance of governmental bureaucracies. But there remains the problem of managing bureaucratic personnel. Like any group of employees, governmental civil servants must be carefully selected and trained, and given proper incentive schemes for maximum results. From this standpoint, the actual management of governmental bureaucracies appears to suffer from a number of common flaws. I limit my observation to three major ones. The first is the generally poor image of the civil service. In North America in particular, the prospect of devoting one's life to the civil service does not rank high in the minds of talented young people. Second, the casual manner in which outsiders slide into the executive offices in governmental bureaucracies probably does more harm than good. Drafting the best talents in the nation for public service without having regard for their occupations sounds good, to be sure. But when the negative effects of this practice, such as a lack of commitment and consistency of the chosen talents, and a demoralization of the long-term workers, are taken into consideration, the net merit of such a practice is highly questionable. Such talents are often chosen on the basis of academic degrees, and as a result advanced degree-holders abound in the civil service. And many of them come in at middle and upper management positions. Implicit in this practice is the assumption that a PhD makes a better public administrator than a BA. Given that a good sense of balance is more important than a narrowly defined skill in public administration, this assumption is suspect. Moreover, given the pattern of self-selection on the part of the PhD's, the very professional skill of those who offer their services is questionable.

Third, North American governments are run on the assumption that bureaucrats are not capable of policy planning. When a policy issue of any significance arises, politicians link up with 'outside experts' and launch a big ad-balloon of ideas, completely neglecting the bureaucratic machine. This practice, I infer, comes from the belief that better qualified public policy advisers exist outside the governmental bureaucracy than within. I find this kibitzer-is-better-than-the-player hypothesis amusing. It is like saying that businessmen are not best suited for running businesses, or that teachers know less about education than others. While it is true that professionals are usually rather poor judges of themselves, it does not follow that they should be replaced by amateurs. Even if a kibitzer may sometimes come up with a better idea than the player, he cannot take the player's place. Even if an academic economist it capable of offering a brilliant idea once in a while, he cannot replace the bureaucracy. The basic problem with the kibitzer-first strategy is, once again, the question of responsibility and commitment. A kibitzer, by definition, is not responsible for the consequence of his advice and therefore cannot be expected to have the degree of commitment commensurate with the importance of the policy proposal involved.

The same thing can be said of politicians using public offices for their personal goals. In a wealthy country like Canada, there is a more than a fair share of such self-serving politicians and experts. Some of the recent prime ministers were not what one might call 'organization men'; they were not good at, or even interested in, the effective utilization of the bureaucratic machine.[2] When self-serving politicians and outside experts team up to form policy ideas, they have the

[2] According to Walter Gordon (1977), Liberal finance minister of the early 1960s, Diefenbaker basically 'was a one-man show. He had no ability to delegate. His government gave the impression of being disorganized' (p. 77); Pearson, 'with all his fine qualities, had little sense of organization and no ability to delegate responsibility. He much preferred to do everything himself . . .' (p. 132). Trudeau was, of course, an even greater one-man show in comparison with his immediate predecessors.

spotlight. But the hard and thankless task of translating the ideas into concrete policy formulas and overseeing their efficient execution remains to be done by others. This is pure public administration, a job that properly belongs to the governmental bureaucracy. But, having been left out of the planning stages, bureaucrats find it hard to carry out their task with dedication, let alone enthusiasm. The governmental bureaucracies in many countries are both overburdened and underutilized: overburdened because business dodges the responsibilities that properly belong to it, and underutilized because most of the more exciting part of policy planning is taken away from them. The result is a large, expensive, and demoralized group of public administrators. No one cares about making better use of the bureaucratic machine. The poor image of governmental bureaucracies in turn discourages the inflow of talent, contributing to the perpetuation of a vicious circle. And society pays dearly for the consequences of such lacklustre work.

The Canadian governmental system is made especially convenient for enterprising amateurs. A case in point is its budgetary rules. In Canada the federal budget (and provincial budgets, for that matter) consist of nothing more than rough estimates of spending plans and revenues. It has some informational value, but no legal power. Although the budget is allocated among the various departments, no one is legally bound by it. It is an honour system. And it is a system that is open to abuses by self-servers.

The recent case of a former Liberal transport minister reveals the vulnerability of Canada's budgetary rules. Between 1 April and early September of 1984, the minister managed to outspend his ministerial office's *annual* budget by $900,000. He more than doubled the size of his personal staff, hired expensive outside experts and advisers, spent a large sum of moey advertising *his* policy, and granted contracts to firms of his choice, in complete disregard of the advice of his department. This sort of thing could not have happened if the budget had been law, as in France, West Germany, and Japan. There, his conduct would have been an obvious breach of trust and possibly would have constituted an embezzlement.

The US system is different from both of these. Spending plans are put forward in the form of appropriation bills which specify the upper limits of spending for specific purposes. Upon sanction by Congress, they go to the President who, as a rule, has the final say. Apart from the fact that individual bills are drafted without regard to the total picture, and that the President is therefore given an enormous power over budgetary matters, the US system is, in the end, much the same as those of France, West Germany, and Japan: once authorized, a budget is a law, and no one can ignore it. It also has the merit of forcing the drafters to be more professional and scientific, thereby reducing room for politicians' vagaries.

In Canada, cost-overruns in public works of two to three times the initial estimates are common. In the case of the 1976 Montreal Olympics, the final cost was *eleven* times the initial estimate. Questionable financial deals involving crown corporations are also routine. The annual cost of such waste to the Canadian taxpayers is easily in billions of dollars. Given the loose budgetary rules and the cost-plus remuneration formula used extensively in public contracts, these abuses of the public purse are inevitable. Related to this problem is the unduly great power given to the ministerial offices. Some observers say that one of the chief functions of these offices is to insulate the ministers from bureaucratic interferences. Another related source of problems in Canada is the country's lenient rules over the conflict of interest of public office holders. The tough US rules prohibit ministers and high officials from dealing privately with their former departments for the rest of their lives, and a violator can face a fine up to $10,000 and a two-year imprisonment. In Canada, in contrast, the only restriction is a mere two-year 'cooling-off period'. Judging from the recurring cases of violation of conflict-of-interest rules, one must conclude that the Canadian honour system is not working well.

Douglas Hartle, a noted Canadian scholar in government, argues that a significant factor causing the persistent growth in government expenditures is the nature of the expenditure process itself; he proposes an improved procedure towards 'less reliance on dubious long-term expenditure projections, more ministerial involvement, less bureaucratic arbitrariness, greater sensitivity to emerging situations, a more informed ranking of competing proposals by ministers, and less likelihood that commitments will be made which preclude superior alternatives or force the government to raise additional revenues' (Hartle 1978: 45). I want to make two comments on Hartle's proposal. First, on world standards, ministers in North American governments already have more power than their counterparts elsewhere. Consider, for example, the following description of the British government:

The day-to-day reality is that officials are often responsible for the actions of their minister. He arrives, for perhaps two years, in a department of which he may well know nothing. Facing him is a permanent secretary, the senior civil servant of his department, who may have spent 20 years there and who embodies departmental experience that goes back years beyond that. His officials know his predecessors' views or, if power has changed hands, what his party policy is, and it is their duty to execute his policy. But the minister has no personal staff, chosen by himself, to provide a fresh perspective, a *cabinet* as French ministers do. His staff come from the department—and will have to make their way in it long after he has departed. It is civil servants who brief ministers on the problems, on the facts of life. It is no huge step from that to telling him what departmental policy is; there is seldom a true distinction between what is technical and what is political. (*The Economist*, 12–18 November 1983: 76)

Second, Hartle's argument reveals his deep sense of distrust of bureaucrats and a matching trust of their political leaders. The issue, however, is not whether ministers *could* make wise choices on public issues, but whether they have the incentive to do so. On the problem of checking the growth of the bureaucracy in particular, a minister who best succeeds in solving this problem will be the most unpopular minister among bureaucrats. The price he pays for his success is the loss of support from his department and possible damage to his political career.

Fnally, I shall comment on the quality of governmental bureaucrats as individuals. Although I have so far taken a sympathetic attitude towards them, and although I honestly believe that they deserve more sympathy, an improvement in the quality of individual members of governmental bureaucracies remains an important social concern. It is evident that, unless bureaucrats are competent enough to win (if they see fit to do so) rational debates with lobbyists and other citizens who come into contact with them a majority of the time, they cannot govern people effectively. In fields where workers' performances are not measurable in money or other quantitative terms, as in public administration, they must be rated on some quality measures. These qualities may be a combination of professional skills, soundness of judgements, devotion, leadership, and a host of other criteria. While difficult to quantify individually, the aggregates of such qualities are relatively easy for colleagues to assess for purposes of comparison. The absolute level of thee qualities, which is what determines the standard of group performances, depends ultimately on the individuals' intelligence and self-esteem. To ensure a high calibre of governmental bureaucrat, society has little choice but to recruit from the very top levels of the younger generation.

In other words, the ideal civil servants are the intellectual élites of society. Most countries adopt systematic method of selecting such élites. Some have one or two universities which historically have served as training centres for civil servants; many use official examinations. The specific selection methods chosen are not as important as the reputation of civil service jobs among the young. If government bureaucracy suffers from a poor image, a conscious effort must be made to change the image. In Canada, where strong provincialism prevails and élitism is a taboo, the task of upgrading the federal civil service seems especially difficult.

Government bureaucrats do not have systematic training institutions comparable to business schools for business bureaucrats. One idea that holds high promise and could overcome this barrier in Canada might be to establish a federally managed national training centre for future high officials, to be occupied by ten top secondary school leavers from (and nominated by) each province with full financial support. The centre could run a special programme towards a BA degree in public administration within an existing university; upon graduation, the students would be listed and hired by the governmental departments. At $10,000 per student per year, such a scheme would cost the federal government a meagre $4 million annually, and the effect would be visible within 15–20 years.

4   ARE INTELLECTUALS GOOD SOCIAL LEADERS?

Large bureaucratic organizations tend to be ineffective in times of change because they are slow to adapt. This has to be one of the chief reasons for the poor performances of many advanced economies since the early 1970s. Both governmental and business bureaucracies today are run by the generation who spent their formative years in the 1950s and 1960s. These were the decades that witnessed one of the most remarkable economic successes in history. World output and trade grew rapidly, with relatively stable prices, and the world escaped a major economic setback. Understandably, it has been very difficult for bureaucrats brought up in such an optimistic atmosphere to come to terms with the hard realities of the 1970s–1980s. They floundered through the seventies, and only in the mid-eighties did the two types of bureaucracies begin to regroup themselves.

When the bureaucracies do not perform, frustration increases and people tend to look to élite individuals for leadership. This tendency, although perfectly understandable, is politically dangerous because society can become too heavily dependent on the chosen individuals, and because the leadership qualities of such élite persons are in doubt. My emphasis here is on the second point. I have already expressed my concern about the idea of letting a kibitzer take over the entire game. Academics and journalists fall into the category of kibitzers so far as economic policy matters are concerned. Needless to say, opinion-leaders can include practitioners such as senior civil servants and corporate executives, but only as individuals.

As an example of the kind of leadership a group of prominent individuals in a society can provide in times of need, let us take a brief look at the performance of the National Economic League of the United States during the 1930s. The evidence presented below is based on Arnold (1937, ch. IV) and Angly (1931). The League was formed in Boston in order to 'create, through its National Council, an informed and disinterested leadership for public opinon'. The National Council was made up of 'men who are nominated as the best informed and most public spirited citizens of the country . . . elected separately from each state by preferential ballot'. The Executive Council of the League for the year 1931, for example, was made up of the following individuals: Charles G. Dawes, former vice-president of the United States; John Hays Hammond, mining engineer; David Starr Jordan, chancellor emeritus, Leland Stanford Jr University; James Rowland Angell, president, Yale University; George W. Wickersham, former attorney-general of the United States; Frank O. Lowden, former governor of Illinois; A. Lawrence Lowell, president, Harvard University; Edward A. Filene, merchant; Nicholas Murray Butler, president, Williams College; and Silas H. Strawn, lawyer. The Yale economist Irving Fisher joined the Council later.

The National Economic League published the results of preferential voting of its members on the 'paramount problems of the United States' annually, and this information reveals much about the nature of leadership of such prominent individuals. Arnold tabulates the results for the years 1930, 1931, 1932, 1934, and 1937. Table 3.1 is a summary of his tables. Although rather concise, it reveals a number of

Table 3.1 Paramount Problems of the United States

Rank order	1930		1931		1932		1934		1937	
1	Admin. of justice	(8.7)*	Prohibition	(8.4)	Economy and efficiency of govt.	(9.3)	Efficiency and economy of govt.	(7.6)	Labour	(9.0)
2	Prohibition	(8.1)	Admin. of justice	(7.8)	Taxation	(6.6)	Recovery measures	(6.6)	Efficiency and economy of govt.	(8.6)
3	Lawlessness	(6.7)	Lawlessness	(6.8)	Reparations	(6.4)	Organized crime	(6.2)	Taxation	(7.1)
4	Crime	(6.4)	Unemployment, economic stabilization	(6.4)	Banking, credit	(6.1)	Taxation, (equalization, reduction)	(6.1)	Fed. constitution	(6.2)
5	Law enforcement	(6.2)	Law enforcement	(6.2)	Arms reduction	(4.6)	Monetary policy	(4.7)	Crime	(5.8)
6	World peace	(4.8)	Crime	(5.9)	Tariffs	(4.5)	Public opinion	(4.0)	Public opinion	(4.9)
7	Agriculture, farm relief	(3.9)	World Court	(4.9)	Restoration of confidence	(4.5)	World peace	(3.9)	Fed. budget	(4.6)
8	Taxation	(3.4)	Taxation	(4.3)	Admin. of justice	(4.3)	Tariff	(3.8)	Monetary policy	(4.2)
9	World Court	(3.4)	World peace	(3.9)	Internat. tariff conference	(3.9)	Veterans' benefits	(3.7)	Democracy	(4.2)
10	Arms reduction	(3.2)	Efficient democratic govt.	(3.2)	Unemployment	(3.4)	Labour	(3.7)	Industry	(3.7)

Total no. of votes cast on top 30 problems

	1930	1931	1932	1934	1937
	25,273	22,256	23,944	15,407	10,610

*The numbers in parentheses are the votes given to individual items as a percentage of the total votes given to the top 30 problems.

Source: Arnold (1937, ch. IV)

peculiarities. First, in the crucial period of 1930 and 1931, economic problems fail to figure prominently, whereas they dominate the scene in and after 1932. Second, the manner in which economic problems were perceived was odd, to put it mildly. 'Unemployment', for example, was ranked fourth in 1931 but only tenth in 1932 and fourteenth in 1934, in the depth of the depression; and while unemployment was recognized as a problem in 1931, such related problems as 'housing', 'health', 'old age pension', and 'relation between capital and labor' were among the items that received the fewest votes in both 1930 and 1931; 'unemployment insurance' was not even mentioned; similarly, 'speculation in stock market' was at the bottom of the list. In 1932, when economic problems rose to the top, the 'economy and efficiency of government' led all other economic problems by a considerable margin, and it continued its domination throughout the period under study.[3] Third, the survey shows little sign of perception of the imminent danger of war. Although 'world peace' and related topics were recognized as a problem in each year, their popularity shows no sign of increasing; indeed, as nationalism rose with the deepening of the depression, romantic ideas like world peace tended to be overshadowed by more urgent domestic problems. Fourth, the very enthusiasm of the members of the National Economic League appears to have tapered off rather quickly, as indicated by the rapid decline in the total number of votes cast on the top 30 problems.

These traits are not peculiar to the particular survey under study, but reflect the basic mental process of intellectuals in general, which may be summarized as follows.

1   Intellectuals despise fortune-telling and speculation for their lack of scientific foundations. For them, problems do not exist until they have appeared. As a result, their advice tends to come too late.
2   Intellectuals prefer abstractions to concrete facts. As a result, their advice lacks detail and consistency and is not readily implementable into concrete policy.
3   Intellectuals' minds are sensitive to new stimuli but at the same

---

[3] In 1937 'labor' took a slight lead. What 'labor' meant was not the welfare of workers but the problems of labour unrest and the need for the tighter control of the unions. In this sense, it was in the same conservative package as the economy of governments.

time are easily bored by repetitions. As a result, their opinion lacks the persistence needed to influence policy decisions.
4 Intellectuals nevertheless keep believing that they have more influence on real-world politics than they actually have. So they remain earnest kibitzers.

Half a century later, the world economy was again in deep depression and 'economy and efficiency of government' was once more the supreme order of conservative politics. And again, most intellectuals approved of this. I wonder whether they understood the fact that the aim of a 'restraint' policy is, purely and simply, to protect business at the expense of labour, as it was fifty years earlier.

But what about our vastly improved data availability and computer facilities, which should have rendered the job of economic forecasting incomparably simpler today than in the 1930s? As Angly brings out so effectively, a major trouble with the 1930s was that the policy-makers failed to anticipate the great depression in time. One would like to think that such a problem could no longer exist. But the fact is that we continue to suffer from the same forecasting problem. Economic forecasting is a big business in North America (and elsewhere), and the forecasters sell their predictions to business and governments for a handsome price. But these forecasts have more often been wrong than right. Bethlehem Steel incurred $768 million operating losses in 1982/3 partly on the investments they made on the strength of a boom in 1981 that was predicted by a forecaster. AMAX, a major metal mining concern, lost $879 m in the same period by heeding forecasts of continued inflation. These are but the tip of the iceberg. Forecasts have generally proved to be wrong, which prompted Feldstein, former chairman of the US President's Council of Economic Advisers, to remark that 'one of the great mistakes of the past few years of economic policy has been an excessive belief in the ability to forecast'.[4]

That economic forecasting has proved to be a 'lemon' poses an interesting economic question: why does such a product keep selling, especially when the sellers refuse to offer guarantees and other insurance policies to go with the product? The answer must lie in the code of rational conduct in bureaucracies discussed earlier. To a

[4] This quote and the preceding episodes were reported in *Time*, 27 August 1984: 47–9 under the title 'The Forecasters Flunk'. For a summary and comparison of the track record of the major forecasting organizations in the USA since 1971, see McNees and Ries (1983).

decision-maker in a bureaucracy, a purchased forecast provides a 'fact', an objective piece of alibi. When he buys a forecast, he is buying the fact of the alibi, and not the quality of it. A decision based on facts is more readily 'rationalizable' than one based on a professional hunch, and this is what counts in bureaucracy. If readers will allow me to venture a forecast about the future of the forecasting industry, I am quite confident that it will continue to prosper, although the quality of its products will remain poor. I am not pleased at this prospect, however. It is deplorable that more and more executive officers of both governmental and business bureaucracies are seeking such an easy and irresponsible mode of decision-making. The old maxim 'caveat emptor' is definitely true in this case.

5 SUMMARY

Governmental and business bureaucracies dominate today's societies. They have developed as the rational solution to meet the need for mass administration and production. They are organizations of professionals, and as such are irreplaceable. Given that the economic performance of national economies depends crucially on the performance of the two bureaucracies, it is important to understand how bureaucracies work and how their performance can be improved. This chapter has stressed the principle of objectified rationality as a guide for bureaucratic behaviour. This pattern of behaviour is rational by any scientific standards, but it has the danger of causing inefficiencies and irresponsibilities in decision-making.

As for potential improvements in the performance of the two bureaucracies, the chapter has emphasized the importance of restoring a sensible balance between the powers and responsibilities of each type. Finally, doubts have been cast about the popular belief that a group of prominent individuals can be effective opinion-leaders for policy-making in today's complex societies.

4

The Central Bank

Monetary policy is made by human beings, often not very 'expert' ones,
in human situations and as part of a complex, operating government.

G. L. Bach, *Federal Reserve Policy-Making*, p. viii

1 INTRODUCTION

Many people believe that the central bank is a powerful authority
governing the monetary affairs of a nation, an institution that
possesses full autonomy and matching technical capabilities. It is,
indeed, an independent public institution, and the level of sophistica-
tion it employs in its monetary control is beyond the comprehension
of lay persons. Why then does the central bank keep baffling the
public with wildly fluctuating interest rates and intimidating
inflation? Are these technical errors? It is possible but unlikely. There
must exist some deeper reasons for its dismal performance which
abstract models of the central bank of our time have overlooked.

In order that we may better understand this (relatively) young
institution and its obscure performance, this chapter will attempt to
bring out an image, or model, of the central bank that emerges from
its history. The approach taken here is as old-fashioned as its theme.
It puts together some basic facts about central banks. While I claim
no originality, I hope that these forgotten facts have a relevance today
and even contain some important lessons.

Money occupies a special status in the world of economic goods. It
is a good created by man to facilitate his social activities called
'exchange'. As such, money is free from the physical constraints of
ordinary commodities: any material can serve as money. The damage
from its oversupply does not fall on its suppliers, as in the case of
ordinary commodities. These facts imply the existence of a huge
potential rent, known as 'seigniorage', accruing to its supplier. Ever
since the first money came into being, people have been aware of the
existence of these seigniorage gains and have endeavoured to pocket

them, small people in small ways and big ones in big ways. But none have seized such gains better than the modern states. Nations first monopolized the coinage business and then proceeded to replace gold and silver with paper money. As this traditional source of seigniorage gains disappeared in the first half of this century, states resorted to another but similar technique of debasement called 'inflation', and the central bank has played a key role in this organized scheme. Many, over the years, have expressed doubts about man's ability to manage money properly. This chapter, unfortunately, tends to support such pressimism.

At any rate, the model of the central bank that emerges from this historical study is very different from the one that academics have popularized. Rather than being an independent and powerful authority in the bureaucracy, the central bank is only a second-rate citizen, struggling to fulfil its sublime duties in the face of overpowering political pressures and technical difficulties. Although popular theory maintains that discretion is the essence of central banking and that working to rule is its antithesis, one could argue with equal force that the central bank is part of the bureaucracy and that discretion is the antithesis of bureaucracy. It is extremely difficult to believe that the discretionary power of the central bank has, on the whole, been used wisely in the past.

This chapter is organized as follows. Section 2 gives a brief survey of the history of the Bank of England, which I shall use as a generic model of central banks. Section 3 reviews certain conceptual issues concerning central banking as they arose in the course of the history of the Bank of England. Section 4 turns to an examination of the current legal and political factors determining the relationship between the central bank and its government. Because this is an extremely important subject in political economy, the section is merely an introduction. The final section collects some of my own thoughts on the subject of central banking.

2 A BRIEF HISTORY OF THE BANK OF ENGLAND

The Bank of England was founded in 1694 during a war with France. To conduct the war, the government of William III borrowed £1 milion in 1693 and another £1 million in 1694 from the public. The

Million Loan of 1693 was the origin of the English national debt, while the Million Lottery Loan of 1694 was the first English state lottery organized by an Act of Parliament. Because more money was urgently required, the government decided to float another loan of £1.5 million. One can appreciate the magnitude of these loans from the fact that the total tax revenue in 1694 was only a little over £4 million. The situation was critical, but the alternative conventional source of money—borrowing from the goldsmiths—could not be relied upon; because goldsmiths had been victims of their misplaced confidence in the Stuart government on previous occasions, their reluctance to lend to the government is understandable.[1] The money market was tight at the time and the goldsmiths were applying exorbitant terms to their clients, causing some distressed merchants to call for the formation of a banking institution that, by virtue of its size and public character, would be able to offer them greater security and more reasonable terms than the goldsmiths.

The time was ripe. Several schemes for such a bank were proposed, but in the end, one designed by a William Paterson prevailed. Paterson correctly estimated that the chance of his bank's receiving parliamentary sanction would be greatly enhanced if it provided a sizeable loan to the government. Consequently, he proposed that subscription should be invited for a sum of £1.2 million on the condition that the subscribers were to be formed into a corporation called the Governor and Company of the Bank of England and that the £1.2 million forming the capital of the Bank, would be lent permanently to the government, for which the Bank would receive an annuity of £100,000 (£96,000 as interest at 8 per cent and £4000 as commission). This proposal was accepted by Parliament and became a law on 25 April 1694 (the Tunnage Act of 1694). The Act gave the Bank the right to issue notes to the amount of its capital on the supposition that the annuity would be sufficient to support the credit of the notes.

The new scheme was gratifying to all the parties concerned, except

---

[1] In 1640 Charles I seized £130,000 worth of the reserve coin and bullion deposited by the goldsmiths in the London Tower, which was repaid only after violent protest and long delay. Charles II, the Merry Monarch, turned to the goldsmiths for advances using anticipated taxes as security, but the amount of advances soon outran his borrowing capacity, and in 1672 he stopped the payment of £1.3 million. The money, though lent to the government by the goldsmiths, belonged to some 10,000 depositors, and its loss spread ruin throughout London. This money was never repaid but was eventually merged into the national debt.

the goldsmiths and Tory MPs. The government got the money it needed. The Bank obtained the privilege of using its capital twice. (Besides earning the 8 per cent interest from the government, it could discount commercial bills to the amount of its capital.) The merchants enjoyed greater security and more reasonable terms on their borrowings from the Bank.[2]

Two features of the new scheme are especially noteworthy from an historical standpoint. First, the scheme was a clear violation of the currency principle prevalent in those days of metallic standard. The capital of the Bank was gone when it was lent to the government; accordingly, all the notes the Bank was allowed to issue were issued against the government debt, an early example of fiduciary note issue. Second, it marked the beginning of the long honeymoon between the Bank and the government. The Bank's charter originally had a time limit, and the Bank had to purchase renewals by aiding the government. In return, the Bank would be authorized to increase its capital and, as a result, its profits.

A quick synopsis of such deals follows. In 1694, as noted, the Bank lent £1,200,000 to the government. In 1697 the government extended the Bank's charter from 1705 to 1710. The Bank increased its capital by £1,001,171, four-fifths of which it directed to the purchase of Exchequer tallies at 8 per cent. In 1709 the charter was extended to 1732. To obtain an extension, the Bank lent the government another £400,000 without interest. The bank doubled its capital to £4,402,343 and purchased £2,500,000 of Exchequer bills at 3 per cent. In 1713 the charter was renewed to 1742. This time the Bank lent the government £100,000 at 3 per cent and purchased £1,200,000 worth of Exchequer bills at 3 per cent. In 1742 the government extended the charter to 1764 in return for an interest-free loan of £1,600,000 from the Bank. And the Bank increased its capital to £9,800,000. The Act of 1742 also established the Bank's right of 'exclusive banking', which lasted until 1826. The bigger the favour, the higher the bribe had to be. A few years later, the Bank cancelled £986,000 of Exchequer bills in exchange for a 4 per cent annuity and reduced the interest on £8,486,000 of the government debt to 3 per cent. As of 1742, the government's cumulative debt to the Bank stood at £10,700,000. In 1764 the government extended the Bank's charter to 1812 and the Bank accordingly provided the government with an absolute gift of

---

[2] If these notes were counted as money, the money supply increased by £1.2 million.

£110,000 and a loan of £1,000,000 on Exchequer bills at 3 per cent. The 1799 renewal extended the charter to 1833. To get the extension this time, the Bank lent the government another £3,000,000 without interest.[3]

The Napoleonic wars marred this sweet relationship. William Pitt, who became prime minister in 1784 at the age of 25, strained it by abusing the convenient machinery, though for understandable reasons. Confronted with the huge and repeated demands for advances as well as loans, the Bank sought to put a lid on advances to the government by having Parliament set a statutory limit to the amount of advances. Pitt took care to omit any clause of limitation from the bill and became armed with the unbounded power of drawing upon the Bank. The following passages indicate the strain the Bank was put under.

So early as the 11th December, 1794, the directors foresaw the ensuing pressure, and made presentations to Mr. Pitt. In January 1795, it became necessary to adopt a firmer attitude; and, on the 15th, they passed a resolution that, a foreign loan of six millions and a home one of eighteen millions being about to be raised, the Chancellor of the Exchequer must be requested to make his financial arrangement for the year without requiring further assistance from them; and more particularly, that they could not allow the advances on Treasury bills at any one time to exceed £500,000. Mr. Pitt promised to reduce them to that amount by payments out of the first loan. He, however, paid little regard to these remonstrances; and, on the 16th April, they were compelled to remind him that he had not kept his promise. . . . Mr. Pitt pretended that he had forgotten the circumstance in the multiplicity of business, and promised that the sum should be immediately paid. Nevertheless, no reduction took place in the amount; another remonstrance was equally ineffectual, and on the 30th July, the directors informed him that they intended . . . to give orders to their cashiers to refuse payment of all bills, when the amount exceeded £500,000. Mr. Pitt was not prepared to comply with this request, and on the 6th August he applied to them for another advance of two million and a half; but they refused to take his letter into consideration until he had made satisfactory arrangement with them for the repayment of the other advances. After some further communications, he persuaded them to agree to the loan for £2,000,000. (MacLeod 1971: 105–6)

Mr. Pitt had never fulfilled his promise so often repeated to the directors that

---

[3] There appears to have been no such favour done by the Bank on the occasion of the 1826 renewal. But one must remember that this Act deprived the Bank of its monopoly power.

the advances on Treasury bills should be reduced to £500,000; on the 14th June (1796) they were as much as £1,232,649. At the end of July he sent an earnest request to have £800,000 more at once, and a similar sum in August. They were induced to consent to the first, but refused the second advance. Mr. Pitt said that the first advance without the second would be of no use to him, and begged them to reconsider their decision. The directors, thus pressed, were driven to assent to it, but they accompanied it with a most serious and solemn remonstrance, which they desired should be laid before the Cabinet. . . . However, in November, Mr. Pitt made a fresh demand on them for £2,750,000 on the security of the land and malt taxes of 1797, which was granted on the condition that the advances on Treasury bills amounting to £1,613,345 were paid out of it. Mr. Pitt took the money, but never paid off the bills. (MacLeod 1971: 108–9)

These loans were used to provide subsidies to England's allies and to pay the expenses of British troops abroad. Subsidies to foreign governments alone amounted to £701,475 in 1793, £2,641,053 in 1794, and £6,253,140 in 1795. The outflows of specie were far greater, reaching £2,715,232 in 1793, £8,335,592 in 1794, and £11,040,236 in 1795. These huge outflows, combined with the unprecedented increase in Treasury bills, created pressures the Bank could hardly bear. In February 1797 a run on the country banks, precipitated by fears of a French invasion, occurred. These banks in turn withdrew a large amount of gold from the Bank of England. The Bank consequently had to ask the Prime Minister for assistance. As a result, Parliament passed the Bank Restriction Act of 1797 forbidding the Bank to make any payments in specie except to the army and navy, or by order of the privy council. This restriction applied until 1821.[4]

To scholars of monetary theory, the first 44 years of the nineteenth century constitute the most exciting period of their studies. First, the famous report of the Billion Committee came out in 1810. The Bank Restriction Act had created an inflationary tendency in the British economy; Bank notes had fallen to a discount compared with gold, and exchanges had turned against England. This tendency was aggravated in 1809 when the restriction on trade and the scarcity of commodities arising from the war caused a speculative mania which the Bank accommodated by rapidly increasing the note issue. Enquiring into the connection between the increase of the note issue on the one hand and the high price of gold and the exchange

---

[4] The Bank was ready to resume cash payments in as early as 1814, but the government did not permit it.

depreciation on the other, the Bullion Committee proclaimed that the excessive note issue arising from the suspension of cash payments caused the high price of bullion and currency depreciation, and that the only remedy was a return to cash payments. Although unsuccessful in gaining the immediate support of either the government, the Bank of England, or the parliamentary majority, the report induced the resumption of cash payments in 1821 and laid the foundation for the 1844 Bank Charter Act.

Second, the propriety of the Bank of England's monopoly became a public issue. The framers of the various Bank Acts had always favoured the Bank's monopoly, as evidenced by the Acts of 1697 and 1709. These Acts, however, had only provided that *Parliament* would not create or permit the creation of any other banks: they did not prohibit private joint stock companies from setting up in the banking business. The Act of 1742 sealed this hole in the legislation, giving the Bank of England an absolute monopoly by declaring that:

it is the true intent and meaning of the act that no other bank shall be erected, established or allowed by Parliament; and that it shall not be lawful for anybody politic or corporate whatsoever, united or to be united, in covenants or partnership exceeding the number of six persons, in that part of Great Britain called England to borrow, owe, or take up any sum or sums of money, on their bills or notes payable at demand, or at any less time than six months from the borrowing thereof, during the continuance of such said privilege of the said Governor and Company . . . (Act Statute 1742, c. 13, s. 5)

As noted, this monopoly lasted until 1826. The stability of the Bank's monopoly throughout this 132-year period should not be interpreted to mean that it enjoyed unanimous support from the public. Passionate defenders and foes existed from the start. The vulnerability of the Bank's monopoly to government abuse is evident from history. Based on the greater demand for banking services arising from the expansion of trade and the unsatisfactory condition of banking in the provinces, another and more positive argument for a freer banking system circulated. The Act of 1742 restricted the right of note issue in England to the Bank of England and to partnerships of no more than six persons, but partnerships had been generally unstable, and frequently failed. In 1822, one Thomas Joplin detected a hole in the Bank's monopoly charter and maintained that joint stock banks of deposit (as against note issue) did not infringe the charter and that such banks might render useful services especially in the provinces.[5] The commercial crisis of 1825 added fuel to the free banking movement. As a result, the Act of 1826 legalized the establishment of joint stock banks with an unlimited number of partners and the right of note issue anywhere outside a radius of 65 miles from London. It also empowered the Bank to establish branches. For a time after the passing of this Act, some doubt remained as to the legality of the establishment within 65 miles of London of joint stock banks with more than six persons but without the right of note issue. The Act of 1833 removed all doubt on this point: it made Bank of England notes legal tender and at the same time declared the establishment of such banks legal.

In the meantime, Joplin's 1822 pamphlet initiated a prolonged and heated public debate on the rationale of central banking. People drawn into the debate were divided into two schools of thought, one supporting central banking with a monopoly of note issue, and the other advocating free banking in which a multiplicity of private banks would be permitted to issue notes subject to the condition of convertibility. The two schools overlapped much with the famous Currency School and Banking School in both philosophy and membership, although notable exceptions existed. The debate covered both historical and theoretical issues concerning the stability of money and credit as well as bank management. The free banking movement was short-lived, for the 1844 Bank Charter Act reconfirmed the status of the Bank of England's central bank.

The Bank Charter Act of 1844 was undoubtedly the most significant legislation in British monetary history. By this Act, the Bank of England became England's central bank in the modern sense of the term (as against a 'Whig finance company'), and it served as a model for the many others to follow. The two most important features of the Act are as follows. First, the Act gave the Bank of England the exclusive right of note issue. (To be precise, those banks that had possessed and exercised this right before 1844 retained it; but should any of these banks relinquish the right, either by ceasing to exist or by merging with other banks within 65 miles of London, the Bank would then have the right of issuing notes against securities to the amount of two-thirds of such lapsed issues.) The Bank's note issue was guided by the currency principle or the gold standard. The Act set a maximum on the amount of fiduciary note issue at £14 million plus two-thirds of

---

[5] The Bank of England had been prohibited from establishing branches.

lapsed issues mentioned above, and required the Bank to hold 100 per cent of gold against the notes issued over and above that amount. It also required the Bank to buy all gold offered to it at the fixed price of £3.17s.9d. and to sell all gold demanded at the fixed price of £3.17s.10½d. The government justified the maximum fiduciary issue of £14 million as an amount that was never likely to be presented for cash payment. It seems more plausible, however, to say that this amount was set to accommodate the existing government debt to the Bank of over $11 million and a little breathing space.

Second, in recognition of its public character, the Act required the Bank to publish its weekly accounts. The Bank was divided into two departments, Issue and Banking. The accounts of the Issue Department showed the amounts of gold and securities held to support the maximum note issue. Conversely, the accounts of the Banking Department were similar to those of ordinary banks, showing on the liability side the deposits of the government and other clients and the Bank's net worth, and on the asset side the governmental and other securities and 'reserves' consisting of reserve notes and coins. (The idea of publishing these accounts was an eminently sensible one; but it was this very publication, revealing the dwindling reserves in the Banking Department, that triggered the crisis of 1847.)

The Act was in full effect until 1914. During this 70-year period Bank note circulation increased at an average rate of less than 1 per cent per annum. The average annual rate of growth of the economy, as measured by the index of industrial production, stood at about 2.5 per cent. As a result, the general price level fell at an average annual rate of 1 per cent.

The Bank Charter Act of 1844 and its record during this 70-year period have long been regarded as the high point of the English monetary history. But how well the new rule actually worked is a moot point. The framers of the Act were confident that the iron-clad rule of the money supply would leave no room for monetary crises because the Bank could not accommodate and foster the speculative manias that usually preceded such crises. Such confidence proved to be totally unwarranted. Three times in the early history of the Act (1847, 1857, and 1866) the Bank stood helplessly by as massive bank and business failures occurred. By suspending the very Act that made the Bank of England Britain's central bank, the government rescued the Bank. On each occasion a great drain of gold occurred, and the reserve of the Banking Department became nearly empty. However, the Bank was unable to issue any more notes because of the rigidity of the Act. As Bagehot (1873: 29) put it, 'In fact, in none of these years could the Banking Department of the Bank of England have survived if the law had not been broken.' As the rigidity of the new rule became evident from experience, an 'elastic currency' became the target for the next monetary reform.

When the war broke out in 1914, although no formal suspension of the 1844 Act took place, two things occurred which altered the nature of the English monetary system. First, both merchandise trade and capital flows were severely hampered, and the cost of shipping gold soared. Second, the government enacted the Currency and Bank Notes Act, which provided for the issue of £1 and £10 notes by the Treasury. These currency notes were legal tender and, although convertible into gold in theory, they were virtually fiduciary. With the Hume mechanism hampered, the conventional Bank rate policy ceased to function. Britain was no longer on an effective gold standard. The fiduciary note issue, which stood at £19,978,000 in 1914 (including the currency notes), rose to a peak of £323,652,000 in 1919 and remained as high as £240,527,000 in 1925. In 1929, when the currency notes were absorbed into Bank notes, the total note issue reached £362,300,000. Gold inflows were also significant. The value of bullion in the Issue Department in 1914 was £45,900,000, but rose to £146,900,000 in 1929. Nevertheless, as far as the spirit of the 1844 Act was concerned, the monetary system had changed dramatically. With the exception of the brief period of 1925–31, the gold standard was abandoned and has never seen the light of day again.

The departure from gold meant a switch in monetary policy from rule to discretion. New techniques, such as open market policy and bank reserve policy, were added to the simple Bank rate policy of the prewar years. These new instruments were aimed at increasing the power of the Bank in its discretionary monetary control. But one major difference between the prewar and postwar environment prevailed. The British economy no longer had the strength and leadership it had enjoyed before the war. The Bank rate policy of the prewar years was simple, for two reasons. First, the British economy in those years had a good command of the world market so that production and employment did not have to rely much on domestic demand, and this reduced the need for a stabilization policy to a minimum. Second, while a gold standard would force a homogeneous action on the part of participating central banks, the strongest central bank had a unique and decisive advantage over others in that, whenever a local or domestic trouble arose, the Bank could use its Bank rate to meet local needs, and at the same time could force others to conform to it, irrespective of *their* domestic needs.

However, both of these advantages were lost after the war. The growth rate of the British economy slowed down significantly, and cycles became pronounced. Also, Bank rate policy became constrained by conditions in the New York market. As if unaware of these changes, the Bank reinstated its Bank rate policy and employed it with the confidence of the power it once had. As soon as the economy pulled out of the severe postwar recession, the Bank started to prepare for a return to the gold standard. The Bank rate was raised and was kept high in an effort to re-establish and sustain the old parity price. The deflationary effect on the economy of this decade-long monetary policy was substantial. When the gold standard was finally abandoned in 1931, the British economy was in deep depression along with many others, but without the benefit of the prosperity of the 1920s. During the 1930s, the Bank rate was kept extremely low, as was the New York rate.

Because the Second World War saw a massive increase in government debt, considerations of debt service deprived Bank rate policy of all its traditional functions. The Treasury bill rate, which was pegged low by official intervention, now set the tune for short-term rates. A mass of accumulated surplus money, which initiated an orgy of inflation, characterized the immediate postwar period. The depreciation of the pound sterling in 1949 from $4.03 to $2.80 aggravated this inflationary tendency. The use of monetary policy was not possible until the rapid rise in prices had adsorbed the redundant liquidity, which was realized in 1951/2.

British monetary policy since the Second World War may best be characterized by a continual struggle to strike a balance between the maintenance of the external value of the pound on the one hand and the maintenance of adequate levels of income and employment on the other, with the former gradually giving in. The $2.80 parity proved impossible to maintain, and another depreciation to $2.40 took effect in 1967. At present the pound is worth less than $2,00. The postwar period has seen a substantial sophistication in the Bank's techniques of monetary control, aided by improvements in data collection and forecasting. Yet, ironically, the Bank seems to have lost control of the money base. Its note circulation rose from an index of 100 in 1929, to

135 in 1938, 314 in 1944, 345 in 1950, 563 in 1960, 898 in 1970, and 2820 in 1980.

3 THE RATIONALE OF CENTRAL BANKING

In reality, central banks did not occur because bankers and business men demanded them: governments created them for their own convenience. This was true of the Bank of England and is even more true of the many others that followed it. The contemporary theory of central banking, in contrast, paints a picture of the central bank as the wise and capable regulator of the nation's money and credit for the attainment of national economic goals, and in particular as the guardian of the value of the national currency. Faced with the glaring gap between theory and history, one wonders where the lofty theory came from. It is indeed difficult to locate textual evidence for such a theory outside of macroeconomic textbooks. Surveying the central bank acts of major nations, one discovers that the Australian Reserve Banks Act of 1959, s. 10(2), is the only act that prescribes the goals of monetary policy explicitly as in macrotexts. The Bank of Canada Act of 1935 comes close to doing so in its preamble but manages to keep the expression much more vague.[6] The majority of the Acts, including the Bank Charter Act of 1844 and the Bank of England Act of 1946, are, rightly and perhaps honestly, silent about the goals. The current Bank of Japan Act is an exception in the opposite direction: Article 2 of the Act stipulates tha the Bank of Japan shall be managed solely for the achievement of national aims, which has been interpreted to mean that the Bank will follow the government's direction. (The current Bank of Japan Act was enacted in 1942, during the Second World War. The Bank launched a massive campaign in the late 1950s to change these articles so as to gain autonomy and in particular to stipulate the stabilization of the value of the yen as its primary policy goal. The campaign would have succeeded but for the vehement last-minute opposition by the Ministry of Finance.) The US Federal Reserve Act of 1913 simply states the aim as the furnishing of an elastic currency. In the almost complete absence of legal authority

---

[6] Except for its peculiar emphasis on the control and protection of the *external* value of the dollar. A few other countries copy Canada's example. They are Costa Rica, Dominican Republic, El Salvador, and Guatemala.

and empirical support for the theory of modern banking,[7] one must be content with a survey of certain key theoretical issues raised in the course of the historical development of central banking. Here I begin with the free banking versus central banking debate that took palce in England during the 1820s and 1830s. The following summary of the debate relies on Smith (1936).

When Joplin opened up the debate in his 1822 pamphlet in support of free banking, he based his argument primarily on an empirical observation that the Scottish banking system, composed of multiple joint stock banks of note issue, enjoyed far greater stability and soundness than the English system, consisting of the Bank of England as monopolist and numerous small banks with no more than six partners as fringes. Encouraged by the partial victory in 1826, the free banking movement, which had its franchise in the Political Economy Club led by Thomas Tooke, gained momentum. Sir Henry Parnell, one of the chief promoters of the movement, published a pamphlet in 1827 stressing the importance of the Scottish banks' practice of regularly clearing each other's notes and paying the balance in gold. This practice, he contended, acted as an efficient check against an over-issue of bank notes. If one bank over-issued its notes, it would be required to pay a greater amount of gold in the interbank clearing sessions, and the consequent loss of gold woud force the bank to contract its note issue. In his own words, 'It is this continued demand for coin, by the banks on one another, that gives the principle of convertibility full effect and no such thing as an excess of paper or as a depreciation of its value can take place for want of a sufficiently early and active demand for gold.' Furthermore, he contended that this internal check should be more effective than the Hume–Ricardo specie-flow mechanism, which would work only *ex post*, i.e. only after actual increases in the note issue and the domestic price level.

The case against free banking was first made in 1831, by J. R. McCulloch, who argued that free banking was conducive to an over-issue of notes. Individual banks would have incentives to increase their note issues (i.e. to discount more bills) for larger profits. If some banks increased their note issue while others remained conservative, the public's demand for gold would be directed evenly to all banks, especially when exchanges turned against the country as a result of the increased volume of circulation. The result would be

[7] To be precise, there was a campaign for universal central banking for the purpose of re-establishing a gold standard immediately after the First World War.

that the banks that increased note issues would tend to benefit at the cost of conservative banks. Realizing this externality, the conservative banks would start expanding their note issues. When all banks did this, a currency inflation would ensue. Against this, the kind of internal check advocated by Parnell would be totally ineffective. Reinforcing McCulloch's argument, S. J. Lloyd stressed the unique feature of banking that, 'while all the evils arising from errors or miscalculations on the part of producers will fall on themselves [in the case of other ordinary industries], the evil consequence of any error or miscalcualtion [in banking] falls in a much greater proportion upon the public than upon the issuer'. Another prominent economist, G. W. Norman,[8] joined McCulloch and Lloyd.

In later years, these three men all became prominent members of the Currency School and adherents of Peel's Act. It was not surprising, therefore, that they opposed free banking. Finding Tooke, the leader of the Political Economy Club and the foremost representative of the Banking School, among the opposition to free banking is, however, unexpected. Tooke believed that 'free trade in banking is synonymous with free trade in swindling, . . . [banking is] a matter for regulation by the state and come within the province of police' (Tooke 1838, vol III: 206). Tooke's objection to free banking was based on an entirely different reasoning than that underlying the currency principle. He pointed to the need for close supervision, by the state, of banking firms, supervision that could be enforced with or without a central bank in the sense used in the present context. However, history has proved that Tooke's fear was fully justified. Throughout the course of modern banking, banks have been plagued by frauds and embezzlements, many of them by their own employees, and these have been a major cause of bank failures. At any rate, the debate ended in the victory of the pro-central bank camp. On purely academic grounds, the case for central banking was far from evident. Even Peel himself swang wildly between the two doctrines:

In 1826 he [Peel] was dead against the monopoly of the bank, which he declared was the root of all the evil in the banking system of England, and recognised the superiority of the Scottish system of a multiplicity of banks. In 1833 he was decidedly in favour of perpetuating the monopoly of the bank. (MacLeod 1971: 70)

---

[8] Grandfather of Montagu Norman. Einzig (1932: 12) describes him as 'representing the ultra-conservative school of thought on banking and currency'.

Although radical arguments disappeared with the passage of the Bank Charter Act of 1844, criticisms of the new scheme lingered on. MacLeod (1866, vol. 2, ch. XII) became one of the earliest and most outspoken critics. He argued that the Bank Charter Act, despite the pretence that it embodied the currency principle, was indeed a variation of (John) Lawism. The aim of the currency principle was to ensure that the quantity of notes in circulation would be exactly equal in amount to what a metallic currency would have been, and that the outflow of bullion would withdraw notes in circulation to an equal amount. According to MacLeod, the 1844 Act did not accomplish this. First, the £14 million-plus fiduciary issue was in itself a violation of the principle. Second, the Banking Department was permitted to create deposits by purchasing bills. Thus, the maximum amount of 'money' the Bank was able to supply was $2 \times £14$ million plus the value of gold, and not just the value of gold. 'To suppose that the Bank Rate does really carry it (the currency principle) out is simply one of the most astonishing delusions that ever deceived the public mind' (MacLeod 1866, vol 2: 208–9).

MacLeod ws correct in pointing out the gap between the principle and the practice. But from our historical standpoint, whether or not the 1844 Act put the currency principle literally into practice is neither a very interesting nor an important issue. The Bank of England could not have survived the crises of 1847, 1857, and 1866 had it abided by the Act, let alone by the stricter principle. Apart from these special occasions, the role of paper currency and credit in alleviating the shocks from specie flows on domestic circulation was so significant that, if domestic circulation had had to move in strict parallel with the gold stock, the consequent instability in domestic money and credit would have been unbearable.[9]

Bagehot (1873) made a more important criticism of central banking and of the 1844 Act. He too thought that 'the natural system—that which would have sprung up if government had let banking alone—is that of many banks of equal or not altogether unequal size (each keeping its own cash reserve)' But, being a man of practical sense, he did not advocate such a decentralized system, for he realized that the country had long been accustomed to the existing system built around the Bank of England. Rather, he wanted to know how best to use the existing system. In his opinion, the centralized

[9] Before 1844, the Bank as a rule maintained its metallic reserve amounting to one-third of its liabilities, according to Hawtrey (1932: 137).

system had a major weakness because the Bank of England was given the sole responsibility of maintaining adequate gold and note reserves for the whole system.[10] Bagehot argued that the actual level of the Bank's reserve was considerably less than what a collection of many banks would hold on their own discretion, and that the increased international role of the Bank called for a much larger reserve. The problem was, therefore, to ensure that the Bank kept an adequate reserve against contingencies of great magnitudes. Recognizing this, Bagehot proposed the following three remedies (1873: 71–4).

1 A clear understanding between the Bank and the public should exist. Because the Bank holds the nation's ultimate banking reserve, it should recognize and act on the obligations that this implies—that it will replenish the reserves in times of foreign demand and lend them in times of internal panic as freely and readily as plain principles of banking require.

2 The administration of the Bank should be improved. Society should diminish the 'amateur' element and augment the trained banking element to ensure more constancy in the Bank's administration.

3 These two suggestions were designed to make the Bank as strong as possible. In addition society should look at the rest of its banking system and try to reduce the demands made on the Bank as much as possible. The central machinery being inevitably frail, society should carefully and as much as possible diminish the strain upon that machinery.

Remedy 1 is significant because it recognizes the public character of the Bank, and in particular the Bank's responsibility as 'the lender of the last resort'—the term coined and popularized later by Hawtrey. The Bank was slow to assume this public responsibility. As it was a private corporation, the primary duty of its directors remained to serve the shareholders. Their concern over the safety of the corporation tended to conflict with their public duty. (The Bank's behaviour during the South Sea Bubble incident illustrates the case very well. The Bank competed fiercely with the South Sea Company for the monopoly licence of the wild eneterprise. One doubts whether

[10] Although Bank of England notes were made legal tender in 1833, the minimum denomination of Bank notes was £5, so that gold and silver coin remained the only hand-to-hand cash. Depending on the nature of the drain, th e pressure fell on either the note reserve or the coin reserve. Bagehot's concern was the latter.

the Bank would have survived to this day had it won that competition.) Furthermore, no legal prescription or public recognition that the Bank of England was the bankers' bank had existed, at least not before 1844. It would discount bills, although most of this discounting business was with merchants rather than with other banks; it was not *re*discounting. The Bank's reluctance to act as the lender of last resort became especially apparent in times of credit crunch. In the crises of 1793 and 1811, for example, the Bank's ordinary discounting facilities were inadequate, but the Bank refused to do more than it already was doing. The government saved the merchants by making advances on merchandise in the form of Treasury bills, which in turn qualified for the Bank's discounts. Even in the mid-nineteenth century, getting their bills rediscounted by the Bank remained a novelty for the London bill brokers.

In this regard, the Bank Charter Act of 1844 did not materially change the Bank's behaviour. Indeed, the Banking Department of the Bank was 'to be managed in the same way as any other private bank' (governor's statement before the Select Committee of 1848). The Bank had no more obligation to lend or discount in times of need than any other private bank. When the tension built up in the spring of 1847, the Bank maintained its conservative stance. The government stopped the crisis by breaking the law, as mentioned earlier. The crisis of 1857 was solved again at the government's initiative. In the crisis of 1866 the Bank finally realized its responsibility, taking the initiative in approaching the government for another 'crisis letter', and making a large volume of advances. Through these events, the Bank learned the importance of Bank rate policy in fulfilling its dual responsibility as holder of the nation's ultimate reserve and lender of last resort. At any rate, this proposal settled the old question of how the Bank should act in times of crisis. Bagehot believed that the Bank was unlike any other bank and that it should face the task of being the lender of last resort. He therefore approved, in principle, the Bank's action in 1847, 1857, and 1866.

Remedy 2 concerns the organizational aspect of the Bank. The Bank of England was a private corporation until 1946. Its governor and other executive officers were elected in the same way as a board of directors in an ordinary corporation. The shareholders of the Bank wanted high dividends and accordingly would apply pressure on the Bank's management. Assuming the grave responsibilities of distinctly public character seemed anomalous for such a profit-oriented corporation: first, the abilities of the executive officers as central bankers were in doubt; second, and more importantly, the pursuit of profits and the fulfilment of the public responsibilities might well collide with each other. Describing one aspect of such conflicts, Bagehot writes:

> In 1844, the dividend on the stock of the Bank of England was 7% and the price of the stock itself 212; the dividend now is 9%, and the price of the stock 232. But in the same time the shares of the London and Westminster Bank, in spite of an addition of 100% to the capital, have risen from 27 to 66, and the dividend from 6% to 20%. Some part of the lowness of the Bank dividend and of the consequent small value of Bank stock, is undoubtedly caused by the magnitude of the Bank capital; but much of it is also due to the great amount of unproductive cash—of cash which yields no interest—that the Banking Department of the Bank of England keeps lying idle. . . . The London and Westminster has only 13% of its liabilities lying idle. The Banking Department of the Bank of England has over 40%. (Bagehot 1873: 38–9)

Herein lay Bagehot's gravest concern: the inadequacy of the Bank's reserves.[11]

Remedy 3 recognizes the necessity for other banks to act prudently and co-operatively with the Bank of England. Many people feared that banks would become less prudent once a central bank existed, especially if the central bank declared its role as a lender of last resort. To keep the demand for rediscounts to a minimum, the Bank had to ensure that the private banks possessed adequate reserves of their own to provide against contingencies. Second, an efficient money market was necessary so that the demand for rediscounts would be an absolute minimum for the banking system as a whole. Third, the central bank had to exercise discretion in deciding how much of which bills to discount and at what rate. The Bank of England's reserve was increased substantially after the 1860s. With the increased reserve and the more conscious manipulation of Bank rate, the Bank of England emerged and remained as the powerful guardian of the gold standard at least until 1914. The 1920 Brussells Conference of international monetary experts passed a resolution that, 'In countries where there is no central bank, one should be established.' The

---

[11] Edgeworth (1888) participated in the debate concerning the adequacy of the reserve of the Bank of England. He argued in his article that the reserve need only increase with liabilities in proportion to the square root of the latter. His argument, based on the law of large numbers, was not applicable to the reserve in times of distress, however, because the core of the problem in such times was the high positive correlation among individual cash demands.

experts aimed at a restoration of the international monetary order based on a gold standard, and for that they regarded the universal existence of central banks as indispensable. The number of small central banks mushroomed in the interwar years, and after the Second World War.

The next major author on the subject was Hawtrey. Having identified the essence of the central bank with its role as lender of last resort, and accordingly recognized the importance of Bank rate policy, he then turned his efforts to reconstructing the theory behind the policy.

The history of Bank rate policy dates to 1833, when Parliament passed an Act exempting the rate of discount on bills of exchange maturing within three months from the usury law, which had set the ceiling on interest rates at 5 per cent. At the same time, the Bank's internal minimum of 4 per cent was removed. These changes gave the Bank rate the degree of freedom needed for policy purposes. The Bank rate recorded peaks of 9 per cent in 1847, 10 per cent in 1857 and 1866, and a low for the period 1844–1932 of 2 per cent as often as 17 times. The Bank manipulated Bank rate within these limits quite flexibly,[12] adopting the so-called Goschen rule of raising the rate by steps of 1 per cent and lowering it by steps of $\frac{1}{2}$ per cent. During all these years, Hume's and Ricardo's naïve quantity theory of money remained the foundation stone behind the policy. According to that theory, the Bank had only to manipulate Bank rate in response to the level of its reserves. Nevertheless, Bank rate policy during this period was on the whole successful, owing to the strength of the British economy. Measured by the index of industrial production, the British economy attained an average annual growth of 2.5–3 per cent with extraordinary stability during the 1844–1914 period, although the growth rate showed a visible slowdown in the latter half of the period. Moreover, the status of London as the world's financial centre reached its peak during this period, making the task of regulating gold flows through Bank rate so much easier. The British economy never regained its strength after the First World War. New York was now becoming a dominant financial centre.

Writing in the 1930s, Hawtrey had the advantage of witnessing the

[12] Hawtrey (1938, App. I) tabulates the complete history of Bank rates and gold reserves during this period. This practice was largely due to the influence of Goschen (1861), who stressed the importance of interest rates in general, and the Bank rate in particular, on exchange rates in place of the then prevalent purchasing power parity theory.

developments during the turbulent 1920s and early 1930s. The British economy was not only worn out by the war, but was damaged further by the severe postwar recession and the subsequent deflationary policy of the Bank of England. Measured by the index of industrial production, the average growth rate fell to 1 per cent in the post-1914 period. Unemployment rose sharply and cyclical fluctuations became pronounced. A high Bank rate policy drew foreign capital into the country, but it also created unemployment. Hawtrey stressed the effect of Bank rate on *domestic* economic activities. When the economy was strong, fluctuations in domestic demand did not affect the production sector much, for enough foreign demand always existed. If so, the old Ricardian theory, which put exclusive emphasis on gold flows, was valid. However, once the economy lost its competitive edge, production, and therefore income, became increasingly dependent on domestic demand. But because demand depended primarily on income, the economy became exposed to greater fluctuations. Recognizing this, Hawtrey proposed his famous inventory theory which focused on 'consumers' income and outlay' instead of the quantity theory of money. According to this theory, a rise in Bank rate tightens short-term credit, which in turn has its major impact on merchants' inventory decisions. The equality between the marginal revenue and marginal cost of holding an inventory of merchandise gives the condition for optimal inventory holding:

$$\begin{matrix} \text{Expected appreciation of} \\ \text{merchandise, or expected} \\ \text{capital gain per unit of} \\ \text{inventory} \end{matrix} = \begin{matrix} \text{Interest charge per unit} \\ \text{of inventory} \end{matrix} + \begin{matrix} \text{Marginal inventory} \\ \text{carrying cost other than} \\ \text{interest.} \end{matrix}$$

Given the left-hand side, a higher interest rate requires a lower marginal non-interest-carrying cost, which, given the convexity of the cost function, calls for a reduction in the inventory level. The excess inventory sets a deflatinary process in motion. As merchants dump their merchandise on the market, prices begin to fall. The revision in expectations in the light of falling prices induces a further contractionary adjustment in inventories. As long as the inventory level is deemed excessive, the rate of produciton will be reduced and kept low. Unemployment rises and remains high, and consumers' incomes and outlay decline.

Unfortunately, the Bank of England maintained a deflationary policy throughout the 1920s. As soon as the British economy began to show a sign of revival in 1923, the Bank raised its rate from 3 to

4 per cent and began to prepare for a return to gold. Bank rate was raised again in March 1925 to an unusual 5 per cent. In April 1925, when Britain returned to gold, the Bank had to struggle to maintain the old parity. Montagu Norman, an exceptionally influential governor in the Bank's history,[13] was the chief architect of the Bank's policy during this period. Norman believed that Bank rate policy was an effective instrument for preserving gold and thereby the convertibility of the pound. In his 1929 testimony before the Macmillan Committee (of which Keynes was a member), he defended his policy as having been forced by international circumstances, but revealed his belief that the adverse internal effects of high Bank rate were 'very greatly exaggerated . . . much more psychological than real'. In the meantime production and employment slid, with the unemployment rate rising to 22 per cent by September 1931, when Norman was finally forced to depart from the gold standard.

Hawtrey concludes:

The conclusion to be drawn is that the Bank of England ought to have been willing to *let gold go*. It ought in fact to have been willing to do so at any time since the return to the gold standard. If it could only retain its gold by a recourse to deflationary measures, and could not otherwise maintain the gold standard, then either the return to the gold standard was premature or the restoration of the former parity was a mistake. It is, I think, not unreasonable to hold that a policy of cheap money and credit relaxation from the beginning would have had a favourable effect on economic activity throughout the world in 1925, and would have made the task of retaining the Bank of England's gold quite easy. But even if that had not been so, if the credit relaxation had been found to involve a serious outflow of gold, an acquiescence in that outflow would have afforded the best prospect of maintaining the gold standard. (Hawtrey 1938: 141)

By 1929 'Sam had a slight headache', but 'John was in bed with pneumonia'.

One must next consider the views that Keynes expressed about the monetary policy of the interwar years in his *Treatise on Money*

---

[13] According to Einzig (1932: 1), 'The history of Great Britain since the war has been characterized by an unusual absence of political leadership . . . If, in spite of this, the British nation has maintained its prestige for its statesmanlike qualities, the credit is due to a man whose sphere of activity has been outside politics. This man is Mr. Montagu Collet Norman. . . . The reason why Mr. Montague Norman has succeeded in making his influence felt in the world of finance as well as in politics lies undoubtedly in the fact that his policy and his opinions have been thoroughly British.' See also Moggridge (1972).

(Keynes 1930). In Chapter 10 of the *Treatise*, he worked out what he called the 'fundamental equations' which were designed to describe the factors responsible for the determinatin of temporary equilibrium prices. Loosely put, these equations state that:

$$\text{Price level} = \text{Unit factor cost (including normal profit)} = \begin{array}{c}\text{Excess of actual over normal value} \\ \text{of aggregate demand per unit of} \\ \text{output (or, the rate of abnormal} \\ \text{profit).}\end{array}$$

Temporary equilibrium means a very short-run equilibrium in which flexible prices equilibrate relative to the existing stocks of goods and factors (including constraints arising from the existing contracts thereof) and the prevailing state of expectations. These temporary equilibrium prices then provide information for the quantity decisions over the short run. Bank rate policy was thought to have its impact on the second term of the right-hand side of the above equation. (Keynes seems to have followed Wicksell, believing that at a certain level of interest, namely the 'natural' rate of interest, abnormal profits or losses would disappear.) A rise in Bank rate, for example, would depress this term (profit deflation), and if it were sustained high enough for long enough, the deflationary effect would slowly spread into the first term (income deflation). In terms of this apparatus, Keynes assessed the period as follows.

In the course of the six months which preceded and the six months which followed Great Britain's return to the Gold Standard in May, 1925, it was necessary to raise the gold-value of sterling by about 10 percent at a time when gold itself was not depreciating in value. This means that the flow of money-income per unit of output, i.e., of rates of earnings generally had to be diminished by 10 percent. . . . In other words, there had to be an Income Deflation in the strict sense of the word . . . Whilst it is arguable that there existed at the end of 1924 a slight tendency to a mild Proft Inflation, the Deflation required for the return to gold amounted to far more than the mere counteraction of this tendency. But the authorities at the Treasury and at the Bank of England knew nothing about the difference between an Income Deflation and a Profit Deflation, with the result that they greatly over-estimated the efficacy of their weapons of credit restriction and bank rate—which had often shown themselves effective against a Profit Inflation—when applied with the object of producing out of the blue a cold-blooded Income Deflation.

By withdrawing credit from entrepreneurs, the power of the latter to give employment was curtailed; by the increased cost of credit, by the fall of wholesale prices, which ensued on the raising of the value of the sterling on the foreign exchanges, and by the reduction of purchasing power at home, profits were diminished and the incentive to production became less. Thus, in the first instance, the use of the Bank of England of its traditional weapons brought about a Profit Deflation. Prices duly fell. The Governor of the Bank of England felt himself able to inform the Chancellor of Exchequer that the task was accomplished.

Yet this was far from the truth. Equilibrium required that the flow of money-incomes and the rate of money-earnings per unit of output should be appropriately reduced. But in the first instance the fall of prices reduced not costs and rates of earnings, but profits. The entrepreneur bore the brunt, and the only means by which the Bank of England's policy could restore equilibrium was to make him smart so severely that he would pass on the pressure to the proper quarters. The entrepreneur, faced with prices falling faster than costs, had three alternatives open to him—to put up with his losses as best he could; to withdraw from his less profitable activities, and thus reduce output and employment; to embark on a struggle with his employees to reduce their money-earnings per unit of output—of which only the last was capable of restoring real equilibrium from the national point of view. In the long run, however, these alternatives might be compatible, if efficiency could be sufficiently increased, with a maintenance of money-earnings per unit of the factor of production.

The entrepreneur tried all three. To a surprising extent, and for a surprising length of time, he submitted to the first, namely the cutting down, or cutting off, of his profits. The leading industries—the old textile industries, the heavy industries working coal, iron and steel, the railways and farmers—just took losses and went on taking them, not merely for months but for years ...

It follows that the full development of unemployment was also longer postponed than might have been expected. But the entrepreneur availed himself from the outset of the second expedient as well—the expedient of curtailing his less profitable activities. Five years after the consummation of the return to gold, the curtailment of employment was still in operation in an unabated degree. (Keynes 1930, vol II: 181–3)

And, more specifically on the high interest rates,

But, looking back, I am inclined to think that the seeds of the recent collapse were already being sown so long ago as 1925. By that date the natural rate of interest, outside the United States, was probably due for a fall. But round about that date there supervened two sets of events, not wholly disconnected, which served to maintain the market rate of interest somewhat regardless of the underlying realities of the natural-rate—namely, the general return to the Gold Standard, and the settlement of Reparations and the War Debts.

For these events, though they had no bearing whatsoever on the real yield of new investment, were a powerful influence on the market-rate of interest.

Those Central Banks which had entered upon the new responsibility of maintaining gold parity, were naturally nervous and disposed to take no risks—some of them because they had just emerged from currency catastrophes attended by a total loss of credit, others (especially great Britain) because they had returned to the Gold Standard at a dangerously high parity probably inconsistent with then existing domestic equilibrium. This nervousness inevitably tended in the direction of credit restriction, which was not in the least called for by the real underlying economic facts, throughout Europe and, sympathetically, in many other quarters. Great Britain played a leading part in tightening the hold on credit and in urging a hurried all-round return back to gold. The inadequacy of free gold supplies much aggravated the position. At this stage, indeed, only the United States was entirely exempt from some measure of credit restriction.

The divergency thus arising between the market-rate of interest and the natural-rate was, therefore, the primary cause of the sagging price level. But once this had proceeded far enough to generate 'slump' psychology in the minds of entrepreneurs, it was, of course, reinforced as usual, by other, and perhaps quantitatively greater, influences. (Keynes 1930, vol. II: 379–81)

Indeed, reading '1979' for '1925', 'conquest of inflation' for 'return to the gold standard', 'oil bill' for 'reparations', 'the United States' for 'Great Britain', and 'Germany and Japan' for 'the United States', one gets a fairly accurate description of the recent state of the world economy.[14]

Sayers (1957) added another, and (thus far) final, page to the historical study of central banking. Sayers had a different background from all his predecessors mentioned in this section. Whereas Bagehot was a lifetime editor of *The Economist*, Hawtrey a civil servant with the Treasury, and Keyes, at least in the present context, more a spokesman for business than an academic, Sayers, in contrast, was a pure academic specializing in money and banking. This difference in background may explain Sayers's relative optimism about the competence of the central banker and his greater sympathy towards the monetary authorities. Sayers declared that 'the essence of central

---

[14] As of 30 November, 1981, the German and Japanese discount rates stood at 7.50% and 6.25% respectively. With these few exceptions, however, the US policy of artificially raising the market rates above the natural rate was a cause for the recent world-wide recession. As is clear from the above quotes, Keynes and Hawtrey were in agreement in their stress on the adverse internal effects of the Bank's policy during the 1920s. Had they combined forces, they might have been able to change the course of the economy. But there is evidence that the two differed in the details of the transmission mechanism and that this difference prevented them from closer collaboration (see e.g. Keynes 1936: 75–6).

banking is discretionary control of the monetary system', and that 'working to rule is the antithesis of central banking' (1957: 1). He found fault with the Bank's policy on a few specific occasions. Nevertheless,

the economic history of this century encourages the view that central bankers can be found to diagnose reasonably accurately, to act quickly, and maintain for themselves the desirable half-way house between ivory towers and the hurly-burly of the market place. And as experience in central banking accumulates, it is reasonable to expect that the inherent weaknesses (e.g., vulnerability to political pressures, danger of misjudgments) will be kept increasingly under control. (Sayers 1957: 3)[15]

Concerning the interwar years that I consider crucial, Sayers believed that the deflationary policy of a very high Bank rate coupled with credit rationing during 1919–20 was too drastic and too late in timing; and that the inflationary policy of 1929–30 was too weak and again too late to sustain prosperity (Sayers 1957: 77–8). As for the policy during the intervening years, he seems to have admitted its deflationary effect but denied the adverse internal effect of high Bank rate as such:

Depression in the export trades and the competition of imports were the powerful deflationary forces at work; it was through these conditions rather than through high interest rates that the gold-standard policy was depressing the British economy. (Sayers 1957: 79)

Before concluding this section, let us briefly review the immediate postwar period and the post-1931 period of floating exchange rates. As evidenced by the 1920 Brussels Conference and the 1922 Genoa Conference of international monetary experts, by Norman's attempt to restore the gold standard, and by the institution of the Bretton Woods system immediately after the Second World War, floating exchange rates were regarded as an anomaly, something that had to be tolerated only in times of major disturbances. The experience of floating rates during the interwar years was not a gratifying one. The wide fluctuations of exchange rates after 1914, the depreciation race following the suspension of gold by the USA in 1933, and the stagnation of world trade renewed the world's interest in the restoration of an international monetary order. Indeed, the same

---

[15] Keynes sometimes expressed a similar optimism (see e.g. Keynes 1930, vol. II: 272). But whether he held the central bankers in high regard is questionable.

feeling prevails in the 1980s, after the turbulent decade of floating rates and world-wide depression.

I have referred to the gap between the theory of central banking and its track record. A similar gap exists between the theory and performance of floating exchange rates. In both cases, theory is responsible for the gap. The theory of rational choice automatically assumes that an expansion of the choice set results in a better, wiser decision, that discretion is better than rules, and that the exchange rate flexibility leads to some additional benefit. Fact disproves the validity of such an assumption. Central banks could do better, but have not. They have often been at a loss as to how to make use of their new freedom, much like the stray individuals depicted by the existentialist philosophers. Their freedom was more a burden than a privilege. Central banks' lack of will and ability to assume their increased power was quickly exploited by governments for their increasingly nationalistic goals, as evidenced by the beggar-thy-neighbour policies of exchange controls and competitive deprecia-tions during the 1930s. A similar tendency has emerged again during the current depression. In both cases, the world was trapped in a highly unsatisfactory Nash equilibrium.

And yet the benefits of national monetary autonomy have always been, and still are, highly valued by national leaders. Academic economists have contributed significantly to the promotion of monetary nationalism. Among the few economists who expressed concern over monetary nationalism was Hayek, who in 1937 correctly foresaw the dismal global consequence of monetary nationalism, including its inflationary bias (Hayek 1964). There is indeed a very close parallel between what the collection of central banks have done at the world level for the most part of this century (and especially during the periods of floating rates) and what a collection of free banks feared to do in the nineteenth century on the domestic scene.

4 THE GOVERNMENT AND THE CENTRAL BANK

In its early history up to 1844, the government exploited the Bank of England constantly and rather heavily as its financial machine. The Bank's initial loan of £1.2 million in 1694 had grown to £11 million by 1844. In other words, the Bank monetized permanently as much as

£11 million of the government debt in this 150-year period. This was nothing compared with what has happened in the twentieth century. The fiduciary note issue rose to £20 million by 1914, to £200 million by 1929, and in the subsequent 50-year period it has grown by more than ten times. The magnitude of the effects of such massive monetization can be seen clearly in the time path of the general price level. As is evident from Figure 5.1 in the next chapter, inflation is a twentieth-century phenomenon. The two world wars are often used as a justification of inflation. This argument, however, is not very convincing. First, inflation has not been limited to war and immediate postwar years. Second, the availability of central banks definitely increased the marginal propensity of countries to engage in wars. It would hardly be an exaggeration to say that military conflicts on the scale of the two world wars would have been utterly impossible without central banks. Today, the reserve assets of most central banks to support their inflated money bases consist largely, and in many cases almost exclusively, of government securities. Why does this sort of thing keep happening? Can't the central bank do something about it? The answer, realistically speaking, must be in the negative.

First, central banks today face no absolute limits to note issue. Where such limits exist, they are set by governments. After the departure from the gold standard in the 1930s, the importance of gold in the reserve assets of central banks has been gradually and deliberately reduced throughout the world. The Glass–Steagall Act of 1932 permitted the Federal Reserve Bank of the United States to issue notes against government securities. The Bank of Japan Act of 1942 made gold and securities perfect substitutes as reserve assets once and for all. In Britain the maximum note issue has remained the amount of gold in the Bank's Issue Department plus a legally fixed fiduciary issue (the Currency and Bank Notes Act of 1954). Since the Bank's holding of gold has drastically diminished, and since the limit on fiduciary issue has been raised accommodatingly, the effect has been the same. Some other central bank Acts, including the Bank of Canada Act, determined that a minimum fraction of reserve assets must be held in gold, but this minimum was gradually adjusted downward, eventually to zero.[16] With the statutory limit for fiduciary note issue adjusting flexibility, central banks have no firm ground on

---

[16] The Bank of Canada Act, for example, had until 1967 a 25% gold requirement, although Parliament always had the power to waive it.

which to resist inflationary pressures, especially when they originate in governments.

Second, there exists another and more profound limitation to the power of central banks as monetary authorities: their statutory as well as *de facto* subordination to governments. The autonomy and the discretionary power of the central bank are sometimes limited by provisions authorizing the government to give directives to the bank (e.g. Bank of England Act 1946, s. 4(1); Bank of Canada Act 1935, s. 14), rules that permit, in certain contingencies, devolution to the government of functions and powers granted by law to the central banks (e.g. Reserve Bank of India Act 1934), and by procedures that ensure that any disagreement is to be resolved in favour of the government (e.g. Organic Law of the Bank of Mexico 1941) (see Aufricht 1965). The following example is drawn from the Bank of Canada Act.

14 (1) The Minister and the Governor shall consult regularly on monetary policy and on its relation to general economic policy.

(2) If, notwithstanding the consultations provided for in subsection (1), there should emerge a difference of opinion between the Minister and the Bank concerning the monetary policy to be followed, the Minister may, after consultation with the Governor and with the approval of the Governor in Council (i.e., the Prime Minister), give to the Governor a written directive concerning monetary policy, in specific terms and applicable for a specified period, and the Bank shall comply with the directive.

(3) A directive given under this section shall be published forthwith in the *Canada Gazette* and shall be laid before Parliament within fifteen days after the giving thereof, or, if Parliament is not then sitting, on any of the first fifteen days thereafter that Parliament is sitting.

To be sure, such directives are seldom, if ever, given. The principle, however, is clear, and the threat always exists. Indeed, a 'difference of opinion' situation has prevailed in the past few years: while the central bank wants to battle inflation or resist currency depreciation, the government is either unwilling or unable to go along with such a policy.

In some countries such as the United States, no stipulations establishing the government's supremacy exist; therefore, the central banks appear more independent than they really are. The Federal Reserve System of the United States is widely regarded as one of the strongest central banks in the world. It actually has some unique organizational features which make it a potentially more independent institution than others (see appendix to this chapter). But, even so, the System has never defied the US President's wishes. Some political economists suggest that its strength, if any, comes not from its being more independent from the government, but from the backing of powerful banking interests (see appendix 1 to Chapter 6).

Our discussion has so far proceeded on the supposition that public budget deficits are the major source of monetary expansion and hence probably of inflation. Historical records offer some evidence in support of such a supposition. The rapidly growing public budget deficits and rampant inflation in the recent past have created a great deal of concern and debate over the economics of public debt in general and the deficit–inflation nexus in particular. As usual, economists have managed to produce a wide spectrum of answers. In view of the great confusion about the public debt problem, it may be useful to briefly review the existing theories of public debt before examining the role played by the central bank in the recent years of large governmental budget deficits.

When writing about public debt, one must draw a clear distinction between internal and external debt. An external debt is a debt to foreigners; its repayment is a loss of a nation's real resources. Thus, an increase in the amount of external debt implies that the debtor nation is that much worse off, *ceteris paribus*. An internal debt, in contrast, is a debt of a government to its citizenry, and its implications are rather subtle. An increase in internal debt does not make the nation any better off or worse off in the above direct sense. Nevertheless it can, and generally does, affect the nation's resource allocation over time. Since the dominant part of government debt is internal debt, this review will confine itself to that category.

Under the maintained hypothesis of full employment of resources, the classical theory of public debt argues that whether a given public project should be tax-financed depends on the nature of the project. If it is of a consumptive nature it should be tax-financed, whereas if it is of an investment type it should be debt-financed, because the burden of the real cost of the project tends to be spread over time in the case of debt finance.[17] The idea behind this theory is the pay-as-you-use principle. Abba Lerner (1944, ch. 24), the most eloquent spokesman of the Keynesian theory, regarded the attainment of full employment

[17] Ricardo (1817, ch. 17) is often interpreted as having denied the difference between tax finance and debt finance. He did indeed state an 'equivalence theorem', but quickly downplayed its practical relevance.

as the sole rational goal of fiscal policy. As long as income is below its potential level, an expansionary fiscal policy in general, and debt-financed fiscal expansion in particular, is a good thing. As income rises through the multiplier mechanism, tax revenues rise and the required size of budget deficit declines. And sooner or later full employment will be reached, at which point deficit ends.

Once the full employment goal is accepted, therefore, no room exists for any other principle, such as the principle of balanced budget. The equilibrium size of the public debt that results from the pursuit of this goal is of no consequence or concern. More recently, however, a number of conservative economists launched a heavy attack on such a Keynesian stand. Buchanan and Wagner (1977), for example, have asserted that the sound principle is that of a balanced budget. They argue that budget balances had been broadly maintained before Keynes came on the scene, but that the Keynesian doctrine brought about an uncontrollable expansion of the government sector and perennial budget deficits which stifled the American and other advanced economies.

True, the rapid growth in budget deficits in the recent past has failed to bring back full employment. The socioeconomic implications of the growing government sector are also profound and alarming, as Buchanan and Wagner pointed out, the most serious being the generally negative effect of higher taxes on people's work and investment incentives. It does not, however, follow that one should therefore subscribe to the principle of balanced budget. First, deficits have been a norm rather than an exception with modern governments, historically speaking. For instance, early eighteenth-century England experienced one of the fastest growths in public debt. English national debt, which started at £1 million in 1693, had grown to beyond £30 million by 1720.[18] This rapid growth in public debt does not appear to have impoverished the British economy. Second, the principle of balanced budget, literally interpreted, would mean balancing the budget each year. One cannot rank such a rigid rule above more flexible ones. Third, and most crucial of all, the notion that budget deficits are unhealthy is based on a mistaken analogy to private debt. A private borrower should be rightly

---

[18] The South Sea Bubble was not unrelated to this large government debt. Both the South Sea Company and the Bank of England offered to take on the debt themselves, and the government was lured into the scheme under the leadership of Mr Aislabie, the chancellor of the Exchequer (see Mackay 1980).

concerned about the growth of his debt. But the public counterpart of private debt is external debt and not internal debt.

Moreover, the debt of private corporate business has been growing steadily. Even today it is growing faster than government debt. Why does no one raise objections to this fast-growing business debt? And why does everyone complain about the more modest growth of government debt? The chief reason for this contrasting reaction by the public is the belief that, whereas business 'invests' the money to build capital, government eats it. But such a belief is unfounded. Government has been building a variety of social capital essential to today's democracies. Schools and roads are the most visible types of a government's 'investment'; medical and judicial aid are examples of intangible but no less important forms of social capital built and run by government. If a proper 'price' were attached to each form of this government-owned capital, the book would probably show a healthy growth of government's net worth comparable to that of private firms. Eisner (1986) finds, for example, that application of the method of capital budgeting used by business to the US federal government reveals a net worth of $382 billion for 1980 and − $58 billion for 1984. Eisner takes into account only tangible capital, however; if he included intangibles, the federal government would look as good as US business.

Turning to the budget deficit–inflation nexus, once again, a number of conflicting opinions have been expressed. The two representative opinions—the monetarist and the Keynesian views, for ease of reference—run as follows. The monetarist view denies any direct connection between budget deficits and inflation. Deficits will cause an expansion in the money supply, and hence inflation, only if they are monetized. But the banking system is under no obligation to monetize the government's IOUs and actually manages to retain the autonomy of the money supply. The Keynesian view, in contrast, admits the nexus in principle, but claims that the actual deficits have always been too small to make an impact on inflation, and furthermore that governments may even have been recording surpluses in the more recent years if proper allowance is made for inflation.[19]

[19] The Department of Finance of Canada's calculation shows, for example, that the $6.5 billion deficit recorded by all governments in Canada in 1980 becomes a $1.7 billion surplus after adjusting for inflation (see Department of Finance, *Economic Review*, April 1981: 87).

Unfortunately, both views dodge the real issue involved. As for the monetarists' claim of autonomy of the money supply, this is merely an assumption; if the assumption is wrong, their argument will crumble to the ground. As a simple test of monetary autonomy, I have regressed the annual change in the money supply against governmental budget deficit, using US and UK data. The results show that, over a short period, the 'monetization function' is quite flat, but it keeps shifting up so that its long-run counterpart becomes much steeper.[20] The implication is that, while the banking systems of these countries do not monetize government debt immediately, they none the less do so gradually and systematically under the guise of open-market operations.

The Keynesian argument takes the inflation rate as given, adjusts the public debt outstanding for inflation, and claims that budget deficits have not been a cause of inflation. This argument would be sound if the government sector were very small in the economy, but this is actually not the case. If budget deficits and their monetization have indeed been the major cause of inflation, then deflating the government debt by the inflation of its own making and belittling the government's contribution to inflation are plainly ludicrous. In short, both these arguments make light of the growing economic role of the government and its institutional advantage over the private sector in commanding a nation's economic resources.

Historically, the connection between budget deficits and inflation has not been very close. The British experience in previous centuries serves as a good example. A steadily growing government debt and its monetization has even been necessary to support the growing world economy at stable prices. We have reason to believe, however, that the connection between deficits and inflation has recently become closer. One reason is the disappearance, in the early part of this

---

[20] For the UK the department variable is $\Delta M3$ and the independent variable is the public sector borrowing requirement, both deflated by the general price level. The sample period is 1952–74. For the USA, I borrowed the data from Buchanan and Wagner's (1977) Table 8.1. The dependent variable is $\Delta M1$ and the independent variable is the federal budget deficit. The sample period is 1947–74. For both countries, the sample period was divided into two periods: pre-1965 and post-1965. For the first sub-period, the regression coefficient for the UK is 0.4763 ($R^2 = 0.1097$) and for the USA 0.1673 ($R^2 = 0.0993$). For the second sub-period, the numbers are for the UK 0.5172 ($R^2 = 0.2455$) and for the USA 0.3034 ($R^2 = 0.1920$). The numbers for the entire period are for the UK 0.7529 ($R^2 = 0.3566$) and for the USA 0.4186 ($R^2 = 0.2832$). These results indicate that the short-run 'monetization function' is relatively flat but keeps shifting up with time, so that its long-run counterpart is much steeper.

century, of the conventional source of seigniorage whereby fiat money could be substituted for gold. So long as this substitution was possible, governments could acquire additional financial resources (by demonetizing gold) without initiating a matching increase in the money stock. As this source of seigniorage dwindled, however, governments have had to rely increasingly on their financial machine.

Another reason is the strong growth trend of the government sector. It is estimated that there are twenty times as many university and college professors per capita in the United States as there were around the turn of the century. A similar trend is observed for civil servants. These trends symbolize the permeation of democracy throughout society, which has proceeded at an unprecedented pace in this century. Governments can no longer be content with the provision of basic services such as protecting their citizens from foreign invasion and maintaining law and order on the streets. They are now given the whole new task of protecting their citizens economically. As the notion of economic protection is unbounded, however, so are their financial requirements.

A third reason is the generally accommodating mode of monetary policy adopted by the central banks in today's democratic political setting. I have already referred to the origin of the central bank as a financial machine for the government, and to its dubious legal power. But above all, the extreme complexities that surround financial policies have prevented the central bank from taking a more resolute stand and earning greater respect and influence in the bureaucracy. In the pre-1914 era, the basic rules of monetary policy were widely accepted by society, and the central bank commanded respect as the enforcer of these rules, but no more. The central banker's aims and the results of his actions are shrouded in mystery. Keynes once described the post-1914 monetary policy as follows:

The prewar system did not do much to stabilise prices or to ward off Credit Cycles—with such acts of God it did not consider itself in any way concerned. But it had one great advantage—everyone knew quite clearly what principles would govern the Bank of England's actions and what they would have to expect in given circumstances. The postwar system has substituted a most efficacious 'management' for the old 'automatic' system—which is all to the good; but, at present, no one knows exactly what objects the 'management' is directed or on what principles it proceeds. It can scarcely claim hitherto to have tried to apply scientific principles to the attainment of the economic optimum, in the light of day and with the assistance of expert discussion and criticism, but proceeds to unknown destinations by the methods described by the hand. (Keynes 1930, vol II: 232)

Hawtrey, aptly calling central banking an 'art', writes:

The art of central banking is something profoundly different from any of the practices with which it is possible to become familiar in the ordinary pursuits of banking or commerce. It is a field within which a certain degree of technical knowledge is necessary, even to take advantage of expert advice. Yet it seems to be taken for granted that a central banker should be like a ship captain who knows nothing of navigation, or a general who does not believe in the 'Staff College'.

The central banker is even reluctant to admit that there exists an art of central banking. If central banks can do these things, what a formidable responsibility rests on those who direct them! Nothing but complete scepticism as to the power of central banks to do anything whatsoever promises a quiet life for their directorates. . . . (Hawtrey 1932: 246–7)

Now, fifty years later, the situation is no better for the central banker. He has no rules to cling to. More critics and self-assumed advisers abound than ever before. Many technical innovations have been instituted in his monetary control, but he has also found that the financial system he aims to control is even more innovative. Every decision faced by the central banker remains a new decision surrounded by a wide margin of uncertainty. And this uncertainty forces the central banker to be silent about his aims and achievements, which merely helps to perpetuate the central bank's subordination to the government.

5 SOME CONCLUDING REMARKS

Central banks do incredible things from time to time. In the summer of 1971, when the yen was certain to appreciate significantly against the major currencies, the Bank of Japan, alone in all the world, kept the Tokyo foreign exchange market open for weeks, bought an unlimited amount of foreign currencies at the old parity prices, glutted the economy with liquidity, and initiated a pure monetary inflation. In 1980/1, the US Federal Reserve Banks managed to stage a spectacular acrobatic show of interest rates. How should one explain such obviously irrational actions of central banks? And, more generally, why have they failed to live up to the general principles of central banking?

Two approaches have been taken by economists in order to solve this puzzle. One is an empirical quantitative approach, in an attempt to identify the central bank's 'reaction function' or the policy behaviour equation for the central bank. The other approach is an application of the theory of bureaucracy in which the central bank is viewed as a bureau having its own objectives (such as prestige and self-preservation) and pursuing these objectives. According to this approach, if the central bank acts in a manner inconsistent with the general principles, the gap is attributed to the discrepancies between the national economic goals and those of the bank.[21] These approaches have two common assumptions. One is that the central bank's intentions can be inferred accurately from the actual outcomes or effects of its policy. The other is that the central bank is an independent institution and pursues its own goals freely. Although these assumptions are basic to scientific analyses derived from the theory of rational choice, the relevance of such a theory to the central bank is questionable, given the great uncertainty surrounding its actions and the dubious nature of its independence. Moreover, declaring that the central bank possesses a preference to aid the government (which is the likely conclusion to be drawn from these approaches) would not be an accurate description of today's central bankers.

The hypothesis behind this chapter is that the central banker has his own goals derived from the general principles of central banking, that he wants to pursue these goals, but that historical and legal constraints limit his freedom of action, expecially in times of emergency, with the result that he is sometimes forced to take an action against his will. The two episodes cited in the beginning of this section illustrate the point. Enough evidence exists to indicate that the Japanese government forced the Bank of Japan to keep the Tokyo market open. The interest rate policy of the USA in the past few years is more difficult to assess. But so far as high interest rates are concerned, it is highly unlikely that the Fed produced them single-handedly. The government must have wanted them, for external reasons (such as to appease those gnomes who own hundreds of billions worth of dollar claims resulting from its abuse of seigniorage rights during the Bretton Woods era).

---

[21] A brief summary of the existing studies of central banking is in Acheson and Chant (1973), who also suggested a hypothesis that the Bank of Canada aims at minimizing the interest costs of government debt.

At any rate, the model of the central bank that emerges from our historical study is not the powerful and capable monetary authority depicted in macroeconomics textbooks, but a rather frail institution trying to prove its *raison d'être* under severe political and technical constraints. If central banks have not done a great job, it is, at least in part, because they are institutionally weak. A more sensible balance of power must be established between them and governments in order for them to have a proper authority over monetary matters.

One way to accomplish this goal might be to strengthen the co-operation among central banks by empowering the IMF to impose rules on the behaviour of its member central banks. Without such rules, unconcerted pursuits of nationalist goals by central banks tend to result in an unsatisfactory Nash equilibrium with volatile exchange rates and high inflation but without visible improvements in production, employment, and world trade. On the other hand, history shows that an international monetary order needs the sponsorship of the leader nation, and that its effectiveness hinges on the strength and morale of the latter. In the absence of an obvious and willing leader at the present time, the future prospect of a new international order is rather dim.

Another way to accomplish the same goal might be to make the central bank a full government department in order that it might have a say in the cabinet on general matters of economic policy. This proposal may sound paradoxical, and may even possess the danger of depriving the central bank of what little autonomy it now has. While no one can deny such a danger, the present problem with the central bank is that it is inferior to the government and that, because of its fictitious independence, the central banker is left out of budgetary deliberations. It might not even be a bad idea to make the opposition leader the *ex officio* head of the central bank, in view of his or her political influence and distance from the government. This latter scheme would also have some collateral benefits, such as getting opposition members more involved in policy decisions in a constructive manner and imposing a higher degree of intertemporal consistency of national economic policy.

Another fundamental lesson to be learned from history is that the proper management of money requires a good knowledge of the real sector of the economy in its historical context. As modern British history shows, the success of a given monetary policy depends crucially on the strength of the underlying economy. It is here that the non-historical dynamic models of theorists lose credibility. In such models, the world is unbounded and stationary, and time is perfectly homogeneous. One year in the 1900s and another in the 1920s carry equal value. In reality, however, mother earth is too small. Every country has its own history, and in its historical process certain times are more critical than others. A mistake made at a critical historical time may never be erased. Take for example British monetary policy during the 1920s. Immediately after the First World War, the British had the chance to rebuild their economy. Had the monetary authority correctly assesed the weakness of the economy and directed its efforts towards its reconstruction (even at the cost of national prestige and external value of the pound), the subsequent course of the British economy would have been quite different. In actual fact, the policy pursued was aimed at restoring the gold standard at the old parity price, and the decade-long restrictive monetary policy dealt a fatal blow to the UK economy. Money was not neutral, even in the long run, in this historical sense.

Thanks to the monetarists' influence, there seems to exist a fairly popular belief that money can be properly managed by watching monetary data alone. This is an illusion, and a very dangerous one. The greatest danger of monetary mismanagement lies in the failure to assess the economy's potential correctly, which results in the economy either being prevented from living up to its potential, or being allowed to live beyond its means. Mindless pursuits of such single targets as the monetary growth rate and exchange rates lack this historical perspective and sense of direction. The conquest of inflation is desirable by itself, and the monetary growth rate may be an important indicator of anti-inflationary policy. But the cost of such a policy can be unduly high, as seems to have been the case with the US recession of the 1980s. Exchange rates are also important, but the long-run course of exchange rates will be set by real forces. The pound sterling, for example, has lost more than 60 per cent of its value against the dollar in the past fifty years, despite Britain's constant struggle to maintain it. Were Britain to relive this period, I do not believe she would wish to pay the same amount of attention to the exchange rate. Canada, I am afraid, has been following the British example in this regard.

In short, no single optimal monetary policy exists which is applicable to all places and all times. What policy is optimal depends on the strength of the underlying economy. In this sense, an ideal central banker is a complete economist, not just a financial expert.

APPENDIX: A NOTE ON THE FEDERAL RESERVE SYSTEM OF THE UNITED STATES

The present chapter has stressed the subordinate status of the central bank to its government. Americans may argue that that is not the case with their Federal Reserve System. In anticipation of such an argument, this appendix offers the view that the 'Fed' *is* rather like the other major central banks studied in the text.

The history of central banking in the United States goes back to the First Bank of the United States, founded in 1791 under the auspices of Alexander Hamilton, Secretary of the Treasury in the Washington cabinet. In Hamilton's opinion, such a bank could stimulate commerce and industry by lowering the cost of credit as well as helping the government with emergency loans and more expedient collection and payments of taxes. The act chartering the Bank for a twenty-year period was signed by President Washington on 25 February, 1791. The Bank was established with its head office in Philadelphia and with a capital of $10 million. One-fifth of this amount, or $2 million, was subscribed by the government and four-fifths, or $8 million, was subscribed by individuals, partnerships, and corporations. Private shareholders paid $2 million in gold and silver and $6 million in federal obligations. The government, on the other hand, borrowed $2 million from the Bank immediately.

The Bank was a success. It provided a safe depository for the public's funds, distributed money around the country, collected public revenues, and made occasional loans to the government. It issued a safe and elastic currency, financed commerce and industry, and provided foreign exchange facilities. It even exercised control over the note issues of the state banks by sending their notes promptly for redemption. However, probably because of this control over the state banks and the ensuing hostility among them, the Bank failed to have its charter renewed and went out of business on 25 February, 1811.

A Second Bank of the United States received the approval of President Madison on 10 April, 1816. The charter was again for a twenty-year period. The Bank's head office was again in Philadelphia. Its capital was set at $35 million, one-fifth of which was subscribed by the government and four-fifths by individuals, partnerships, and corporations. Private subscribers were again required to pay for their stock one-fourth in coin and three-fourths in coin or federal government obligations, while the government was permitted to pay its share in coin or in its own obligations. The Bank was empowered to issue notes up to the amount of its capital. The Bank acknowledged this favour with a gift of $1.5 million to the government.

The Second Bank's record was smeared by imprudent management. It granted loans with great liberality, routinely on mortgages and the Bank's own stock. Its Baltimore branch was seized by stock speculators who, through fraudulent transactions, caused the Bank a loss of $1.5 million. Lacking discipline itself, the Bank lost control over the state banks. It regained shape, and even began to look like a central bank, under the leadership of Nicholas Biddle, who assumed its presidency for the period 1823–30. Biddle recognized the Bank's role as holder of the nation's specie reserves and maintained these reserves in adequate ratio to the Bank's liabilities. He cleaned up the mess left by his predecessor, stressed short-term commercial credit, and expanded foreign and domestic exchange operations to promote interregional and international trade. He regained control of state bank note issues. Moreover, he deliberately engaged the Bank in counter-seasonal and counter-cyclical policies.

Despite Biddle's great work, however, the Bank was denied renewal of its charter by President Jackson (who vetoed the bill to recharter the Bank). Its earlier misconduct was partially responsible for its failure to earn the renewal of the charter; in addition, foreign elements in the Bank's ownership stirred nationalist resentment. The location of its head office (Chestnut Street, Philadelphia) was a source of constant irritation on the part of the Wall Street financiers. All these factors, along with the public's deep-rooted distrust of paper money and federal control of banking, contributed to the Bank's demise.

From 1836 to 1913, the task of central banking was back, if by default, in the hands of the federal government. The Independent Treasury Act of 1846 provided for a self-contained system for the management of federal government funds. This system was designed primarily to increase the efficiency of the government's cash management (the alternative system of keeping the funds with state banks, as employed during the periods 1811–17 and 1833–46, had proved very costly), but also had the unfortunate feature of making conditions of the money market susceptible to the government's fiscal operations. A budget surplus, for example, would reduce the monetary base of the economy automatically. In order to relieve stringencies in the money market arising from its fiscal operations, the government found it necessary to engage in various monetary policy actions. The use of private banks as depositories of federal funds was soon resumed. Purchase of silver bullion for new coinage and a prepayment of the federal debt were made from time to time. In addition, the National Currency Act of 1863 gave birth to national banks with the power to issue notes against federal obligations. These national banks would have been an important source of 'elastic' money supply but for the fact that the federal debt outstanding was rapidly declining from its Civil War peak throughout the rest of the nineteenth century.

All in all, the history of banking reform from 1791 to 1913 was 'long and tortuous', in the words of Beckhart (1972), who enumerates the following three traits as constituting the major defects of the US banking system prior to 1913:

1 inelastic note issues by the national banks: their failure to meet the panic demands for currency led to suspensions of cash payments in 1873, 1893, and 1907 and to payments of heavy premiums for currency;
2 absence of a lender of last resort: the national banks in the three central reserve cities (New York, Chicago, and St Louis) served as depositories of reserves for the national banks in other cities and country towns. As a result, funds flowed from other cities and country towns to the central reserve cities, and especially to New York, where much of these funds were turned into unsound loans such as those made to stock exchange brokers;
3 defective exchange and transfer system: the collecting of out-of-town cheques remained so awkward and expensive that the interest rates were often high and the currency was often at a discount in remote cities and towns.

By the turn of the century, industrial growth in the US had outpaced that of the banking sector; money was lagging behind goods. There was therefore a need for a banking system capable of providing efficient financial services to the industries that had attained an unprecedented growth both in scope and space. It was in such an environment that the idea of a new central bank was formed.

In 1908 a 16-member congressional commission on central

banking, headed by Senator N. W. Aldrich, travelled to Europe to study practices there. In 1912 the commission recommended adoption of a system of centralized bank reserves, centralized note issue, and central banking facilities for the rediscount of commercial paper to provide commercial bank reserves in times of stress. But the recommendation was received by the public with considerable distrust and antagonism. Newly elected President Wilson and the Democrats pledged themselves against a central bank or central reserve association. The result was a compromise: a federally established regional banking system with a degree of loose central control, known as the Federal Reserve System. The System had certain centralizing features, such as monopoly of note issue, pooling of the reserves of the banking system, rediscounting services, and policy formulation and supervision by a central board located in Washington, DC (originally called the Federal Reserve Board and later renamed the Board of Governors of the Federal Reserve System); but it also had some decentralizing features, such as the 12 regional banks (instead of one) comprising the System, and a balanced regional representation in the board.

Unlike the earlier banks of the USA, the Federal Reserve System was an explicitly public institution built for the task of central banking under the Federal Reserve Act of 1913, despite its 100 per cent private ownership. (Each of the 12 Federal Reserve banks is owned by the member banks in its 'district', and the expenses of the Board's operations are paid by assessments on the 12 banks in accordance with the statute. The major source of the Reserve banks' revenues is the interest on government securities and on funds advanced to member banks. These earnings are used to pay the operating expenses of the Reserve banks themselves and of the Board, to pay a fixed 6 per cent dividend on stocks held by member banks, and to build up the surplus accounts of the Reserve banks up to a limit. The banks' 'profit', on the other hand, has always been paid into the Treasury in one form or another. Earlier it was taxed; since 1947 the System has been paying in voluntarily.) As a public institution, the System is subject to general congressional supervision.

Turning to the specific issue of the independence of the central bank, one can safely say that the Federal Reserve System of the USA is one of the most independent central banks in the world, at least in the legal sense of the term. First, the System has always been 100 per cent privately owned and free from budgetary restrictions. This fact alone makes it look more independent than most other central banks. Second, the System has been recognized as an independent bureau and as such was not under the jurisdiction of the Treasury Department from the start. (Such was the opinion rendered by the attorney-general of the USA in 1914.) Third, government's involvement in the Board of Governors, the System's principal policy-making body, has never been substantial. The seven board members are appointed by the US President each for a 14-year term (in such a manner that one member is replaced every two years), subject to the consent of the Senate. The members are to be chosen to represent the interests of various fields and regions evenly. One of the members is designated as chairman and another as vice-chairman by the President each for a four-year term (which begins in the final year of the presidential term, by accident). In the early years (up to 1935), two of the seven seats had been occupied by the Secretary of the Treasury and the Comptroller of the Currency as *ex officio* members. They were removed partly because these government members were often too busy with other important duties to tend properly to monetary affairs, and partly because their presence on the Board could be too political and dominating. (According to a testimony given to the House Banking and Currency Committee in 1935 by a long-time member, the Secretary of the treasury acted as a spokesman for the banking interests of New York in 1929, which made the checking of unsound credit extension impossible.) Fourth, the System has gained power and expertise over the nation's monetary affairs. The 1935 revisions to the Federal Reserve Act and other related laws gave the System the power to alter the reserve requirements within certain statutory limits and also the margin requirements for security purchases. They also gave the Open Market Committee a legal status. Through its constant efforts, the System has cultivated a significant franchise of its own in the banking community and the economics profession to fend off political pressures.

But is the Federal Reserve System really more independent than other central banks? Although this is not the kind of question that has a ready answer, I can safely say that the System has never had the degree of *de facto* independence commensurate with its legal independence. First, legal independence means an independence only from individual departments within the government, but not an independence from the government as a whole. It gives the System at most the same status held by the other departments within the government, but in reality something less. The central bank is not a fully fledged governmental department. Civil servants do not hold the same sense of kinship towards central bankers as they do among themselves. This may be because central bankers' salaries do not come from taxes, because central bankers do not speak the same language as other civil servants do, or because central bankers are free from the political hustle and bustle with which civil servants must cope day in and day out. The legal independence of a central bank contributes more to its isolation than to its gaining power within the government. The private ownership of the Federal Reserve System works negatively in this regard.

Second, monetary policy and fiscal policy cannot be independent of each other because of the various monetary implications of fiscal policy. It is well-known, for example, that government's debt policy takes precedence and emasculates monetary policy during wartimes, a situation the Federal Reserve System found itself in during and after the Second World War (up to 1951), and also during the Vietnamese War to a degree. The continued large budget deficits in the 1980s impose a similar constraint on monetary policy. Although the System does resist excessive demands from the fiscal side (as it battled the Treasury into a successful 'accord' in 1951), the existing laws and congressional procedures dictate that the central bank is responsible for a smooth execution of the government's fiscal plan as sanctioned by Congress and that, should any unexpected events develop, monetary policy must bear the burden of adjustments. By the very nature of fiscal and monetary policies, and by the very order in which they are formulated, fiscal policy comes before monetary policy. To reverse the role would require Congress to approve a detailed itinerary of monetary policy actions before approving governmental budget, a practice that is neither feasible nor desirable.

Third, the fact that the System is headed by President-appointed board members and is subject to congressional supervision is a reminder that it is not above the government and that its Board is but a small part of the complex governmental decision-making machine. It is a perception like this that induces the Federal Reserve System to act co-operatively and deferentially with the government, its legal independence notwithstanding. The fact that the legal independence of the central bank has been formally eliminated in most major countries except the USA is not a definitive proof that the Federal Reserve System is more independent than the other central banks.

Rather, it means that the relation between the federal government and the Federal Reserve System has been relatively good, so that the government has not felt the need to formalize its supremacy over the central bank. But a more serious conflict may prompt the government to have Congress write it into law.

At any rate, what constitutes a proper relation between the central bank and the government remains an unsettled issue in the United States (as in some other parts of the world). For example, there have been proposals to restore governmental representation in the Board of Governors, to shorten the term of the board members, to make the chairman's office co-terminous with the President's, and to increase governmental supervision of the System in general. These proposals have been countered by proposals defending the System's independence. One such proposal, made in 1950 by a subcommittee of the Joint Committee on the Economic Report, went so far as to recommend that the two houses of Congress resolve that

primary power and responsibility for regulating the supply, availability, and cost of credit in general shall be vested in the duly constituted authorities of the Federal Reserve System, and that Treasury actions relative to money, credit and transactions in the Federal debt shall be made consistent with the policies of the Federal Reserve.

This proposal comes close to making the Fed the Supreme Court of Finance.

Sensible or not, these proposals hint at the great deal of politics that is going on behind the scene. When the issue is as big as central banking, that is, a monopoly of a nation's note issue, politics is inevitable. Senator Aldrich, whose report led eventually to the Federal Reserve Act of 1913, was John D. Rockefeller's son-in-law, and no doubt acted in the interests of the few big New York banks which saw in the monopoly of banking a greater source of profits and power than, say, in oil monopoly. The opponents, having discovered that they were no match for the power and resources of the banks, strove to put into the new institution as much public character (congressional and governmental control and supervision) and decentralization of power as possible in order to alleviate the possible evil of the gigantic monopoly. From the beginning, the influence of the Rockefeller family on the Federal Reserve management has been visible. (The outgoing chairman Paul Volcker is a former personal aide to David Rockefeller.) The point is that in all likelihood, the alternative to subordination to government is not a neutral and rational central bank, but a monopoly acting on behalf of some private interests. As remarked above, if a stronger central bank is judged desirable, the solution lies not in a further distancing of the bank from the government, but in making it a more visible and influential bureau within the governmental bureaucratic structure.

5

The Political Economy of Inflation

1 INTRODUCTION

Inflation is somewhat like war. Although every political leader denounces it as a social evil, it shows no sign of disappearing. This embarrassing fact calls for an explanation. In this chapter I shall argue that inflation is the product of the political dynamics ingrained in today's democratic capitalism.

The economists' conventional explanation, which boils down to some version of the quantity theory, attributes inflation to an ever rapid growth of the money supply. It follows from this that curbing the rate of monetary growth should cure inflation. But this simple explanation—if an explanation at all—generates more questions than answers. First, there is the question of causality, well known from the time of the Bullion Committee controversy. Even though an economy, when disturbed by a sudden and large increase in the money supply, will produce price increases, not all price increases are caused by such exogenous monetary shocks. Shortages of goods or exogenous increases in input prices, for example, can also trigger extensive price hikes. Second, and more importantly, in explaining inflation one must go further than establishing the money–inflation nexus, which is indeed no more than identifying the weapon in a murder case. Just as who did it and why are central to any murder mystery, so here one must ask: Who causes inflation, and why?

Such questions are addressed in this chapter, which follows the spirit of Chapter 1, in which I suggested that macroeconomic dynamics, including those of policy actions, are chiefly the outcomes of the political games played by the several major groups in our system, rather than a quasi-natural process typical of conventional economic models; that each policy affects these groups differently; and that, by studying the differential policy impacts on different groups, one might gain insights into the working of our macroeconomy. More specifically, in order to answer the questions of who causes inflation and why, we must investigate who benefits from it and who suffers; in other words, we must study its effects.

Although the chapter follows many other studies in examining the redistributional effects of inflation, it differs from most in stressing the inflationary bias inherent in twentieth-century capitalist economies. Inflation is not a random event. Rather, it is created by those who hold power in the economy. The main feature of today's capitalism is that the savings of the public are directed, not by choice but by necessity, towards the purchase of IOUs issued by either business firms or governments. The result is an accumulation of huge debts by the business and government sectors. Given the monetary nature of these debts, the real value of the public's claims on the two sectors is affected by monetary factors. Specifically, inflation hurts the public and benefits the debtors. Moreover, although business firms and governments are theoretically mere 'agents' for the public, the operation of today's sophisticated system of mass production and administration necessitates that these agents be the virtual 'bosses' in our society, in that they make the major decisions for the 'principals', including the management of money. When power is in the hands of debtors, inflation can become their favourite choice, and apparently it has. As a matter of fact, today's 'debt capitalism' cannot function in a deflationary environment. A permanent 5 per cent deflation would destroy it. In a society dependent on the good health of the debtors, the choice is not between inflation and deflation, but of the magnitude of inflation needed to keep both debtors and creditors in relative peace. As a result, inflation stays and anti-inflationary efforts are half-hearted.

The chapter is organized as follows. Section 2 provides an historical perspective to today's inflation. It supports the hypothesis that inflation is a twentieth-century phenomenon and an integral part of today's corporate or debt capitalism. Section 3 lists the principal actors in the inflation drama, studies the differential impacts of inflation on them, and examines their behaviour in the dynamic process of inflation. A dominant pattern of development of the dynamics of inflation is identified from broad historical observations. Section 4 presents a critique of the existing pure theories of inflation, and in particular of the Chicago theory, which proposes a permanent deflation at a rate equal to the agents' rate of time preference as monetary optimism. I argue, however, that such a theory, based on the eighteenth-century family capitalism, does not apply to today's world, and that the policy prescriptions derived from the theory lack credibility. Section 5 turns to the international aspect of inflation. It suggests that monetary nationalism has a tendency towards inflation, that only a very powerful international monetary order could curb such a tendency, but that the world may lack a credible and willing leader to enforce such an order. The sixth and final section concludes with a brief summary.

2 INFLATION AS A TWENTIETH-CENTURY PHENOMENON

On a broad historical scale, one can safely say that inflation is a twentieth-century phenomenon. Figure 5.1 charts the path of British prices since the 1660s. The graph was constructed by connecting the cost-of-living indices by Schumpeter, Rousseau, and Sauerbeck for the older periods and similar official indices for more recent years. It shows that no trend between 1700 and 1914 exists apart from the disturbance during the Napoleonic wars, and that all the significant increases in British prices have occurred since the First World War, which put today's prices approximately twenty times as high as those in the pre-1914 era. Although I claim no in-depth knowledge of how these cost-of-living indices were constructed or how reliable they are,

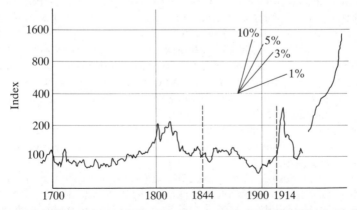

Fig. 5.1 British prices, 1660–1978. *Sources:* B. R. Mitchell, *Abstract of British Historical Statistics*, 1962; CSO, *Economic Trends*, Annual Supplement, 1975; and IMF, *International Financial Statistics*, more recent issues.

for the purpose of extracting a rough historical trend of prices, no serious problems exist. The US historian Walter Haines (1981, Fig. 5) has produced a similar chart on the same time scale using US wholesale prices. The shape of his curve is almost identical to this. Any thoery aiming to explain today's inflation must recognize this historical nature of inflation and must equip itself with proper twentieth-century features. Any theory that fails to draw a distinction between the present and past centuries must be deemed inadequate.

What, then, are the essential features of the twentieth-century capitalist economies that distinguish them from their predecessors? A number of major events and institutional changes come to mind. First, during the twentieth century, the world moved from gold to managed currencies. The gold standard came to a virtual end in 1914, except for a brief revival between 1925 and 1931. 'Gold standard' means that only gold (and possibly some qualified foreign exchanges) qualifies as reserve assets against note issue; 'managed currency', on the other hand, means that any financial claims, and claims on government in particular, qualify as reserve assets. As a result, central banks no longer have any external constraints on the amount of bank notes they can issue.

Second, the two world wars permanently altered the fabric of our society. For one thing, they were total wars, requiring the full mobilization of national resources; they required more military expenses than governments could collect either through taxes or bond issues, resulting in a rapid expansion of money supply. For another, these wars required, for the first time in history, the participation of the traditionally 'lower' classes of citizens. To persuade them to join the military services, governments had to promise these classes increased legal rights and economic rewards. Fulfilling this promise has become a major fiscal burden on governments. Furthermore, both of these wars generated many new nations. Just as the domestic permeation of democracy has increased the strain on the public purse of a nation, so the international permeation of democracy has added to the financial burden of wealthier nations.

These changes certainly paved the way for larger governments and more expedient ways of financing their fiscal needs, thereby contributing to inflation. None the less, a more fundamental change in the nature of capitalism between the nineteenth and the twentieth centuries, namely the transition from family capitalism to corporate capitalism, has had a profound influence on inflation. In American history, the railway and telegraph companies of the nineteenth century marked the beginning of corproate capitalism which still dominates business today. Besides the well documented technological superiority of large corporate firms over the traditional family businesses, corporate capitalism has brought with it certain profound changes in the structure of our economy. Two changes are especially relevant to this chapter's theme. First, unlike family businesses, which relied on the limited financial resources of the family for capital, corporate firms are designed to live on the financial resources of the masses of people, not only for initial capital but also for maintenance and growth. In this sense, one can alternatively call corporate capitalism debt capitalism. Second, unlike the small single-unit enterprises under family capitalism, corporate firms are typically multi-unit enterprises. The need for co-ordination among these units has given rise to a new breed of management professionals who, over the years, have become an influential group in our political economy. (For a comprehensive discussion of the character and status of modern corporations, see Chandler 1977.)

Corporate firms are legal 'persons', formed specifically for business purposes. In order to facilitate their large-scale operations, a large and sophisticated financial infrastructure, among other things, has had to be developed. First, the ownership of corporations by the public in the form of shares was devised (although this was not a twentieth-century invention); furthermore, in order to encourage such capital participation, the share owners were given the privilege of limited liability, and the transferability of shares was facilitated by the establishment of well organized stock markets. Second, in order to meet the corporations' growing demand for other forms of funds, ranging from short-term commercial credit to long-term investment funds, a wide variety of financial intermediaries developed to channel the public's savings efficiently into the type of loans the corporate firms want.

By looking at the stock of financial assets existing in these economies, readers may appreciate the magnitude of the financial infrastructure of today's developed economies. In Canada at the end of 1985, for example, the gross total value of financial assets stood at $2491 billion, more than five times the country's 1985 GNP of $454 billion (see Table 5.1 below).[1]

---

[1] Throughout this chapter, Canadian figures are used for illustration. The Canadian economy is approximately one-tenth of the size of the US economy.

Needless to say, not all of these financial assets are business-related, but as we shall see later, the corporate firms are the most important participants in the nation's financial markets. In particular, they are the single largest debtor group. Although financial assets are the liabilities of some agents within the system, and hence net out to zero in the aggregate, they are not insignificant. On the contrary, that the various groups are related through the financial markets, and that the major portion of these financial assets are fixed in monetary terms, makes today's economies structurally different from those under family capitalism. Ever since Keynes stressed these features of the modern economy and called an economy with such features a 'monetary economy', macroeconomists have been grappling with the problem of modelling such an economy, without great success (*pace* Sir John). Monetarists, in the meantime, have steadfastly refused to recognize this major structural change, clinging to their timeless, institution-free, and largely real theory. When it comes to understanding today's inflation, however, the choice seems obvious. More on this point later.

The emergence of the professional corporate managers as a new élite class has marked another very significant change from previous centuries. Although these managers are a natural consequence of the separation between ownership and management, they have proved to be much more than just hired professionals. They differ from the hired managers of traditional haciendas, for example, because they have established themselves as a group of leaders in society with enormous political–economic power. A number of factors have contributed to their gaining such power. First, the widespread ownership of corporate firms has reduced the owners' power. As owners have become passive dividend-recipients, power has naturally shifted to the managers. Second, the establishment of formal training institutions—business schools—has solidified a new élite club by ensuring that all the members are trained alike—that they read alike, think alike, and remain loyal to the club. Third, corporate firms have always been actively involved in politics; with their large financial resources, they have exerted a great influence on the choices of the political leaders both at home and abroad.

The chief implication of all these structural changes for inflation is that the two major debtors—business and government—hold power in today's economies. Of the two, government has had a much longer history of financing its needs by money and debt. In the days of family capitalism, *rentiers* and owner–managers of firms held political

power. Their concern to preserve their wealth checked the government's excessive demand for resources, that is deficit finance. The shift
of power from the *rentiers* or wealth-owners to the corporate
managers, however, has displaced the political balance towards
another that is more inflationary. As carriers of huge monetary debt,
corporate firms fear deflation. In an economy capable of growing at
3 per cent per annum, a 5 per cent deflation is certain to destroy
corporations. Conversely, inflation tends to benefit them. To the
corporate firms, borrowed funds are a necessary input, and inflation
tends to lower its cost. Moreover, they are all speculators with a 'long
position': they precommit themselves to the purchase of inputs in the
hope of selling the resulting output dear at a future date. As a result,
corporate firms must find inflation attractive.

From this it follows that today's economies, which are controlled
by the debtors, have a definite inflationary bias, and that this bias is
far stronger now than in centuries past. A moderate rate of inflation
may well be the price economies must pay today for the enormous
productive power of the corporate firms, without which today's
standard of living is inconceivable.

Governments and businesses cannot, however, start inflation any
time they choose. First, inflation is perceived negatively by the public.
Second, policy-makers must maintain a pretence to rationality.
Third, inflationary gains to the debtors are limited in both magnitude
and duration. For these reasons, some credible cause is usually
needed to start an inflation. Once started, the inflation is kept within
tolerable limits and is brought under control, sooner or later, to set
the stage for another. However, the average inflation rate over such
cycles will remain significantly above zero. Many appear to think that
inflation is a thing of the past now that it has calmed down and
stopped making headlines. But this certainly is no proof that inflation
is gone for good: a major change in the US monetary policy or a third
oil shock, for example, would bring it back. Judging from the recent
historical trend, one may say that the current 4–5 per cent inflation is
probably the lowest we shall ever see.

3 THE ANATOMY OF INFLATION

In order to study the differential impact of inflation on various groups
in our economy, we must first list the principal actors in this drama
according to the conventional functional classification of agents in a

monetary economy. More specifically, we can follow the basic format used in the compilation of the Canadian national financial flow accounts. The 1985 year-end picture for Canada is shown in Table 5.1.

Households

Although households as economic agents play multiple parts, the role most relevant to the present discussion is that of savers. As is evident from Table 5.1, households as a group are the single most important suppliers of funds in the Canadian economy, a feature common to all advanced economies. Without a constant flow of savings from households, debt capitalism could not function. Despite this and the other vital parts they play, and despite their large numbers in society, households have the least political power of the several groups on the list. This fact has puzzled and exasperated social scientists since the beginning of capitalism. The classic debate was over why the masses of suppliers of labour services should be subordinate to a handful of capitalists. That today's households, who combined are the single largest creditor in the economy, lack political power is even more difficult to answer, for we can no longer resort to the haves-versus-have-nots argument. We could, however, argue that households do

Table 5.1 Financial assets and liabilities, by sector ($b)

	Financial assets	Liabilities	Balance
Households[a]	753	239	+514
Corporate firms[b]	268	651	−383
Banking system[c]	828	856	−28
Government[d]	285	561	−276
Rest of the world	357	184	+173
Total	2491	2491	0

[a] Persons and unincorporated buisness.
[b] Non-financial private corporations.
[c] The monetary authorities, chartered banks, near banks, insurance companies and pension funds, and other private financial institutions.
[d] Federal government, provincial and local governments and hospitals, social security funds, non-financial government enterprises, and public financial institutions.
Source: Statistics Canada, *National Balance Sheet Accounts*, 1986.

not really 'own' financial wealth in the sense of having control over it, but rather that they, along with their savings, are 'owned' by the system. In an economy where the debtors regulate money and credit, creditors maintain a rather vulnerable existence.

Corporate Firms

Firms are the specialized agents for the production of goods and services, according to the economists' usual definition. Although indisputable as a technical definition, this not only understates the political power of corporate firms, but also fails to capture the essence of business activities in a monetary economy. First, we cannot readily maintain that today's corporate firms are merely 'agents' for the shareowners. They are increasingly accepted as legal 'persons', in both theory and practice. Besides, the proportion of corporate shares owned by individuals is not high: it is about 50 per cent in many Western countries; in Canada it was 40 per cent in 1985; in Japan, where corporate power is strongest among all the capitalist economies, the proportion has fallen from 70 per cent in the prewar period to less than 30 per cent. Probably reflecting the increased corporate autonomy, the Japanese dividend rate in recent years has been in the order of 1 per cent as against 5 per cent in Western countries. Needless to say, these figures are somewhat arbitrary, since the growth of pension funds and dummy holding corporations has certainly reduced them. Nevertheless, one can expect them to decline in future, as corporations seek increased autonomy. If one of the main features of modern corporations has been the 'internalization of markets', as Chandler concludes, corporate managers will seek to reduce their exposure to the vagaries of the stock market and the interferences by individual shareholders.

Moreover, business firms are speculators. They do not live on a commission for their technical services: they live on speculative gains. The public does not seem to understand this point. A widespread public outcry occurred in the autumn of 1973 against oil companies charging the new, higher, price for oil they had acquired at the old price. To disapprove of such speculative gains is to deny the capitalist system in principle. In fact, millions of firms throughout the world must have made fortunes during the first oil crisis, at the expense of the public. In Japan, where the shock was hardest, one corporate president called it 'one chance in a millennium', urging his employees to make the most of it. Another corporate president, attempting to reduce profits, paid out unscheduled bonuses to his employees, advising them not to tell outsiders. Inflation, even when it spells disaster to the economy, can be a boon to business.

Lastly, corporate firms constitute the largest single debtor sector in our system. Their debt has grown hand in hand with the growth of their activities. Their borrowings have become so essential to their livelihood that the public have come to equate their strong demand for funds with good times. No one expects corporate firms ever to pay off their debt. Society wants them to borrow more. The attitude of the public towards corporate debt is in sharp contrast to its attitude towards government debt.

The Government

Here 'the government' means the consolidated government, although the emphasis is on national or federal governments. In this classification, the central bank is combined with private banks to form another group called the 'banking system'. The government, in economic theory, is a faceless and egoless character always acting to maximize the value of a given social welfare function. Reality is of course far more complex. First of all, the form of such a social welfare function is unknown. Without an adequate specification of the function, the theory is rather void of content. In explaining the growth of the government, for example, the theory might assert that the government's share in our economy has grown because public goods are luxury goods having higher income elasticities than private goods. But the theory could have 'explained' the shrinkage of the government with equal ease. Moreover, because different political parties represent the interests of various groups differently, one cannot suppose that the preferences of the citizenry as basic human data dictate the government's behaviour.

Second, the government, like any other organization, has its own goals. While the politicians in power are concerned primarily with the survival and prosperity of their government, the bureaucrats compete for greater power among themselves. Power means money—the amount of financial resources under control. When various governmental departments are ranked in terms of power, the economic departments occupy the top spots. From a high office in the government, the entire private sector is beneath the clouds, or so it seems. Such a perception is quite prevalent in government, as a matter of fact. The notion that the government exists to serve its populace is a myth. A warm heart is the least important asset, and indeed often a liability, for a successful career in the civil service or politics. All this is sad, but it is only human nature.

At any rate, given the power structure of today's government and the mentality of the career civil servants, one can easily understand why governments are always hungry for money and why the downsizing of the public sector would be their last choice. In many countries governments' shares in the GNP have been rising constantly and dramatically during the past hundred years. In order to command an ever-increasing share, governments have exploited all the available means of raising revenues. Taxes of all forms have been increasing. Internal and external borrowings have been on the rise. Governments have been implementing social programmes such as public pensions to raise extra revenues.[2] Last but not least, governments have relied consistently on the inflation tax, a tax that is hardest to avoid and easiest to collect.

As of the end of 1985, the governments of Canada had a combined (net) debt of $276 billion. The breakdown of this total was: the federal government, $160 billion; provincial and local governments, $33 billion; public corporations, $125 billion; and social security funds, a net credit of $42 billion.

The Banking System

For Canada this group includes the Bank of Canada, the chartered banks, trust companies and credit unions, insurance companies and private pension funds, and other private financial institutions. Although many minor differences among these financial institutions exist, they have one thing in common: they are all financial intermediaries bringing the ultimate lenders and borrowers together. As intermediaries they have very little equity of their own. Their combined net liability was $28 billion, as shown in Table 5.1. However, the total (gross) amount of assets they owned was

---

[2] While both the US and Canadian social security programmes are 'funded' in theory, the US programme has become virtually 'pay-as-you-go', enabling the government to exploit the entire equity value of the fund. The Canada Plan is much younger and is still recording surpluses. But the surplus cash in the fund has been lent out to the provinces without any restrictions on the uses the provinces may put the loans to. It is quite plausible that the scheme is *de facto* pay-as-you-go.

$828 billion, making this sector a particularly influential group in the economy. The central bank and the chartered banks are of special importance. Their combined assets were $318 billion, or 38 per cnt of the above total. (If the so-called 'near banks' are added, the asset share jumps to 53 per cent.) Moreover, they are the suppliers of money. Their behaviour is consequently an important key to our understanding of the inflationary process.

Anyone who studies the behaviour of the banks is bound to be struck by the glaring gap beween the general theory of banking and its track record. The theory of central banking holds that the stabilization of the value of the currency is the chief goal of monetary policy. This is not just a textbook theory. Central bankers avow themselves to be the guardians of the value of the currency. Yet inflation is everywhere. Quite apart from the money–income causality, continued inflation implies an accommodating pattern of behaviour of the banking system. The question therefore is why the banks accommodate inflationary pressures and thereby validate inflationary expectations, against the basic principles of banking.

In dealing with this question, two important features of our banking system deserve attention. One is the subordinate status of the central bank to the government. In Canada, as in the UK, the Central Bank Act stipulates that it is the government, and not the governor of the central bank, that bears the ultimate power and responsibility for monetary policy. Although other central bank Acts do not state the relationship between the two very explicitly, the government is the boss, as was discussed in Chapter 4. As a result, the central bank is institutionally incapable of fighting inflation without the approval of the government. Moreover, the banking system is unwilling to counteract inflation in its initial phase because of not only technical factors, but also political reasons. As for the technical factors, the initial phase of the inflationary process is invariably characterized by sharp increases in the prices of materials. During a 12-month period in 1919–20, the average price of materials increased by 40–50 per cent in Britain. A similar phenomenon was observed during the 1920s in the USA and many other economies. In Canada, the three major inflationary surges in 1946–7, 1950–1, and 1973–4 were each led by a rapid increase in materials prices, according to Letourneau (1980: 57–8). On each occasion the banking system held its lending rates very low. In the first British case Keynes (1923: 19) reports that the banks' lending rates never exceeded 7 per cent. During the 1920s the

US rates stayed below 6 per cent. The same was also true in Canada on each of the above three occasions. During the 1970s, in particular, Canadian chartered banks' prime corporate paper rate stayed below the inflation rate for as long as four years from 1973 to 1977.

These long lags in interest rate adjustments have been recognized in the literature. Wicksell's (1934, vol. II: 190–208) famous cumulative process and Gibson's Paradox (Keynes 1930, vol II: 198–208; Wicksell 1934) both refer to this phenomenon. Fisher (1930: 43–4) also noted the lag in interest rate adjustments in his discussion of the real interest rate, observing with disbelief that the real interest rate in the USA from March to April 1917 fell below −70 per cent, and in Germany in the summer of 1923 it fell to the absurd level of −99.9 per cent.

In his discussion of the same phenomenon, Keynes (1930, vol. I: 254–5) recognized a fundamental 'dilemma' that banks faced. If banks take too stern an attitude when the speculative demand for money is strong, they might choke off more essential activities of production and distribution; too lenient an attitude, on the other hand, would merely validate the inflationary expectations. Keynes advised banks to accommodate both the speculative and the transaction demand for bank credit, but at appropriately discriminating interest rates. This sounds like a perfect solution, and undoubtedly it is, except for one problem. Banks cannot always be sure which demand is for which purpose—the same only problem the ancient Real Bills doctrine had faced. The problem becomes especially serious when business firms ask for more credit in order to build up their inventories for business purposes. As mentioned earlier, business activities are inherently speculative in nature, and one cannot tell who is an 'investor' and who is a 'speculator'. The banks' inability to distinguish between speculative and transaction demands forces them to offer a single interest rate to all. The situation becomes one of adverse selection and moral hazard. Those banks who charge higher rates tend to attract only high-risk speculators, creating consequences not beneficial to them. Their profit-maximizing interest rates tend to be below the market-clearing levels. See Stiglitz and Weiss (1981) for an illuminating analysis of this issue.

On top of these technical problems, other, more political, problems such as pressure from the government exist. A boom is always pleasant, and usually beneficial, to an incumbent government. A government is naturally loath to see a boom nipped in the bud, while banks are not willing to take the blame for doing it. Moreover, banks are concerned about their public image; they do not like to be called 'profiteers', which would happen if they raised their lending rates sharply in order to arrest the speculative mania. These considerations lead me to conclude that the banking system has a built-in tendency to fail to counteract inflation when it is most effective to do so. In this sense money is an important accomplice in the political dynamics of inflation.

The Foreign Sector

At the end of 1985, Canada owed $173 billion to the rest of the world in paper form, and this external debt cost 3 per cent of her GNP to service. The chief reason for including the foreign sector in the list of principal actors, however, is its significance not to the Canadian economy but to the US economy and US monetary policy.

As is well known, the dollar standard under the Bretton Woods system gave the USA a monopoly of seigniorage rights. Americans could purchase foreign goods and services by merely printing money. In other words, a continuous transfer of real purchasing power from the rest of the world to the USA occurred over the quarter-century up to the early 1970s. The end of the official dollar standard and the shift to the floating regime meant an end of the US monopoly, but not the end of her seigniorage rights, for the US dollar has continued to serve as a leading reserve currency. However, the status of the US dollar has since declined steadily in relation to other major currencies. The proportion of the US dollar in the official foreign exchange reserves of the rest of the world declined from 85 to 70 per cent over 1976–86. The number of countries pegging their currencies to the US dollar has also fallen, from 42 in 1978 to 35 in 1983. Such a decline in popularity reduces prospective seigniorage gains and increases threats by foreign creditors. The tight money policy adopted by the USA since the late 1970s may indeed be thought of as the US reaction to this new uncomfortable environment.

The depressive effects of this high-rate policy are well known. In the first half of the 1980s, interest rates have been considerably above the inflation rate—indeed, so much so that the implicit real rates have been out of line with the 'natural rate', which, judged by the recent growth trend of the major economics, is probably in the range of 2–3 per cent. Given this fact, the policy must have already cost the US economy hundreds of billions of dollars' worth of potential GNP. There will be much more to pay over a longer period of time when the current depressed investment activities affect international competitiveness. Following the USA's lead, the rest of the world has also paid a similar price—although reluctantly. Especially hard-hit have been the non-oil developing countries. Their major suffering came first with the 1973 oil shock, as industrial countries shifted away from their products to oil. Second, the slower growth of the world economy since 1973 has lowered the growth rate of the world trade from 9.1 per cent per annum for 1965–70, to 5.6 per cent for 1970–5 and to a meagre 2.9 per cent for 1976–81. This has aggravated the hardships of the non-oil developing countries. Their terms of trade, which were improving slightly throughout the 1960s, started to deteriorate at an annual rate of over 2 per cent since then,[3] causing a further stagnation of their real incomes. The high interest rate policy of the USA has simply added to their agony by increasing their burden of debt service. Poland, Brazil, Mexico, and the Philippines are just a few examples of virtual national bankruptcies. Given that the total debt of the non-oil developing countries stands at over $600 billion, we can expect to see a few more countries making similar headlines in the near future. The problem with these external debts, however, is not limited to the debtor nations: the lenders, 80 per cent (by amount of credit) of whom are private banks, are in serious financial trouble, serious enough to endanger the functioning of the world-wide financial network.

The observation above on the recent deflationary policy may appear to contradict the main thesis of this chapter, that today's political economy has a definite *inflationary* bias. This, however, is not necessarily the case. The high interest rates of the late 1980s are an anomaly, chiefly the result of the USA's choice to maintain its dollar as a leading reserve currency in the face of increased competition from the other major currencies. The nature of the competition involved is the same as that in any ordinary oligopolistic industry with product differentiation. Although the US dollar is still the number 1 reserve currency, the USA can no longer safely rely on clients' brand loyalty. The large dollar balances held abroad would present a serious problem to the USA if they were dumped in the market. America has

[3] IMF, *International Financial Statistics*, Supplement series no. 4 on Trade Statistics, 1982.

had to appease foreign creditors with a higher rate of return on its dollar. The recent high interest rates are not the necessary consequence of the dynamic process of inflation described earlier, but the product of an unusual and artificial policy action by the leader-nation refusing to pay off the bill accumulated from its own past actions. The global effect of this policy has been very similar to the effect of the artificial deflationary monetary policy adopted by Britain during the 1920s in order to force the world back to gold.

Turning to the analysis of the dynamic process of inflation, it must be noted that savers hold their savings in the form of paper assets, most of which are titles to a stream of payments fixed in money terms. From this basic feature of the system, it follows that a 10 per cent increase in the general price level for one year results in a 10 per cent loss to the creditors and a 10 per cent gain to the debtors, so far as the capital accounts are concerned. We can appreciate the significance of these transfers by using the Canadian figures cited earlier. We would be talking about a $38 billion transfer from households to businesses in just one year. This figure can almost be compared to the direct taxes that households paid to the federal government in 1985. The magnitude of such transfers between any two dates is determined by the difference in the price *level* between them. The mere ending of inflation does not restore the initial distribution of wealth.

Needless to say, these actual transfers or redistributions are modified by what happens to the Income Account, namely, the way certain flow variables react to inflation, the most notable ones being interest rates and wages. The reaction of these variables depends on the proximate cause of inflation and on how well it is anticipated. Simply put, once the interest rates have fully adapted to the inflation rates, no further redistribution between household and business through the interest variables occurs, for the inflation component of the interest rates is just enough to cover the loss in the capital account mentioned above. Similarly, once the nominal wage rate has fully caught up with the inflation rate, no further gains or losses between the two sectors take place. While the behaviour of these variables is bound to differ in detail from one inflation to another, as a rule, the variables adapt to inflation with some lags, so that each inflationary process causes a substantial transfer from households to corporate firms. Between 1973 and 1977, such transfers in Canada may have been as much as $60 billion in 1982 dollars, most of which is attributable to the slow adjustment in interest rates.

Wages also tend to lag behind prices in the initial stages of inflation; that is, real wages have a tendency to decline. First, a recognition lag exists. Second, there is an inherent inertia in group behaviour such as that of labour unions. Even if individual members are fully aware of inflation, group decisions take time. Third, wage contracts come up for renegotiation only gradually. As a result of all these factors, wage-earners lose in the initial phase of the inflationary process. In this sense, households may incur an additional loss. Empirically, however, the behaviour of real wages is more difficult to identify than that of interest rates. First, data on wage rates are scant. Second, wages have their own trends, so that the 'decline' in real wages need not be observed. Third, because labour services are heterogeneous non-traded goods, the impact of inflation and other shocks on real wages tends to vary widely between sectors of an economy and between economies. In 1973–5, for example, the oil shock caused a sharp increase in materials and other prices and a drop in the real income of many oil-consuming nations. These forces should have applied a downward pressure on real wages in general, but the business of some oil-related industries boomed, while some nations like Canada managed to use their own energy resources to tide them over the difficulties without a visible dent in real wages. In any case, both interest rates and wages may be expected to catch up with inflation after several years, if the inflation continues.

The Income Accounts restore a balance between sectors in real terms when interest rates and wages have fully adjusted to inflation. This is a kind of flow equilibrium. Economists, who are accustomed to think in terms of hydraulic models of flow variables, tend to believe that all the injustices of inflation have been eliminated once such an equilibrium is established, focusing their attention on the economy-wide welfare loss arising from the perpetual, 'fully anticipated' inflation. This approach is too simplistic, however. Before interest rates and wages have fully adjusted to inflation, the real transfers have been taking place continuously from creditors to debtors in a manner described above, though at declining rates. The cumulative transfers are at their maximum at that point, and the flow equilibrium merely preserves them.

When both interest rates and wages have caught up with inflation, however, an important change in the political dynamics of the system tends to occur. Business no longer sees any further gain from inflation. Its alliance with government ends. While the government can keep commanding additional resources in the form of an inflation tax without end, business becomes weary and critical of inflation. It even begins to promote the notion that it is a victim of inflation, putting aside the benefits it has reaped in the preceding phase of inflation. The government, while perfectly capable of continuing its lucrative venture in an inflationary environment, encounters some difficulty, now that the household and business sectors have united in opposition; and at this stage it begins to talk about anti-inflationary measures, though with less than full enthusiasm. Business begins campaigning vigorously to promote the view that government budget deficits and rising wages are the major evils besetting the economy, and therefore that their growth must first be curbed. The government agrees but labour resists. Academic economists tend to side with government, because in their hydraulic models the state of the flow equilibrium described earlier appears to be a perfectly legitimate equilibrium and the prevailing inflation appears to be an obvious nuisance to all the parties concerned. To economists, curbing inflation by direct control or any other means seems only too natural.

But as soon as we look at what has happened during the preceding years, we recognize that the current state is hardly an equilibrium, if 'equilibrium' is interpreted in any sensible socio-psychological sense. A massive redistribution among the sectors has been validated. This redistribution remains in effect even if inflation were to be brought down to zero overnight. Households are justifiably angry and demand redress, although no appeal procedures exist or are available to them. As if unaware of their feelings, government implements measures to curb the growth of wages and prices, which has the effect (among others) of denying households' appeal for redress. Whatever the short-term benefits of such policies, they must be weighed against the long-term costs arising from the rift they create between the winners and losers. Or so it seems. The fact of the matter, however, is that households as a group are incredibly forgiving and co-operative. Only their poor understanding of economic affairs and their short memory can account for such generosity.

But whether or not society would be better off with more enlightened households is a moot question. If one believes that today's affluence has been made possible by debt capitalism, and that the debtors need occasional breaks in the form of inflation, the implied trade-off may well have been worth exploiting.

4   A CRITIQUE OF THE PURE THEORIES OF INFLATION

Inflation is widely believed to be an evil. But if one seeks a solid analytical proof that it is, one is struck by the paucity of such attempts. Even Schumpeter's encyclopaedic *Analysis* (1954) does not list inflation as a separate entry in its 30-page subject index. Although this may seem remarkable to people who have lived through fifty years of continual inflation, it is consistent with the view that inflation is a twentieth-century phenomenon.

Another reason for the paucity of inflation theories is the strong bias in orthodox economic theory towards 'real analysis' as opposed to 'monetary analysis'. The victory of real analysis at an early stage in the development of economic thought was so complete that monetary analysis had to 'lead a lingering life . . . in an "underworld" of its own' (Schumpeter 1954: 282). This bias led to the conventional general equilibrium model in which the monetary equation (the quantity theory formula) hangs like an appendix to a system of elaborate real equations. The model embodies a belief in neutral money. The paths of real variables are determined by 'real forces' and independently of monetary forces; interest rates on money loans tend towards their demand price, the marginal productivity of capital. In this sense interest rates themselves are real variables (in sharp contrast to Keynes's theory, in which interest rates are essentially monetary variables). The only monetary influence on interest rates works through inflationary expectations, which raise the nominal interest rates on money loans so as to keep the 'real' rates on money loans at par with the marginal productivity rate of return on capital. Once income and interest rates have been determined, one has only to ascertain the form and stability of the demand-for-money function, expressed as a function of the predetermined real income and interest rates. The Chicago theory of inflation, to be discussed shortly, is built on this neoclassical framework.

As for the *effects* of inflation, the only theory worth remembering appears to be that of forced saving. Put simply, the theory stresses the reallocative effect of inflation from consumption to investment. If, in a fully employed economy, investors receive new bank credit and claim additional real resources of the economy with it, the sacrifice must come from the consumption goods industry, as the resources of the economy flow into the investment goods industry. With the consumers' money incomes and their spending plans in money terms unchanged, this means higher prices of consumer goods and less consumption in real terms. Inflation thus stimulates the formation of capital. This reallocative effect of inflation is sometimes called the 'Cantillon Effect', after Richard Cantillon (1755).

The theory of forced saving has been all but forgotten in the past fifty years. But the idea behind it is important, and is capable of applications in a more general setting. One could relax the assumption of full employment and assume that the government rather than business were the recipient of the extra credit, in which case one would have a theory of inflation tax. Furthermore, the extra credit need not come as a surprise but could be partially or wholly anticipated by the consumers, thereby causing voluntary revisions in their spending plans and asset portfolios. Changing assumptions certainly leads to different results. If business gets the extra credit, we would expect some increase in business investment. If government gets the extra credit and spends it, the economy should receive some stimulus. In any case, this line of reasoning does not lead to an effective demonstration that inflation is a social evil.

Examining contemporary works, we find the first clear demonstration of the anti-inflation proposition in the writings of some Chicago economists, notably Sidrauski (1967) and Friedman (1969). They constructed and analysed a stylized model of capital and money with the following results. First, the long-run capital stock and real output are independent of the growth rate of the money supply; that is, money is neutral in the long run. Second, money yields liquidity services to its holders, but the amount of real balances desired by society decreases as the inflation rate increases. Inflation, therefore, forces society to consume less of the services of money. Given their assumption that money is costless to produce, it then follows that it would be socially optimal to reduce the opportunity cost of holding money to zero and let society consume the maximum amount of the liquidity services of money, in the form of less frequent trips to the bank and more flexibility with which to meet uncertain cash needs, by setting the rate of deflation equal to the rate of time preference of the populace of the society. Using a simple demand-for-money function and 1968 US data, Friedman calculates the hypothetical welfare gain resulting from a move from 2 per cent inflation to 5 per cent deflation at \$2.3 billion per year, or 0.33 per cent of the US GNP of that year. He also indicates that, if society's discount rate were raised to 17 or 33 per cent, the gain could be much larger. In short, he concludes that inflation imposes real costs to society even in the long run.

From an historical and institutional standpoint, the analysis of the Chicago economists is severely flawed and their verdict biased. One must begin a critical analysis of their work by reviewing some of the key assumptions underlying the Chicago capital theory. First, their neutrality result is the direct consequence of their assumptions that the people's rate of time preference is an immutably given human datum, and that the people are immortal. When these assumptions are combined, the long-run capital stock of society is determined by the equality between the rate of time preference and the marginal product of capital, and nothing can affect it. With the population and labour force growth exogenous and full employment assured, the long-run output or real income is determined. This enables Friedman to ignore the real sector and concentrate on the monetary aspect of the model.

But what if people are mortal, or if their rates of time preference are influenced by the economic conditions surrounding them? First, given the mortality of individuals, their rates of time preference and the equilibrium marginal productivity of capital need not equal each other. Individuals save and dissave over their life-cycles. The aggregate volume of savings forthcoming from such a society is a demographically weighted sum of individual savings, which may fall or rise with an increase in the individual rates of time preference. This, in turn, implies that society's rate of time preference is an amalgam of taste parameters of individuals, demographic parameters, and such institutional factors as lifetime wage profiles, and need not even be positively correlated with the individual rates. Second, in all likelihood, individuals' rates of time preference are not magical constants, but are influenced by the future prospects of the economy and more generally by the 'mood' prevailing in society. Hard times tend to raise these rates and vice versa. Future consumption is, after all, a luxury good in relation to present consumption, and it is hard to see how a parameter relating them should be a constant immune to outside influences.

Recently governments have drastically cut spending on long-term projects such as education and public investment. This may be interpreted as an increase in their rate of time preference. If the discount rates of supposedly far-sighted and rational governments are already so volatile, it seems safe to conclude that the individual rates are, if anything, more capricious. What is questionable is not the equality between society's rate of time preference and the marginal product of capital, but the causality from the former to the latter as asserted by the Chicago economists.

A second and more serious criticism concerns the authors' total neglect of the institutional features of today's capitalism. Their model economy contains 'wealth-owners' alone: no debt-owners, except the government, exist. They have a model of family capitalism, not corporate capitalism. Government debt (in the form of money) aside, their supposition that family capitalism is neutral to inflation rates is acceptable as a first-order approximation. But this same claim cannot be justified for corporate capitalism. Corporate capitalism has generated separate debtor and creditor sectors, which are related to each other by monetary IOUs. Inflation affects these two sectors differently, and the range of inflation rates compatible with the viability of the two sectors is quite limited, especially from below. If readers are not convinced, imagine a permanent deflation at 10 per cent per year. Suppose you put aside a $1000 bill today: in just 208 years, it would be able to buy the entire current Canadian GNP of $454 billion! No debtor could stand that.

Over the past hundred years, the average annual real growth rate of the US economy has been in the order of 3 per cent. One may take this to be the long-run marginal productivity of capital, which, in turn, may be interpreted as the revealed rate of time preference of the US economy. What would be the consequence of imposing a 5 per cent deflation on such an economy? At the minimum, the capital stock would have to contract in order to earn the higher marginal productivity rate of return. If one uses a simple Cobb–Douglas production function with the capital exponent of 0.25, raising the marginal product of capital from 3 to 5 per cent means that the capital stock would have to be cut by half, and output by 16 per cent. True, Friedman's welfare gain would still exist, but it would be smaller than his estimate and most certainly would be swamped by the welfare loss coming from the huge decline in output.

Figure 5.2 depicts the situation under discussion. In this figure the curves DD and $D'D'$ are the demand curves for real balances under a 2 per cent inflation and a 5 per cent deflation, respectively. The $D'D'$ curve lies inside of DD because the output under a 5 per cent deflation

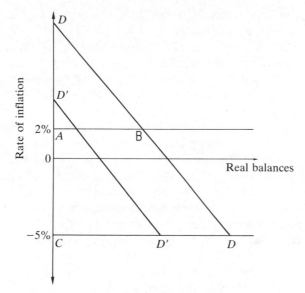

Fig. 5.2   Inflation and long-term economic welfare.

is smaller than that under a 2 per cent inflation, and because the demand for real balances is an increasing function of output.[4] Friedman's welfare gain described above refers to the area $ACDB$, whereas the correct gain is the difference in area between $\Delta D'CD'$ and ΔDAB, which may be positive or negative. If we allow for the negative welfare effect of reduced output and real wages arising from the smaller capital stock in the deflationary economy, it is quite plausible that a 2 per cent inflation equilibrium is superior to a 5 per cent deflation equilibrium. In other words, a mild inflation tax may very well be an efficient tax in the sense of enhancing the economic welfare of society. Yet this would probably be only a minmum estimate of the welfare loss, for in reality a total collapse of corporate capitalism and a return to the era before Henry Ford and Gustavus Swift would occur. The consequence of a move to a more drastic rate of deflation such as 17 or 33 per cent would be even more disastrous. Incidentally, Friedman never mentions the dire consequence of deflation to the government, whose monetary debt would be outgrowing the

---

[4] Tobin (1965) has developed a model in which the long-run capital stock depends positively on the rate of inflation.

economy in real value. How the government would propose to honour its debt, I don't know.

Ever since the appearance of the above essay by Friedman, I have always suspected that Friedman really was a socialist. For, according to his prescription, the government should fully use the faith and credit given to it by its citizenry first to create real balances, and then to render the entire seigniorage gain to the citizens instead of pocketing it, even if this meant the end of the corporate capitalism which many other Chicago economists cherish. At any rate, it follows from these observations that our system is one in which the debtors have taken the creditors hostage, that its survival and prosperity depend on the health of the debtors, and that a mild inflation probably offers the most favourable environment for it.

As a matter of 'feeling', one cannot deny that inflation is exciting. It has destroyed many family and business fortunes, but has created many more. If there had been no inflation since the turn of the century, far fewer changes in the list of millionaires would have occurred.[5] If a dozen eggs were to sell for six cents and a loaf of bread for three cents for ever, business might be very stable, but it would also be very dull. In other words, a non-inflationary environment would be very conservative and stifling to entrepreneurial activities.

5 INTERNATIONAL ASPECTS OF INFLATION

No analysis of inflation is complete without an examination of the global constraints, both physical and psychological, under which national economies operate. Economists argue that small open economies have only limited control over their inflation rates. This is true under a fixed exchange rate, in which the world has a single currency. If the real parts of the system are assumed exogenous as a first approximation, the world inflation rate is then essentially

---

[5] It is a fact of life that large individual wealths are created increasingly through speculative activities in various asset markets. During 1987 in Japan, for example, as many as 77 of the nation's top 100 personal incomes were based on capital gains from sales of real estate, according to the National Tax Agency. The top income-earner paid an income tax of over $15 million. Konosuke Matsushita, Japan's leading entrepreneur/capitalist, was ranked 24th, with a modest tax liability of $5 million. Real estate booms are not the same as general inflation, to be true. However, goods prices are known to become more flexible and volatile as rate of inflation increases. In this sense, inflation creates more opportunities for quick and large profits and losses.

governed by the growth rate of the world money supply, which in turn is a weighted average of national monetary growth rates, where the weights are the individual shares in the world money stock. A small open economy, having a small share of the world money stock, is naturally rather powerless to influence the world inflation rate.

More relevant and interesting to the present theme is a floating regime. Under this regime, each nation can in principle choose its own inflation rate, barring major and lasting changes in the terms of trade. For example, if the US economy were to inflate, Canada could maintain a tight money, letting the exchange rate absorb the inflationary pressure coming from the USA. History indicates, however, that the Canadian authorities have, on the whole, been reluctant to let the dollar appreciate. They may fear the speculative capital movements that fluctuating exchange rates can produce. Indeed, this fear can be justified for a country like Canada, whose financial markets are closely tied to those of the USA, because capital gains and losses from exchange rate changes could easily swamp small interest rate differentials, given the high substitutability between US and Canadian securities. From a more general viewpoint, however, this cannot plausibly explain why so many small open economies should have chosen to peg their currencies to those of the major trading partner (see Table 5.2). Rather, these countries may believe that a currency appreciation will weaken the competitiveness of their export industries and thereby cause increased unemployment.

An argument based on this idea is often used in favour of a currency depreciation when exports slump and unemployment rises. Implicit in this argument is a belief that every change in the exchange rate has a direct impact on the terms of trade or the 'real' exchange rate. However, this belief is not well founded. First, the real exchange rate is protected from a monetary shock from abroad to the extent that the flexibility of exchange rates serve as an insulator. Second, for small open economies, most if not all of their traded goods are priced in the world market in the units of key foreign currencies such as the US dollar. In such circumstances the exchange rate is merely a number translating foreign prices into domestic prices. No manipulation of the exchange rate can alter the real exchange rate, i.e. the relative price of exports over imports. In such a situation an expansionary monetary policy would merely result in an equi-proportional depreciation of the exchange rate. Recall the famous and much oversold advice that a small open economy operating under a floating regime could use monetary policy beneficially. This conclusion depends crucially on the 'homemadeness' of domestic prices. For many small open economies, prices have a low domestic content, and consequently the link between the nominal and the real exchange rates must be weak. That people believe the opposite is due largely to the influence of the Mundell–Fleming model of the early 1960s, which assumes, among other things, that domestic prices are 100 per cent homemade. For many small open economies this is a poor assumption, and the policy conclusions derived from it must be assessed with caution.

In reality, since 1973 a great majority of the IMF member-countries have opted to limit the flexibility of their exchange rates. Table 5.2 shows the current classification of the member-countries by type of exchange rate policies, suggesting that the world today still centres around the US dollar, with the rest of the countries making

Table 5.2   Classification of the IMF member-countries by type of exchange rate policy, 30 September, 1983 and 30 September, 1986.

	1983	1986
Currencies pegged to:		
US dollar	35	31
French franc	13	14
Other currencies	5	5
SDR	12	10
Other currency composites	27	31
Co-operative exchange arrangements[a]	8	8
Flexibility limited in terms of single currency[b]	9	5
More flexible:		
Adjusted according to a set of indicators	5	6
Other managed float	23	20
Independent floating[c]	8	20
Total membership	145	151

  [a] Members of the European Monetary Union, namely, Belgium, Denmark, France, Germany, Ireland, Italy, Luxembourg, and Netherlands.
  [b] All in terms of the US dollar.
  [c] Canada, Israel, Japan, Lebanon, South Africa, UK, USA, and Uruguay in 1983; Australia, New Zealand, and a host of small nations have since joined this group.
Source: IMF, *International Financial Statistics, November 1983, November 1987.*

efforts, singly or in groups, to moderate the fluctuations in exchange rates. Even the relation among the major currencies is not one of independent float, as evidenced by the recent joint attempt by the USA and other major countries to regulate the external value of the US dollar.

In a global system operating in this manner, two principal sources of inflation exist. One is inflation initiated by the key currency nation; for, once the leader nation inflates, the others are more likely to follow it than fight it. The other is the tendency for the smaller countries to inflate away their problems of a real and often structural nature.

The world inflation problem is complicated further by the indeterminacy inherent in any game situation, of which the international money game is one. As history shows, it takes a strong leader to keep tight control over the world money/moneys. But there is no assurance, as at the present time, that a widely acceptable leader exists, and that such a potential leader would in fact want to lead. Should either of these two conditions be lacking, the world would be left without a leader, the consequence of which would be a rather unsatisfactory non-cooperative equilibrium, at best. The rampant world-wide inflation during the past decade may be thought of as one such equilibrium, with a higher inflation rate than anyone wanted.

Figure 5.3 attempts to depict this sort of equilibrium. It is based on a simple two-country monetarist model under fixed exchange rates. Each country is assumed to possess preferences concerning the (common) inflation rate and the balance of payments, which peak at a prescribed 'target' combination of inflation rate and balance of payments. The world inflation rate is assumed to be a weighted average of the national monetary growth rates, whereas the balance of payments of one country is assumed to depend on the difference between the domestic monetary growth rate and the world inflation rate. In symbols, the welfare function of each nation is assumed to be of the form

$$U_i(p, b_i) = -(p - p_i^*)^2 - a_i(b_i - b_i^*)^2, \quad a_i > 0, i = 1, 2,$$

where $p =$ the (common) inflation rate, $p_i^* =$ the target inflation rate for country i, $b_i =$ the balance of payments of country i, and $b_i^* =$ the target balance of payments of country i. Denoting the monetary weights of the two countries by w_i, they of course satisfy the conditions $w_i > 0$ and $w_1 + w_2 = 1$. Using these weights, we can write

$$p = w_1 m_1 + w_2 m_2$$

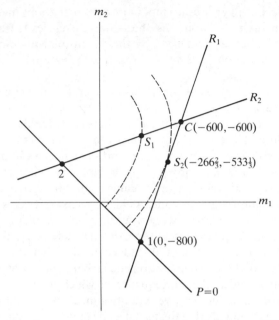

Fig. 5.3   The non-existence of a stable Stackelberg equilibrium.

and

$$b_i = p - m_i = (1 - w_i)(m_j - m_i), \quad j \neq i, \, i, j = 1, 2,$$

where m_i is the monetary growth rate of country i.

Figure 5.3 is based on the above model with $w_1 = w_2 = \frac{1}{2}$, $a_1 = a_2 = 2$, $p_1^* = p_2^* = 0$, and $b_1^* = b_2^* = -10$. In other words, the situation is one in which two countries of equal size (the USA and the EEC, for example) are vying for leadership, each desiring a zero inflation but wanting to run a balance of payments deficit to alleviate domestic hardship. In Figure 5.3, points 1 and 2 are the target or optimal position (p^*, b_i^*) for country 1 and country 2, respectively, C denotes the Cournot solution, S_1 is the Stackelberg solution with country 1 as leader and country 2 as follower, S_2 is a similar solution with the roles of the two countries reversed, and the paired numbers in parentheses represent the utility levels of country 1 and country 2 in that order. Each country's indifference curves are concentric ellipses with centre at (p^*, b_i^*) and major and minor axes of slopes $+1$ and -1, respectively. The two broken curves in the figure are part of the indifference map of country 2. The figure is completely symmetric with respect to the 45° line $m_2 = m_1$.

Now, the point of Figure 5.3 is that, in the situation depicted therein, each country finds itself better off being a follower than a leader. In this sense, it is a situation in which there is no leader. It is a situation Stackelberg called *gleichgewichtlos* (Stackelberg 1952: 202) and the probable consequence of that would be that the world would settle into the Cournot point, which unfortunately means a greater welfare loss for each country and a higher inflation rate than at a Stackelberg point. This feature of the model is preserved irrespective the values of the targets, so long as the weights and the form of the utility functions remain unchanged. When the latter conditions are altered, the Stackelberg solutions may be shown to become 'stable' for certain ranges of the parameters, but the above non-existence or instability remains a possibility. Given the overwhelming historical evidence that every world leader resigned totally exhausted, and that no nation has ever regained leadership, the job of being a world leader is probably not a profitable job, and is definitely becoming more all-consuming as membership of the world community increases and democracy permeates international politics. If so, the future of the international monetary order appears bleak, and so does the prospect of counter-inflationary policies.

6 SUMMARY

The thesis advanced in this chapter is that inflation in today's societies is, par excellence, a political phenomenon. Societies in which debtors hold political power have an inherent inflationary bias. This bias is not something that can be removed or reversed by the whim of political leaders. Today's monetary economies carry financial assets or debts several times as large as annual gross national products. If these debts were to appreciate in real value owing to deflation, the health of the debtors would be seriously endangered. Even a zero inflation would inhibit their activities. On the other hand, debtors must rely on a continuous flow of loanable funds from creditors, and this need may set a limit to the rate of inflation. Within these bounds, however, inflation can go on, and it will.

Is inflation a social evil? To the extent that it is caused by the abuse of seigniorage rights by the government, it goes counter to our notion of justice. Inflation can cause a massive redistribution of wealth from the creditors to the debtors. This too defies our sense of justice. Inflation causes further inconveniences and nuisances to all. In this sense also it is an evil. But if today's high productivity and expanded economic democracy were made possible by the constant growth of monetary debt, and if the loosening effect of inflation has been instrumental in fostering economic minds and activities in general, and if the alternative were a return to the family capitalism of past centuries, a mild or sporadic inflation may well have been a price worth paying.

In other words, inflation is more like air pollution than war. It must be controlled. But only within sensible limits. A monomaniac anti-inflationary policy would do more harm than good.

6
Money as a Source of Power

With the Mafia, they shoot you; the banks let you shoot yourself.
Ronald Derrickson, chief of the West Bank Indian band

1 INTRODUCTION

There exists a significant 'credibility gap' between academic economics and the real world. This is an old problem, and one that exists more or less in every field. Academics operate within a model, or more broadly a paradigm, and seek answers to real-world problems within it. The model or paradigm provides academics with a framework for systematic thinking and analysis, and is therefore absolutely necessary for any scientific investigations. But the answers that academics derive from it are naturally only as good as the paradigm itself. When the object of investigation is as complex and evolutionary as a national economy, it is not possible to identify a single 'true' paradigm. There is usually room for several alternative paradigms competing with one another. On the other hand, the rapid institutionalization of academic economics in the past fifty years or so makes it increasingly difficult for the alternative paradigms to compete freely, because the institution of academic economists has endorsed one paradigm as the orthodoxy. Once the orthodoxy is identified by the institution, its members feel the presssure to abide by it, or otherwise risk their membership. Without this institutionalization and the group dynamics under it, it is very hard to explain the 110-year reign of neoclassical economics, itself a spin-off from Newtonian physics. Although I cannot claim to have good knowledge of the present state of the art in other branches of the social sciences, it seems that the dominance of neoclassicism for over a century is itself a rather unique social phenomenon.

Needless to say, that it is old does not necessarily mean that it is bad. There are indeed many good things one could say for neoclassical economics, including its amenability to formal analysis.

But it has a few indefensible drawbacks, which in my opinion constitute the major cause for the credibility gap mentioned earlier. The first is its preoccupation with competitive markets. The notion of competitive equilibrium is a direct import from the natural sciences. It is a state of balance to which physical objects tend; it is a state of equalized pressure or heat. But it is *not* what an economy, made up of actively rational agents, naturally tends to.

Figure 6.1 serves to make this point. In the figure, a competitive exchange equilibrium is shown by point *C* in an ordinary Edgeworth box. *E* is the initial endowment point, and the two broken curves labelled *PEP* are the price expansion paths, or offer curves, of the two price-taking agents, A and B. The solid curves labelled *U* are of course the indifference curves. Now suppose the market is in competitive equilibrium at *C*. Agent A can see that he could do better by displacing the equilibrium from point *C* to some point on that portion of the PEP_B, B's offer curve, bordered by points *C* and *D*. Having sensed this possibility, it would be *irrational* for agent A to be content with the competitive equilibrium. He would naturally do everything within his means to improve his lot. The monopolist solution is one well-known outcome of such a move. Agent A could even lie about his preferences (which would shift his *PEP* up), so that the new 'competitive equilibrium' is on the arc *DC*. But what is true of agent A is also true of agent B, who also would sense and try to seize the opportunity to improve his own lot.

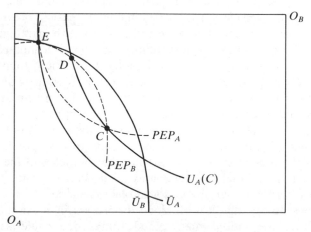

Fig. 6.1   The non-viability of competitive equilibrium.

The result of such interactions would not be as determinate as the mechanical competitive equilibrium bcause it would depend on the information, power, and many other attributes of the agents. No matter what the actual outcome would be, it is clear that the conventional competitive equilibrium would *not* be a viable equilibrium for an economy composed of rational agents. True, economists are becoming increasingly aware of the despairingly demanding conditions under which competitive markets lead to a socially efficient outcome. Yet they continue to use stylized competitive equilibrium models in theoretical and empirical analyses. They do so primarily because their institution approves of such a practice. Practitioners, in the meantime, remain unconvinced of the economists' models. They know that economic competition is like the game of musical chairs, and that the key to economic success is to outsmart the others, by means ranging from haggling to winning government favour.[1]

The second major drawback of neoclassical economics is its failure to properly recognize the role of money in a capitalist economy. As Schumpeter (1954) noted, economic theory has always had a bias towards 'realist' theory. Classical economics were already realist in nature; but its sin was minor compared with that of neoclassical economics. Quesnay's *Tableau Economique* of 1759, for example, is capable of a monetary interpretation. His 'advances' were a 'fund', i.e. a money form of capital; and the landlords' decisions to invest or advance their money capital depended essentially on the prospective rate of return on the fund. If the landlords' desires to invest were weak, then farmers and artisans would face the danger of being unemployed. In this sense, the *Tableau* foreshadowed the 'monetary' analyses of Malthus (1836), and Keynes (1936). Marx, in 1867, identified one of the central features of a capitalist economy as its money–goods–money sequence, compared with the pre-capitalist goods–money–goods sequence, the point being that, whereas in the pre-capitalist system money was a mere agent intervening between the produced bundle of goods and the bundle of goods to be consumed, under capitalism it becomes an end itself (see Marx 1906).

---

[1] The literature on core theory shows that competitive equilibrium is the only core of large economies, that is, that competitive equilibrium is the only equilibrium that withstands all possible collusive attempts at destruction. While the theoretical significance of this theorem is indisputable, it does not make competitive equilibrium any more plausible, because its fulfilment depends on unrealistic assumptions, such as the free dissemination of information and zero bargaining and transaction costs.

Marxian money has two important characteristics: first, for the capitalist, which goods intervene between monies is inessential; marijuana is just as good as bread; second, capitalist activities must start with money, so that whoever has access to it has a definite advantage over those who do not.

As this brief survey indicates, classical economists generally had the right perception of money and were much more receptive to the monetary influences on the economy than neoclassicists. When neoclassical economics took over, money was reduced to an innocuous medium of exchange. Its combined assumptions of perfect information, competition, passive rationality of individuals, zero transactions costs, the timelessness of economic activities, and the backward-looking notion of capital as machines has made money totally irrelevant. The real side of the model economy is completely determined by 'real forces'. The only role of money is to determine the absolute price level; but why should anyone be interested in the absolute price level when no one's welfare depends on it? Having set out to work within a framework so ideal and smooth as to make money superfluous, economists naturally have had a difficult time monetizing their model economy in a logically sound and meaningful way. The most popular way of theorizing a monetary economy has been to postulate certain costs, physical or psychic, which an agent must incur if he is out of money. Walras, in 1900 invented the notion of the 'service of availability' (see Walras 1954); Patinkin (1965) talks about the 'embarrassment' one feels if one fails to have enough money when presented with a bill; more recently, it has become fashionable to speak of the 'cash-in-advance' economy *à la* Clower (1967), in which an agent cannot discharge his debt by any means other than cash.

Although money undoubtedly has the kind of effects as perceived here on individual choices, these formulations are far too *ad hoc* and incomplete, and far too narrow in their perception of the role of moey in capitalist economies, to be a satisfactory theory of a monetary economy. Money has in fact changed the organization and the power structure of the economy; it has resulted in the shift from family capitalism to corporate capitalism, the households' new role as suppliers of investible funds, the great power exercised by the banks and other financial intermediaries, the constant exploitation of the seigniorage gain by the states, and the rise of the new élite agents who thrive in this environment. Indeed, one interesting aspect of today's political economy is that power is distributed not in accordance with real wealth but rather in accordance with the ability to command monetary resources. This suggests that there is something special about money. But why? This chapter intends to find the answer.

No one disputes the fact that wealth is power. History provides enough proof of this. In pre-monetary economies the wealthy owned the means of production and used others to produce more wealth. Those who supplied labour to the wealthy were typically tied down to the manor as serfs or slaves. Even when the labourers were not 'owned' by the landlord, they were under very long-term contracts, often extending over generations. The landlord's control of his labourers was direct and *real*. This real control of the poor by the wealthy did not change, even after the economy moved into the first stage of capitalism, 'family capitalism': money was still relatively insignificant. The economic theory of the firm as we know it today was modelled after this mode of capitalism. Not surprisingly, the theory is totally devoid of monetary features.

Although virtually everyone equates wealth with power as a matter of fact, some economists contend that it is not self-evident. Production activities require both capital and labour. Why should capitalists be bosses of labourers, and not the other way around? Why shouldn't the labourers hire capital and be their own bosses? Eswaran and Kotwal (1985) offer an explanation as to why capitalists should be bosses. The gist of their argument goes as follows.

Consider two individuals who face the same uncertain income prospect but differ in the sizes of their wealth. Let us say that one individual is rich and the other, poor. Let the expected utility of the poor facing this uncertain prospect by $\bar{U}_p$. If we assume that the two individuals have the same tastes, including the degree of risk aversion, then the rich individual's expected utility of the uncertain income prospect must be the same as $\bar{U}_p$. But, being rich, he need not be content with this utility level. He can use his wealth to smooth out his income. As a result, his expected utility $\bar{U}_r$ becomes higher that $\bar{U}_p$. In other words, the cost of risk, or the risk premium of the rich individual, becomes smaller than that of the poor person. The rich, having a smaller risk premium, can now gainfully purchase the labour of the poor for a certain wage w at which $U_p(w, L) > \bar{U}_p$ and at the same time $EU_r(Y-w, 0) > \bar{U}_r$, where L is the amount of labour, Y is the (random) income, and E is the expectation operator over Y. In other words, thanks to the reduction in risk owing to wealth, there emerges room for a Pereto-superior contract in which the poor works for the rich for a certain wage, and the rich, released from labour, can now devote his time to managerial tasks or simply to leisure.

One interesting implication of the Eswaran–Kotwal study is that individuals' 'tastes' become affected by wealth; the rich individual behaves *as if* he has a lower degree of risk aversion than the poor, contrary to the supposition of the model. Eswaran and Kotwal also argue that the same results would obtain if one individual had access to commercial credit while the other did not, although the ability to obtain commercial credit may well be correlated with wealth.

Thus, the Eswaran–Kotwal model explains why wealth is a source of power. But it has no monetary characteristics. In this sense, it is a model of family capitalism, and not of today's corporate or *debt* capitalism. Corporate capitalism is organized in a very different way from family capitalism. Banks and other financial intermediaries siphon off the public's savings and loan them to corporate firms. The firms use these borrowed funds to purchase the physical assets needed for their production activities. For example, at the end of 1985, Canadian (private non-financial) corporations had a net liability of $383 billion, while the households had net financial assets amounting to $514 billion, roughly the same as Canada's GNP of the same year. In terms of the ownership of wealth, the households are the wealth-owners and should therefore be the 'bosses'. But they are not. If anything, the corporations are bosses. Moreover, within the corporate sector, the financial intermediaries, which own no net financial assets, reign over the non-financal corporations, which own several hundred billion dollars' worth of physical assets and control the production of goods and services in the economy. This massive shift of power from individuals to corporations, from creditors to debtors, and above all *from goods to money* is what distinguishes today's economies from those of the previous centuries. But how has this shift of power been brought about? I offer the following observations in lieu of a definitive answer to this question.

In terms of the broad historical time scale, it is only a very recent phenomenon, perhaps over the last century, that the wealth and savings of the general public have become significant. The increased wealth of the public made its members attractive to capital for two reasons: their purchasing power was greatly increased, and their savings represented a source of investment funds. The preconditions for mass production were met. Mammoth corporations were first formed from capital made available by working men and women in the fields of rail and telegraphy; subsequently, they spread into other areas. Corporate demand for commercial credit also came to be financed by the savings of the public through the agency of the financial intermediaries. With the growth of the corporate sector, the significance of the ownership of such organizations by members of the general public also increased. But, owing to the several detrimental characteristics of the general public as a social group, such as the smallness of the average per capita size, the large size of the membership, the heterogeneity of the members, and their generally poor knowledge of the corporations they own, individual owners of stocks and shares have been unable to acquire the power commensurate with their wealth. Today these people are not all-powerful, not even important in society. They are as much owned by the system as they were in the past. Their potential power as wealth-owners has been aborted, and the slot has been taken over by the debtor-corporations.

Within the corporate sector, banks and other financial intermediaries have come to occupy a central place. The reason for this is not hard to see. To the corporations engaged in produciton activities, bank credit is their life-line, but its stopcock is under the control of the banks. Following the line of argument by Eswarian and Kotwal, one may say that commercial credit expands a firm's real opportunity set and increases the value of the firm over and above the explicit cost of borrowing. There is a positive borrower's surplus. The bank that supplies credit knows and uses this fact to gain control and power over the borrower. Again, this power never accrues to the individuals who loaned their money to the bank in the first place.

The unique power of the money-lender must derive from the versatile nature of money as an economic resource, but also, and more significantly, from the indivdualistic character of loan contracts. What is traded for ready cash in a loan contract is a stream of future sums of money or, more precisely, the borrower's promise to deliver such sums. The asset the lender acquires in this transaction is thus essentially personal or borrower-specific. It is chiefly this peculiar nature of loan contracts that gives the lender the power to control the borrower. To the loan applicant, what is at stake is not only a significant prospective profit but also often his life, whereas to the lender, an applicant is no more than one of many clients. Moreover, when opinions differ between the lender and the borrower, the opinion of the lender prevails. Hence the lender's power.[2]

Today's businesses are more or less subordinate to the money-lenders, who can easily kill small businesses by calling their demand loans. Even the largest of large corporations are not free from the lenders' control. Chrysler would have been long gone, had it not been for the lenders' decision to keep it alive. Even some sovereign states would have to die, should the creditor banks decide to terminate their credit.[3] As a result, the money-lenders exert an enormous power in domestic and international politics. But for the billions of dollars of loans by the US banks to the Marcos regime, for example, President Reagan would not have hesitated to withdraw his support of Marcos after the scandalous election of 1986. Similarly, his stubborn opposition to an economic sanction of South Africa against the will of the Congress hints strongly at pressure exerted by the large US banks with heavy investments in that country.

Besides the money-lender's control over the borrower at the micro level, another important source of power of money is the seigniorage right, namely, the right to create money. By monopolizing this right, the modern states have fully exploited it, first by pocketing the full commodity value of gold and silver once used as money, and then by continually issuing more and more paper money under the present managed currency system. In a monetized economy, where the public hold their savings in the form of monetarily denominated debts of others, a monetary tampering by the state can affect the real values of the public's savings drastically in a short period of time. Money has indeed been a covert but very potent means of affecting the agents' 'endowments' themselves. In terms of Figure 6.1, the endowment

[2] According to a 1982 study of Canada's business loan market cited by Crawford (1985), 25% of all loan enquiries by small businesses were rejected by the chartered banks before reaching the formal application stage; the actual loan size was 90% of the amounts requested on formal loan applications on average; and one-third of the 400 small businesses surveyed had been denied a loan request at some time during the preceding three-year period. Crawford estimates that the dominant part of total credit rationing by the chartered banks in this market is 'equilibrium', or discretionary, rationing, as against 'disequilibrium' rationing. These facts depict the enormous power exercised by the money lenders over the borrowers, potential and actual.

[3] For an excellent historical account of the power of the money-lenders, see Sampson (1981). Of course, the sense of fear and hatred the public holds towards money-lenders is legendary; the Shakespearean personality Shylock epitomizes it.

point E is itself susceptible to every monetary tampering. In a monetary economy, resource allocations are inherently political. It is in this sense that members of the public are owned by the system along with their savings. Not only that: the state uses the newly acquired monetary resource to carry out its various policy goals. Intentionally or unintentionally, it exercises a great deal of discretion and power in this allocation process in much the same way as a private lender does to his borrowers.

All in all, money in today's economies is much more than a unit of account and a medium of exchange; it affects the real opportunity sets of individuals and even the course of development of a national economy. Those who produce money or credit exert a great influence in today's political economy. This is not necessarily all bad. If one holds, as I do, the view that competition and price mechanisms are not enough to keep an economy on even keel, let alone produce a winner in the global economic race, there is clearly room for the rational will of the state in economic planning carried out through its monetary power, with the banking sector assiting it. But this is a risky choice for society; for those in power tend to act irresponsibly. Moreover, economic theory has so far failed to teach policy-makers what the optimal rules of monetary management are. Chronic inflation and budget deficits all over the world in the postwar period attest to the difficulty of using the power attached to money wisely.

I have said above that monetary theory is devoid of the human or political element. Given the natural scientific bent of neoclassical economics, this is understandable. Efforts have been made to build models in which money matters. The cash-in-advance model is one such example. To the extent that the cash constraint is self-imposed, the model fails to capture the political dimension of money. Nor will the mere recognition of bargaining between the lender and the borrower do the job, because the key feature of a loan contract lies in the fact that the lender's judgement is final.[4] What are the macroeconomic consequences of replacing the historical entrepreneurs with Midas and his men as the major decision-makers of the system? This seems to be one of the important socioeconomic questions as yet unanswered.

---

[4] Stiglitz and Weiss (1981) show why the interest rate might not be much of a bargaining variable for borrowers.

2 THE WORLD MONEY GAME

Another important area in which money influences real activities is
world politics as it affects the international monetary rules. For a
quarter of a century after the Second World War, the US dollar
reigned over the free world as the international currency. At the end of
the war the economies of both Axis and Allied countries were
fatigued, with the exception of the USA. With her dominant military
strength and abundant gold holdings, she was able to construct a new
international monetary order known as the Bretton Woods system.
During the first two postwar decades, the USA recorded a cumulative
trade surplus of over $50 billion, which translates into over
$600 billion in today's prices. Because the scale of the world economy
was much smaller then than now, US chronic trade surpluses of this
magnitude created a serious global shortage of the dollar, despite US
efforts to loan out these surpluses. Other countries' economies
behaved much like the cash-in-advance model economies of recent
origin. Black market prices of the dollar were often greatly in excess of
IMF parity rates. Americans could merely print money, take it
abroad, and buy foreign goods and services freely—a model case of
seigniorage exploitation.

In the meantime, however, the economies of Europe were
recovering rapidly. By the late 1950s, the major European economies
were able to compete freely in the international markets and the
convertibility of their currencies was restored. As the European
economies regained strength, there emerged a rivalry between them
and the USA. Europeans were never enthusiastic supporters of the
dollar standard and the US monopoly of the seigniorage gains.
Although they never revolted against it, they were always eager to
accumulate gold rather than dollars. The US holdings of monetary
gold declined and those of the European nations, especially of the
continental ones, increased rapidly (see Figure 6.2). This had the
effect of shaking the foundation of the US-sponsored Bretton Woods
system. By the beginning of the 1970s, US holdings of monetary gold
were at an alarmingly low level, which was soon to force the country
to sever the tie between the dollar and gold. This act stopped the
further loss of gold, but also deprived the dollar of its monopoly
power as the key international currency. Since then, several major
currencies have been vying for the international seigniorage gains,

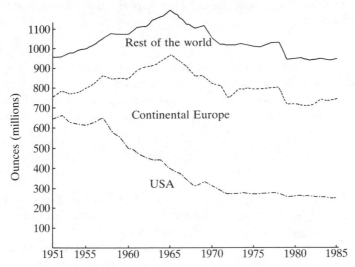

Fig. 6.2   Monetary gold holdings, 1951–1985. *Source:* IMF, *International Financial Statistics.*

which Aliber (1983) has aptly likened to the oligopolistic competition in the soda pop industry. The USA has found this competition unpleasant. In order to maintain the popularity of the dollar, US policy-makers have been forced to support high interest rates at the expense of jobs and capital formation at home.

In the mid-1980s the US economy was still running large trade deficits (to the order of $150 billion a year), while the dollar lost about 30 per cent of its value against other major currencies in 1985–6. Faced with large chronic trade deficits, the Reagan administration was naturally inclined to let the dollar depreciate. But Federal Reserve chairman Volcker registered a strong opposition to such a move. In his opinion, using the dollar to correct the trade imbalance had already run its course; more importantly, he felt that any further fall could do an irreparable damage to the dollar as a key international currency by destroying the world's confidence in it; he feared that the recent fall in the external value of the dollar might have already brought it near danger level in terms of market psychology. In contrast to the Reagan administration's simple model of 'fundamentals', Volcker's was clearly one that emphasized the speculative forces in the foreign exchange market.

The following simple model may capture the concern held by Volcker. Let

$$\dot{e} = a - be + c(\dot{e}/e).$$ (1)

In this equation, e is the external value of the dollar, $\dot{e}$ is its rate of change, and the coeffcients a, b, and c are all positive. The right-hand side may be thought of as the excess demand for the dollar, which consists of the fundamental part, $a - be$, and the speculative part, $c(\dot{e}/e)$. Solving (1) for $\dot{e}$, we obtain

$$\dot{e} = \frac{e(a - be)}{e - c}.$$ (2)

which implies that e goes to zero once it enters the 'danger zone', $e < \min(a/b, c)$. This region is so called because, once e enters, it is driven to zero by the market forces built into the above equation. This equation also implies that, if the speculative forces are strong, i.e. if $c > a/b$, the exchange rate that equilibrates the trade accounts, $e = a/b$, may be impossible to establish. This latter case is depicted in Figure 6.3.

The new Bush administration and Federal Reserve chairman Greenspan face a tough choice between prestige and comfort, between keeping up the value of the dollar to maintain its reputation as an international currency, and lowering its value to stimulate the economy, but at the same time running the risk of losing the seigniorage rights for good. History shows that national prestige tends to carry weight in such major political decisions, as the case of Britain in the 1920s showed. An emotional speech by Greenspan may well tip the balance in favour of the strong dollar, despite his lack of political power, especially if he can bring business to his side. But the choice may not be up to the USA alone. There is a political battle going on between the USA and other industrial nations, especially the continental European states. This is a battle between the dollar and gold, or between the Rockefellers and the Rothschilds, as some people put it. Gold is far from being dead. Indeed, the unstable international monetary condition in the 1980s has increased its importance. With their large holdings of monetary gold, European nations could dethrone the dollar if they wanted to. (The current US holding of 262 million ounces (on 1986) is worth $100 billion at the current market price of gold, which amounts to only a small fraction of the dollar claims held abroad.) The future course of the international

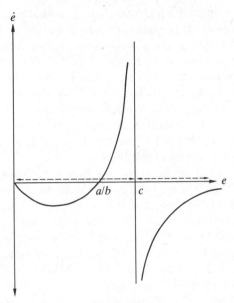

Fig. 6.3 'Fundamental' equilibrium in foreign exchange markets made unstable by speculative forces

monetary system and of the world economy itself will depend critically on the outcome of this monetary battle. (For a lucid and comprehensive survey on the subject of international monetary rules, see Hamada 1985.)

APPENDIX 1: 'THE ROCKEFELLER MEN RUN THE UNITED STATES'

Henirich Heine is reported to have said, 'Money is the god of our time and Rothschild is his prophet', and a Rothschild endorsed this statement when he said, 'Give me the right to issue a nation's money; then I do not care who makes its laws.'

The Rothschilds built an international banking house in the eighteenth century. Its network extended to all the major European financial capitals—Paris, Vienna, Naples, London, and Frankfurt —and it constituted a dominant political power in Europe for over a century. The Rothschild family first gained fame when it effectively circumvented Napoleon's blockades using its financial resources and an efficient network. European governments came to depend on the Rothschilds for emergency funds. The British government was particualrly dependent. It managed to pull itself through the Irish famine, the Crimean War, and the purchase of its share in the Suez Canal, thanks to money advanced by the Rothschilds. The Rothschilds were also behind Cecil Rhodes's development of diamond and gold mines in South Africa. The family's visibility as a power source diminished toward the end of the nineteenth century as it became assimilated into European high society.

Today, one finds a similar political power in the Rockefellers in the USA. The Rockefellers are similar to the Rothschilds in that their power stems from their financial resources, but the Rockefellers exert a far greater political pwoer than the Rothschilds through their supreme organizational abilities. The following brief account of the Rockefellers' position of power in the US politics relies on Allen (1976), Elias (1973), Lundberg (1975), Maisel (1983), Sampson (1981), and Sklar (1980). These authors, though arguably a biased sample, put forward the hypothesis that US politics since the mid-1950s has been shaped by the will of the Trilateral Commission, David Rockefeller's brain trust, including the choice of President and other key cabinet posts, and the basic policy direction in both domestic and international areas. Some authors even go so far as to implicate the Commission for the oil shocks and the subsequent speculative mania and high interest rates, all at the expense of jobs and growth of the US economy.

The Trilateral Commission is an outgrowth of the international group knowns as the Bilderberg Conferences, organized in 1954 in order to promote trade and international banking between Europe and America. The Bilderbergers were drawn from the most prominent political leaders, bankers, and intellectuals of both sides of the Atlantic, and the group included David Rockefeller as one of its founder-members. In 1973 the Bilderberg Conferences were reorganized and renamed the Trilateral Commission to include Japan.

But the idea of a brains trust on a global scale goes back even further, to some of the other Rockefeller organizations. The Council on Foreign Relations, founded at the end of the First World War in New York, is particularly relevant. The Council 'is composed of 1400 of the most élite names in the world of government, labor, business, finance, communications, foundations, and academics. It has staffed almost every key position of every administration since that of FDR', according to the *Christian Science Monitor* (1 September, 1961). David Rockefeller's father and David himself have been generous donors to the Council. David became its chairman in 1969. The Council had previously been chaired by John McCloy, an ex-Chase Manhattan man and World Bank governor, and lawyer for the Seven Sisters. Another Rockefeller organization, the Commission on Critical Choice for America, has 42 prominent Americans as members under the chairmanship of Nelson Rockefeller, one of David's brothers. Members of the Trilateral Commission overlap with these other organizations. The Commission has 300 members, 100 each from the USA, Western Europe, and Japan.

One remarkable feature of the Trilateral Commission is its global scale and élite membership. It obviously transcends party politics (both Democrats and Republicans have been in it), and every member is a star in his or her respective field. This feature makes it difficult for a charge of conspiracy or rent-seeking to stick. Yet, the Trilateralists' domination of key public offices in the US government makes the Commission suspect. For example, in the Carter administration, the Trilateralists included Jimmy Carter himself, Walter Mondale (Vice-President), Cyprus Vance (Secretary of State), Henry Kissinger (special adviser), Harold Brown (Secretary of Defense), Michael Blumenthal (Secretary of the Treasury), Samuel Huntington (National Security Council), Anthony Solomon (Under Secretary of the Treasury for Monetary Affairs), Robert Bowie (Deputy to the Director of the CIA), the three chairmen of the board of governors of the Federal Reserve System (Arthur Burns, G. William Miller, and Paul Volcker), and a host of other high officers. The Reagan administration included somewhat fewer Trilateralists. Reagan himself was not a Trilateralist. But George Bush (Vice-President), Casper Weinberger (Secretary of Defense), and Zbigniew Brzezinski (special adviser) were, to name just a few. And Volcker continued to chair the board of governors of the Federal Reserve System until the summer of 1987.

When so many key offices are occupied by Trilateralists, there is a probability that the US politics, domestic and international, reflect the will of the Commission, whose leadership and power emanate from its mentor and sponsor, David Rockefeller. Another important feature of the Commission is its strength in the field of money and finance: 24 out of the 50 largest banks in the world, as well as several central banks, are represented on it. This adds credibility to the theory that the Trilateral Commission strongly represents the interests of bankers around the world. Although David Rockefeller would be the last person to accept such a theory, the Rothschild statement quoted lends support to it.

Now, what has been the track record of US economic policies of late? Where, if at all, have the policies gone against the general economic welfare of Americans? The area in which the will of the policy-makers has been put to practice most rigorously and consistently throughout the 1970s and 1980s has been that of monetary policy. The early 1970s saw the rise of monetarism as the guiding principle behind monetary policy. Monetarism is strongly neoclassical (as against Keynesian) in its belief in markets and price mechanisms. More specifically, it places price stability before full employment as a policy goal. There was therefore a clear breaking away from Keynesianism, which had ruled postwar economic policy in the USA up to that date. In the meantime, the Bretton Woods system had collapsed and the First oil shock shook the entire world. The growth rate of income and trade volume dropped, and the world economy fell into a prolonged recession. The unemployment rate shot up and so did the inflation rate, triggered by the sharp increases in oil-related products and the speculative mania in real estate and certain raw materials.

On the other hand, the US government, like that of any other democratic country, felt the pressure to create more jobs by an expansionary policy mix according to the conventional wisdom of the postwar era. But the monetary policy did not relent. After an unsuccessful battle agaisnt inflation for a number of years, tight money began to make its effects felt in the economy in the form of high real interest rates. President Carter is reported to have wanted an easy money to stimulate the economy personally, but he could not have his way under the terms stipulated by the Trilateral Commission. Once inflation came under control, fiscal policy, and especially the budget deficit, became the next target of attack by the Trilateralists. Tight money and fiscal restraint have been the order of the day ever since.

In summary, the Trilateral Commission has been the driving force behind the new conservatism, which on the whole, has served well the interests of capital, and of the banking community in particular, at the expense of labour. The influence of a global body like the Trilateral Commission on economic policy-making is likely to icnrease in future as international conferences of national policy-makers gain popularity.

The apparent rationale behind the new conservatism is the trade-off between present enjoyment and future prosperity. While the cost of the conservative policy package is immediate and concrete, its future benefits are highly uncertain. For example, tight money and fiscal restraint have already pushed the US economy back a few years in terms of capital formation and productivity gains. This could have important long-term implications. A more serious doubt arises concerning the Trilateralist strategies that emanate from a desire to sustain the dominant status of the dollar in future as a source of long-term profits, and the power of the dollar barons. The status of an international currency is eventually determined by the real strength of the economy. If the potential of the US economy is high, the future status of the dollar is secure without contrived efforts; if its potential is low, on the other hand, any attempt at preserving the status of the dollar will be ineffectual, leaving only the heavy current cost on the book.

APPENDIX 2: TOWARDS A THEORY OF MONEY GAMES

'Business? It's quite simple; it's other people's money.' 'Pay as you go, but not if you intend going for ever.' 'I do not regard a broker as a member of the human race.' 'Corporation: an ingenious device for obtaining individual profit without individual responsibility.' 'Nothing is easier than spending public money. It does not appear to belong to anyone.' 'Capital formation is shifting from the entrepreneur who invests in the future to the pension trustee who invests in the past.' 'With the Mafia they shoot you; the banks let you shoot yourself.' 'Every Republican candidate for President since 1936 has been nominated by the Chase Manhattan Bank.' 'A "sound" banker, alas!, is not one who foresees danger and avoids it, but one who, when he is ruined, is ruined in a conventional and orthodox way along with his fellows, so that no one can really blame him.'

These are some characterizations of today's monetary economy by acute observers from all walks of life. Collectively, they capture quite well the added dimensions of the corporate capitalism of this century as opposed to the family capitalism of the previous centuries, and the expanded scope for rational choice that people exercise in the new environment.

This appendix studies one aspect of today's firm behaviour, namely, optimal exits by firms. It is motivated by a number of intriguing facts. First, business firms are as mortal as individuals; every year 0.5–1 per cent of existing business establishments go bankrupt, while two to three times as many new ones enter. Second, an overwhelming majority of bankruptcies is 'voluntary', in the sense that the action is initiated by the bankrupt. Granted that voluntariness is probably overstated (remember, the banks like to let you shoot yourself), a significant portion of voluntary bankruptcies is nevertheless a consequence of deliberate decisions on the part of the debtor firms. Stock up the goods on credit, put on a bargain sale, grab the money, and run. This 'scam' operation is well known in the retail business. The recent case of Texaco is a reminder that such dubious actions are not limited to petty retailers. (Indeed, statistics show that the failure rate among very small businesses is much lower than average, presumably because they are mostly proprietorships and partnerships doing honest business with their own money.)

Third, bankruptcy laws have become increasingly lenient towards the bankrupt; they allow the bankrupt to exempt certain assets and to extend or reduce parts of its debts. As a result, bankruptcies, both business and personal, have increased dramatically in recent decades. Texaco filed for bankruptcy in April 1987, under Chapter 11 of the US Federal Bankruptcy Act, in order to avoid the payment of $10 billion in damages to Pennzoil for interfering with Pennzoil's attempt to buy Getty Oil, as ordered by a Texas court. According to media reports, Texaco was not broke; it had a net worth of $13 billion. The Bankruptcy Act as amended in 1978 no longer requires proof of insolvency to file for bankruptcy. It also permits the management to retain much of its control even after filing. Moreover, Chapter 11 of the Act allows the bankrupt to write off unsecured debts. Texaco apparently exploited the haven provided by the Act. (In December 1987, the federal court ordered Texaco to pay a total of $5 billion to clear its debts, of which $3 billion went to Pennzoil.) Fourth, today's businesses are highly marketable; professional corporate business brokers buy and sell businesses routinely. In this sense, today's corporate businesses are very different from the old family firms in which business and family life were one. They are much like financial assets, created and destroyed with ease. Knowing when to close out a business is therefore an integral part of today's corporate business strategy. Fifth, the incidence of business failures does not exhibit a high negative correlation with the business cycle; for example, a positive correlation, if anything, was observed in Japan between 1975 and 1984, which calls for an explanation.

A Theory of Voluntary Exit

In the usual neoclassical formulation of the firm, the firm is modelled as a maximizer of the present discounted value of its net income over an infinite time horizon. This assumption of an infinite time horizon is unduly restrictive in the light of the observations made above and generally leads to a suboptimal solution. Deciding when to exit should be one of the important choices the firm is entitled to make. Moreover, the infinite horizon assumption obscures the fact that today's firm is a debtor, as will be seen shortly.

Consider a retail firm which buys a certain good X from a wholesaler on credit from a bank at interest r. Assume this wholesale price to be 1. Then a purchase of x amount of the good increases the firm's debt by x. Assume further that the loan is made on a long-term commitment by the bank to supply the credit needed by the firm subject to the condition that the firm repay δ per cent of its outstanding debt on a continuous basis. Let us denote the firm's debt by D. Then the above assumptions imply the following motion of the debt:

$$\dot{D} = x - \delta D, \quad D(0) = D_0 \geq 0 \tag{A1}$$

where D_0 is the amount of debt existing at time 0. (Hereafter time 0 is taken to be the decision time.) Assume also that the (expected) price of the good is given by $p(t)$ and that the selling cost $c(x)$ is an increasing convex function of the rate of sale x.

An Infinite Horizon Optimization
First let us consider the conventional infinite horizon case. In this case, the firm's problem is to maximize

$$V(x) = \int_0^\infty \{px - c(x) - (r + \delta)D\}e^{-rt} \, dt \tag{A2}$$

subject to (A1). The Hamiltonian function is given by

$$H(D, q, x, t) = e^{-rt}\{px - c(x) - (r + \delta)D + q(x - \delta D)\}, \tag{A3}$$

from which the following first-order conditions are obtained:

$$p+q=c'(x), \quad \text{or} \quad x=x(p+q); \quad x'(p+q)>0 \qquad \text{(A4)}$$

$$\dot{D}=x(p+q)-\delta D \qquad \text{(A5)}$$

$$\dot{q}=(r+\delta)q+(r+\delta) \qquad \text{(A6)}$$

$$\lim_{t\to\infty} q(t)e^{-rt}=0. \qquad \text{(A7)}$$

Given the concavity of the profit function, the solution of these first-order conditions is indeed optimal. Note that (A6) and (A7) imply that

$$q(t)=-1 \quad \text{for all } t\in[0, \infty), \qquad \text{(A8)}$$

as it should be ($q=-1$ means that the firm acknowledges its debt to the full).

But why should the firm stay in buisness for ever? Clearly, the answer is: only if it pays to do so. Let $V(t)$ be the value of the firm realized in $[0, t]$ when the firm follows the above solution. Plot $V(t)$ against t. For an infinite horizon to be the optimal length of time to be in business, it is necessary and sufficient that $V(t)$ keep increasing with time, except possibly in the very first phase of the firm's history. What is the chance that this condition will be met in the real world? Very small, because fluctuations are the basic fact of life. Take $p(t)=\bar{p}+\sin t$, for example. With everything else remaining constant, $V(t)$ becomes the sum of a convergent upward trend $\bar{V}(t)$ corresponding to $\bar{p}$ and a cyclical part involving e^{-rt} times $\sin t$ and $\cos t$ and their higher-order terms. This means that the function $V(t)$ is most likely to reach its global maximum at some t in the rather near future unless the growth trend is so strong as to eliminate downturns altogether. If a global maximum is to be reached at a finite t_0, it is irrational to stay in business thereafter, because by exiting at t_0 and banking the profits up to that time, the firm can maintain a constant value $V(t_0)$ for ever.

The 'Scam'

Suppose a global maximum is expected to occur at sime finite time. Assume that the firm learns of this fact in advance and prepares for an exit. The optimal exit problem is now formalized as one of maximizing

$$V=\int_0^{t_1} \{px-c(x)-(r+\delta)D\}e^{-rt}\,dt, \qquad \text{(A9)}$$

subject to (A1), with t_1 and $D_1 = D(t_1)$ as free choice variables. The first-order conditions are (A4), (A5), (A6), and the following:

$$q(t_1) = 0 \tag{A10}$$

$$px(p) - c\{x(p)\} - (r+\delta)D|_{t_1} = 0. \tag{A11}$$

Conditions (A10) and (A11) are obtained as follows. Let the maximized value of V in (A9), subject to arbitrarily fixed parameters t_1 and D_1, be $V(t_1, D_1)$. Since t_1 and D_1 are choice variables, optimality calls for vanishing partial derivatives. But since $\partial V/\partial D_1 = -q(t_1)e^{-rt_1}$ and $\partial V/\partial t_1$ is the value of the Hamiltonian function along the optimal path at t_1, (A10) and (A11) follow. The second-order condition is that p must be falling at t_1. The most conspicuous difference between this solution and the previous infinite horizon solution is that the shadow price of debt q is now raised above -1 and reaches 0 at the time of exit. From equation (A4), a higher q means a greater volume of purchase of merchandise and an increased rate of borrowing, given $p(t)$. The firm planning a fraudulent exit adopts this strategy. Condition (A10) means simply that the firm intends to default entirely on $D(t_1)$.

An Honest Exit

To see the fraudulent nature of the above solution more clearly, consider an honest firm planning a clean exit. Being honest, the firm intends to pay off its debt at the time of exit, which means that its objective functional is now of the form

$$V = \int_0^{t_2} \{px - c(x) - (r+\delta)D\}e^{-rt}\,dt - e^{-rt_2}D(t_2). \tag{A12}$$

The side constraints are the same as before. Again, first fix t_2 and $D_2 = D(t_2)$ arbitrarily and solve this fixed endpoint problem, ignoring the last term in (A12). Denote the maximized value of this subsidiary problem by $V(t_2, D_2)$, which is the same function as $V(t_1, D_1)$ in the scam solution. Now the maximum value of V in (A12) is equal to $V(t_2, D_2) - D_2 e^{-rt_2}$. Choosing t_2 and D_2 independently to maximize this expression, we obtain

$$q(t_2) = -1 \tag{A13}$$

$$(p-1)x(p-1) - c\{x(p-1)\}|_{t_2} = 0, \tag{A14}$$

which compares with (A10) and (A11). Again, $p(t)$ must be falling at t_2. Note that (A13) implies $q(t) = -1$ for all $t \in [0, t_2]$. In this sense, whether or not q is equal to -1 is the crucial test of honesty. (Readers will recognize (A14) as the familiar critical condition for firm survival in the conventional theory of the firm which precludes dishonesty.) But q is not directly observable to outsiders. It is here that the lender is placed at disadvantage. The bank can observe x. But x does not in general permit an accurate inference on q. To make such an inference, the lender must also know the (expected) price p. The simple model used here abstracts from inventory policy and other speculative aspects of firm behaviour, and fails to convey a good perception of the noise in the link connecting x to q. But in reality, such a noise must be quite serious.

More Realistic Exits

The above 'scam' solution assumes that the exciting firm can evade its debt obligation completely. This is patently unrealistic. Even though the lender's monitoring is not very close, the lender usually imposes some restrictions on the debtor's disposition of assets. Securing of collaterals is a common practice. Bankruptcy laws, though increasingly lenient, impose restrictions on the dispositions of assets by the bankrupt and other costs. (For example, the head of a bankrupt firm cannot be the head of another firm with limited liabilities for a certain number of years after bankruptcy.) On the other hand, the creditors of a dishonest bankrupt usually shoulder some of the bankrupt's debt. Realistically, therefore, a more sensible formulation would be to assume that a typical voluntary bankrupt intends to pay off a fraction of its debt when it exits. If this fraction is α, the ones appearing in (A13) and (A14) will be replaced by α's. It is plain that a higher value of α discourages scam attempts. Raising the interest rate, on the other hand, may have the effect of encouraging fraudulent exits.

Honesty and Infinite Horizon

For firms exiting in a finite time, honesty is characterized by the condition that q remain at -1; any q above -1 implies a fraudulent intent on the part of the debtor firm. Alternatively, the mark of honesty is the subtraction of the term $D(t)e^{-rt}$ from the present discounted value of the net cash flow in calculating the value of the firm. How do these criteria work for a firm with an infinite horizon? Unfortunately, neither criterion can be an effective check on the honesty of the debtor in an infinite horizon case. As for the $q = -1$

criterion, a firm with an infinite horizon, honest or dishonest, will voluntarily meet this requirement. But q is not directly observable. Besides, even with $q = -1$, the debtor can negotiate the parameter δ down to extend its debt without bound. As for the subtraction of the terminal debt, we have

$$\lim_{t \to +\infty} D(t)e^{-rt} = 0,$$

provided only that the firm is committed to keep its debt from growing exponentially at a rate equal to or greater than r. The problem with this criterion is that it is not possible to evaluate such a limit properly on the basis of finite observations. In short, there is no foolproof method of checking the honesty of a debtor with an infinite horizon, because paying off one's debt in an infinitely long time and never paying it off are indistinguishable.

Involuntary Exits

Not all business exits are voluntary. Although relatively few in number according to statistics, involuntary exits do occur. When a bank is a dominant supplier of credit to a firm, it has a degree of control over the life of that firm. This is largely due to the fact that the commercial credit supplied by a bank to a going business concern is typically based on a standing loan commitment made by the bank to finance the firm's needs automatically at flexible rates, the type of loans called 'demand loans'. Such a practice is absolutely necessary to reduce the transaction costs on regular clients. At the same time, however, the flexibilities implied by this type of contract give the bank an additional degree of control over the debtor. Most of such credit is callable at any time, at least in theory. If the bank exercises this power and calls its loan on short notice, the debtor may be unable to repay it on time, which gives the bank a valid excuse to initiate bankruptcy procedures if it sees fit. Even if the bank does not abuse this power, the threat is always there. This is probably the reason why a typical firm does business with several banks.

For the purpose of discussion, let us assume that the bank exercises this power only after the debtor has fallen into arrears. Since the firm under consideration is an honest going concern, such a default occurs only in times of distress, that is, when the value of the firm has fallen to an unexpectedly low level. For concreteness, assume that the first default occurs immediately after the net value of the firm, $V_n(t) = V(t) - D(t)e^{-rt}$, hits zero. Call this time t_3. The bank could force the firm to bankruptcy at this point. If it chose to do so, it would finalize the loss at $(1-\alpha)D(t_3)$. Alternatively, the bank could help the firm through the hardship to t_4, where t_4 is defined as the first time that V_n moves up to zero, by relieving the firm of the debt service cost. If this strategy were chosen, the firm's debt would be larger at t_4 than at t_3, but the prospect of recovery would be better. One of the peculiar features of today's debt capitalism is that goods in the hands of a receiver are worth much less than the same goods in the hands of a healthy firm: 30, or even 50 per cent discounts are common. Depreciation of firm-specific assets is even greater. This fact suggests that the bank has a strong incentive to help the debtor firm out in hard times.

Assume the bank has chosen to keep the firm alive. If things go as expected, the firm will recover at t_4 and resume regular payments, which is clearly a better outcome for both parties. But this is not the bank's only choice. Between t_3 and t_4, the bank gains a virtual control of the firm. Using this control, it can force the firm to bankruptcy. The reason for doing so may be to prevent the losses from increasing. But this is not the only reason. By supervising the firm's management into recovery and then removing the management, the bank may have in possession a firm of greater value than if it had been terminated at t_3. The bank therefore faces an intertemporal problem of whether and when to dispose of the firm. This is the same old problem as when to cut trees or sell a vintage wine. Clearly, the best time to do so is when the bank can profit most. Given that the bank gains control of its debtor firm after the firm has fallen behind in debt payments, the optimal time for the bank to kill and sell the firm is more likely to be t_4 than t_3, since t_4 is the time when the firm has exerted its best effort towards recovery under the bank's supervision, and is on the verge of self-support. At that time, the demand for the firm by prospectors would also be the strongest because demand likely depends on the difference between what the firm is worth in the near future and the cost of acquiring it. Assume that the selling price of the firm, S, depends in part on the current gross value of the firm, V, and in part on the demand factor, which may be represented by $\dot{V}$, so that $S = S(V, \dot{V})$. Assume further that the bank gets a fraction $(1-\beta)$ of S. Then the bank's profit from the disposition of the firm, discounted back to t_3, will be

$$\pi = \{(1-\beta)S - (1-\alpha)D\}e^{-r(t-t_3)}.\tag{A15}$$

So the bank will choose that t between t_3 and t_4 which maximizes this expression. If such an optimum time exists between t_3 and t_4, it will satisfy $d\pi/dt = 0$; or

$$(1-\beta)(\dot{S}-rS) - (1-\alpha)x(p) = 0,\tag{A16}$$

where it has been assumed that the firm makes no debt-related payments during this rehabilitation period so that its debt grows according to $\dot{D} = x(p) + rD$. Since it is reasonable to assume $x(p) > 0$ (the firm can always make profits if it can ignore the purchase cost of the goods), the optimal time will be the time when the selling price is increasing sufficiently rapidly. And this is most likely to occur around t_4.

Business Cycles and Business Failures

Business failures have conventionally been associated with business cycles. Bad times cause businesses to fail. This simple account of bankruptcies may have been fairly accurate in the old days of family capitalism. But things are more complex today. Capital markets are much more fluid. Businesses can be bought and sold. Corporations are created and destroyed for purely financial reasons. Moreover, corporations operating on borrowed money and under the limited liability rule have a different attitude towards business than the old owner–managers. Business is more a money game than a means of subsistence. The analysis presented above predicts that exits will occur around the peak of the value of the firm (voluntary exits) and around the trough (involuntary exits) of the value of the firm. If the business cycle is defined in terms of the price p, voluntary exits tend to concentrate in the downturn, and involuntary exits in the upturn, phase of the cycle. Given the diverse pattern of exits, today's bankruptcies are expected to spread more widely and to have a weaker correlation with the business cycle than those in the old days.

Figure A6.1 charts the rate of change in the number of business failures in each month over the same month of the previous year during the 1975–84 decade in Japan. The peaks and troughs of the cycle by diffusion indexes are shown by vertical lines denoted P and T. The graph shows an almost pro-cyclical pattern. Granted that many factors contribute to business failures, this puzzling fact suggests that

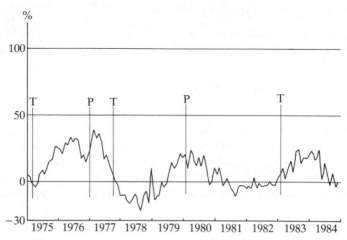

Fig. A6.1   Business cycles and business failures in Japan, 1975–1985.
Source: Economic Statistics Almanac, 1986, Toyo Keizai Shimposha, Tokyo.

we must look more seriously into the microeconomic causes of such failures.

Table A6.1 summarizes some micro information about the bankruptcies of Japanese businesses, the only group for which micro data of interest have been available. The top panel of the table reports the frequency of bankruptcies by type of industry. Wholesale and retail businesses lead with 40 per cent, followed by the construction and manufacturing industries. These frequencies are not the correct measure of the 'riskiness' of business, however; they may merely reflect the relative size of membership. A more accurate measure of riskiness is shown by the numbers in parentheses, which denote the proportion of firms that failed in each industry category. According to these figures, the construction industry has the highest failure rate, with the wholsesale/retail industry a distant second.

The middle panel tabulates the number of bankruptcies by firm size as measured by capital. A heavy concentration of bankruptcies is observed in the small- to medium-sized firms. To see what this really means in terms of riskiness, we must again look at the membership size, which is shown by the numbers in parentheses. These figures confirm the fact that firms of capital size ¥1 million–50 million indeed have the highest failure rate. That larger firms fail less frequently is not surprising. But that smaller firms should also fail less

Table A6.1   Japanese business failures[a] by industry, firm size, and cause (%)

	1970		1985	
By industry				
Wholesale/retail	39.0	(0.85)[b]	40.6	(1.09)[b,c]
Construction	22.1	(1.73)	28.3	(1.89)
Manufacturing	28.0	(0.78)	16.2	(0.71)
Service	4.2	(0.16)	7.5	(0.26)
Transport/communications	2.5	(0.56)	2.4	(0.72)
Other	4.2	(2.00)	5.0	(3.19)
By size of capital				
Proprietorships	19.7		28.0	
Less than ¥1 million	13.9		2.9	(17.1)[c,d]
¥1–10 million	58.8		53.8	(65.1)
¥10–50 million	6.7		14.1	(15.5)
¥50–100 million	0.5		0.9	(1.3)
Over ¥100 million	0.4		0.2	(0.9)
By cause				
Mismanagement	64.6		38.3	
Poor sales	0.0		34.1	
Bad debts	0.0		9.4	
Industry-wide slump	5.6		8.3	
Competition	22.9		5.5	
Other	6.9		4.4	

[a] Debt of ¥10 million and over.
[b] Fraction of firms that failed.
[c] 1984 figures.
[d] Distribution of existing firms other than proprietorships.
Source: Economic Statistics Almanac, 1986, Tokyo Keizai Shimposha, Tokyo.

frequently is more difficult to accept. For example, firms with capital of less than ¥1 million have a markedly lower failure rate. Moreover, proprietorships account for two-thirds of the total business establishments, which makes them a relatively low-risk group also. The reasons why proprietorships and the smallest firms, most of them partnerships, have a lower failure rate are probably complex. But some obvious reasons are that they are run by owner–managers, that they are largely excluded from the limited liability rule, and that they are more prudent in planning. In short, they are much like the family firms of old days. In contrast, the firms with capital of ¥1 million--50 million are those that have gained entry into the debtors' club and play the modern corporate game with an expansionist mentality. Besides, their size makes them most marketable.

The bottom panel shows the causes of business failures. It reveals a few intersting features of business failures. First, mismanagement (loose or overly aggressive management, wrong planning, etc.) is the single most important cause of failure. This, along with a relatively small contribution from industry-wide slumps, suggests that business failures have a large microeconomic content. Second, the importance of poor sales and bad debts (inability to collect receivables) indicates that bankruptcies are caused largely by cash-flow problems. Third, the causes of bankruptcies vary greatly between good times and bad. In 1970, one of the last good years, mismanagement and competition were the major causes of business failures; in 1985, when the environment was much more sober, mismanagement reduced its weight significantly but cash-flow problems loomed large. The actual number of bankruptcies due to 'mismanagement' and 'competition' was 8457 in 1970 and 7970 in 1985. When normalized by the total number of firms in the respective years, the failure rate arising from these causes becomes 0.86 per cent in 1970 as against 0.48 per cent in 1985. These facts suggest that bankruptcies occur in both good times and bad, but that the causes and motives are different. Many of the bankruptcies occurring in good times that are due to mismanagement and competition may be regarded as a new type of bankruptcy induced by the permissive rules of today's corporate capitalism.

Exits and Owners' Risk

Separation between ownership and management creates potential conflicts between the owners and managers of the firm. The hired managers can pursue policies that benefit them rather than the owners. For example, managers may put growth before profits; they may seek luxurious office facilities and generous expense accounts rather than cost savings. This principal–agency problem in modern corporate firms has long been recognized in the literature.

The increased marketability of firms and the ease of exits in recent years seem to have aggravated the problem. Just as voluntary exits by debtor firms created an additional monitoring problem for creditors, so certain planned exits by managers have increased the headaches suffered by shareholders. In mergers and acquisitions (M & A), the shareholders of the firm being acquired are, in principle, consulted by their managers and are usually compensated for by the acquirer in the form of a premium on their shares. In some recent cases of M & A, however, these presumptions proved false. When the Bank of British Columbia, one of the dozen federally chartered banks in Canada, was bought out by the Hong Kong-Shang'hai Bank in 1987, for example, not only were the shareholders of the Bank of British Columbia not consulted by management, but they were paid less than $1 for their shares which stood at $6 before the deal. Toda (1984) finds a broad tendency in Japan for the managers and employees of failing firms to help themselves to generous pay raises towards the end. Sato (1987) reports on recent cases of M & A in the USA where managers of the exiting firms retired happily on 'golden parachutes' arranged by the acquirers and the brokers. These examples show that the freedom to exit encourages malfeasance on the part of management at the expense of the shareholders. Sato also notes that M & A are pro-cyclical; that is, they occur more in good times than bad. This is so presumably because in good times more money is available for such financial deals, and because the appreciation of firms' assets such as land (in alternative uses) tends to make them undervalued in the market. These M & A may be thought of as a form of voluntary exits discussed above.

The Role of the Financial Intermediaries

Throughout history, man has considered it shameful to be in debt. Going bankrupt meant the end of a person's social existence. Things started to change drastically a hundred years ago. A new way of organizing and running business on other people's money was popularized and soon came to dominate the business scene. Individuals also learned to emulate corporate firms with a half-century lag. True, many individuals still attach stigma to being in debt, but the stigma is rapidly disappearing, as the sellers of goods and the money-lenders join forces to pressure the masses to buy-now-pay-later. The result has been a sharp increase in people's debts and the number of bankruptcies, both personal and corporate, with part of the bankrupt's debt regularly and legally discharged and shifted on to the creditors and the rest of society, a typical case of negative externalities and overborrowing.

What about the actual cost of going bankrupt? A pursuit study of bankrupt individuals by Stanley and Girth (1971) reveals that it is, on the whole, rather negligible. First, there is a considerable range of assets that are exempt by law. Second, a majority (70 per cent) of the bankrupts found credit availability no worse than before; some (8 per cent) even found their credit availability improved. The situation facing bankrupt businesses is much the same. Stanley and Girth found that two-thirds of the debts discharged in the bankruptcy courts in 1968 belonged to businesses.

These facts suggest that the money-lenders today are the helpless victims of the irresponsible and often dishonest behaviour of the debtors. This is apparently not the case, however. Large financial intermediaries enjoy unmatched power and prestige in today's political economy. But why? In seeking answers to this question, we must first realize that the financial intermediaries are themselves debtors. The money they lend belongs to the public. As debtors, the financial intermediaries are similar to the debtor firms described earlier. They too are anxious to turn over the money borrowed at cost fast enough to stay ahead of the debt service costs. They too are prone to take fraudulent actions against their creditors and sprinkle negative externalities. Commodity and stockbrokers make frequent news headlines for their fraudulent use of clients' money and securities and illicit insider transactions. The banks issue credit cards liberally in competition with one another, despite the alarming 5 per cent default rate. The major banks all over the world have loaned huge amounts of money to proven high-risk foreign states, some such loans amounting to over twice their capital. Apparently, imposing tighter lending rules and closer monitoring of borrowers is not the popular strategy of the banks today. Like any other debtors, banks have learned to play the game of musical chairs.

Another point to be noted in this context is that the public in today's monetary economy have little choice but to supply their savings and temporary excess cash to some financial intermediaries. The large numbers and relative naivety of the public make them uniquely uncritical money-lenders. As a result, the financial intermediaries are able to exercise all the power and authority of the true owners of money when they face their borrowers.

But the more fundamental source of power enjoyed by the large financial intermediaries is the informational edge they have over the other participants in the financial markets. A bank knows a large number of clients and their economic conditions. A security firm or a trust company keeps a complete list of customers' accounts as well as updated information about the security-issuing corporations it represents. Much of this information is 'inside information', that is, information obtained through business but not shared with the rest of the market. Although the information the intermediaries have of their individual customers may never equal the information possessed by the customers themselves, as has been stressed in the economic literature, the amount of information the financial intermediaries have over many individual customers is much more valuable to market transactions than the information known only to the individual customers. This, along with the fact that much of the transaction between an intermediary and a customer is of a bargaining (as opposed to auction) nature, places the intermediary in a dominant position in the money game.

Financial intermediaries utilize this informational edge in a number of ways to make money. One way, which is considered legitimate, is to sell inside information in the form of financial advice and counsel to their customers. Security firms rely heavily on this type of business. In many cases, however, the customers who purchase these services will never know whether they are getting honest advice. Another way, which is illegal but not easily detectable, is for a financial intermediary to utilize the informational edge to profit at the expense of unsuspecting customers or, less directly, to earn profits for a favourite customer at the expense of others, the practice known as 'insider trading'. Historically, insider trading was so rampant and their consequences so disastrous during the 1920s and 1930s that the US government has since instituted one of the toughest rules in the world against the abuse of insider information by financial interme- diaries in conflict-of-interest situations. Specifically, banks are prohibited from the security business; they are required to set up an informational barrier between their banking and trust businesses; and insider trading is banned and violators given stiff penalties, among others. Yet, as the never-ending investigations by the FBI of security firms for suspicion of insider trading reveal (in 1986 some fifty members of the NYSE including Merrill Lynch were the targets of such investigations), the temptation to profit from insider trading seems too much to resist.

Currently, the world is witnessing a tide of globalization and reregulation of the financial industry, which indicates that the conventional fences that have defined different types of financial institutions such as banks, building societies/savings and loans associations, trust companies, insurance companies, and security companies are soon to be removed in the name of international competition and increased efficiency. It is possible, for example, that the licensing of banks will end; that policy controls by the central bank such as the legal reserve requirements will soon be scrapped; and that banks will be allowed to go freely into the trust and security business. The lessons learned in the 1920s and the reforms instituted in the 1930s are about to be unlearned and undone. If anyone with capital can run a bank as a side-business, and if the bank can simultaneously deal in trusts and securities, the way is open for unlimited opportunities for conflict of interest and insider trading. For example, the bank can force an ailing debtor-firm to issue bonds, can sell these to the unsuspecting public, and can then keep the proceeds in lieu of the debt payments. In this way, the bank can shift the burden of bad debts to the public. A bank owned by non-financial capital can divert the funds to help the parent business.

In short, freer financial industry can and will greatly increase the incidence of conflict-of-interest and fraudulent insider trading. And among the variety of financial firms, the largest and most powerful ones stand to gain most from deregulation because of their superior informational network, their better access to the global financial markets, and the wider range of financial services they can offer. If deregulation is put into practice without qualification, the result will be less healthy, less efficient, and less credible financial firms in the long run. Financial markets where debtors and creditors trade promises for money are far too imperfect to be left to market forces for a desirable social outcome.

7

Labour

It is not plausible to assert that unemployment in the United States in 1932 was due either to labour obstinately refusing to accept a reduction of money wages or to its obstinately demanding real wages beyond what the productivity of the economic machine was capable of furnishing. Wide variations are experienced in the volume of employment without an apparent change either in the minimum real demands for labour or in its productivity. Labour is not more truculent in the depression than in the boom—far from it. Nor is its physical productivity less. These facts from experience are a *prima facie* ground for questioning the adequacy of the classical analysis.

J. M. Keynes, *General Theory*, p. 9

1 INTRODUCTION

In 1932 the US economy was in deep trouble, and the downward trend was continuing. With the 1929 figures set at 100, the following indexes depict the state of the US economy in 1932: real GNP = 73; labour input = 73; CPI = 80; hourly wages in manufacturing = 80; real government spending = 113; high-powered money = 109; the money stock (M2) = 75. In the meantime, the prime commercial paper rate fell from 5.85 to 2.73 per cent, while the Baa (medium-ranked) bond yield shot up from 5.90 to 9.30 per cent.

These were the facts that prompted Keynes to invent a new framework for macroeconomic analysis. Keynes described this state of the economy as a highly unsatisfactory but rational (in the individualistic sense of the term) equilibrium, given the way decentralized markets worked and given the prevailing market psychology. It was a type of non-cooperative game solution known as the 'prisoners' dilemma': businesses would hire more workers and produce more if the markets could take more; households would spend more if more jobs were available; but the way things were, neither side dared to be the first to stimulate the economy. In Keynes's opinion, it was the task of the government to get the economy out of this dilemma by injecting an additional demand for goods and services. As a means of carrying out this task, he favoured fiscal policy over monetary policy for its more direct and reliable influence on aggregate demand.

In 1932 Keynes's *General Theory* was still in the making. Social security programmes as we know them today were non-existent. For example, there was no unemployment insurance, no public pensions, no deposit insurance. The sufferings of the unemployed and the elderly were great. Yet labour was under attack. The US Republican administration, which took full credit for the 6 million increase in employment during the 1920s,[1] refused to take the blame for the massive rise in unemployment in the 1930s.[2] A poll taken of the leading intellectuals of the nation urged that a tighter control of labour unrest and union power be one of the high-priority public issues. Reflecting this opinion, a popular columnist wrote: 'labor that objects to wage reductions may find some comfort in the fact that a ten percent reduction may mean before long one hundred percent increase in general prosperity'.[3] Henry Ford, while claiming that the hard times saved the nation from the evils of false prosperity and therefore were good times, shut down his Detroit factories in 1931, throwing at least 75,000 men out of work. In the meantime, all levels of government were busy with their own measures to cut deficits and reduce debts. On the international scene, defaults of sovereign debts surged, and nations set up protective tariff walls in competition with each other.

A half-century later, in the supposedly enlightened 1980s, the unemployment problem is again a social problem of top priority. Many of the industrialized economies suffered from unemployment of

---

[1] 'When we [the Republican Party] assumed direction of the Government in 1921 there were five to six million men upon our streets. Wages and salaries were falling and hours of labor increasing. . . . The Republican Administration at once undertook to find relief to this situation. . . . Within a year we restored these five million workers to employment. But we did more; we produced a fundamental program which made this restored employment secure on foundations of prosperity; as a result wages and salaries and standards of living have during the past six and a half years risen to steadily higher levels.

This recovery and this stability are no accident. It has not been achieved by luck. Were it not for sound governmental policies and wise leadership, employment conditions in America today would be similar to those existing in many other parts of the world' (Herbert Hoover, campaign address, 17 September, 1928).

[2] 'The depression has been deepened by events from abroad which are beyond the control either of our citizens or our government' (President Hoover, radio address, 18 October, 1931).

[3] Arthur Brisbane in his syndicated column, 'Today', 24 September, 1931.

over 10 per cent for four to five years in a row since 1982, with the unemployment rates among youths running at twice the national rates. To be sure, today's societies are much more civilized about the problems of unemployment than those of the 1930s. Democratic governments have professed the economic protection of their citizens as one of their prime duties. They have accepted the Keynesian notion of stabilization policies; they have instituted various social security programmes as well as job training and placement agencies. Gathering and processing of economic information has seen vast improvement. Moreover, international policy co-ordination has become a reality. But despite all these improvements, today's societies are suffering from high rates of unemployment, and the situation is not improving. Many economists are alarmed by the rising trend in the 'natural rate' of unemployment.

In terms of general attitude, today's societies are indeed much the same as those of the 1930s. There are in power a number of conservative governments whose chief goal is to restore budgetary balance; businesses continue to undo their past mistakes by dismissing workers at no cost; labour continues to be blamed for the nation's economic ills; the economists are at their wits' end, unable to find enough room to manoeuvre between the actual unemployment rate and the non-accelerating inflation rate of unemployment. In short, today's societies find themselves in essentially the same kind of prisoners' dilemma as that which prevailed half a century ago; the conventional trap that catches business and labour has caught national governments as well, and all are waiting for someone else to take a bold initiative.

Faced with this impasse, economists are coming to realize that something more fundamental and less costly to government than the conventional short-term stabilization policies merits a closer attention if we are to cope effectively with the persistent unemployment problem. One such solution, or direction of solution, is the regaining of a higher rate of economic growth than that prevailing since 1975. The importance of economic growth is unquestionable. An economy with a 3 per cent annual growth will expand 4.4 times in 50 years, while an economy with a 5 per cent annual growth will expand by a factor of 11.5 in the same time span. And one need not wait fifty years to enjoy the benefit of higher growth: the benefit begins to be felt immediately in the form of more active investment and a faster rate of job creation.

A faster rate of growth has many other benefits. It makes short-run stabilization easier by prolonging the upturn and shortening the downturn of business cycles; it helps government revenues to grow faster, thereby easing the strain on the public purse and the current debt problem itself; moreover, it enables government and business to correct past mistakes and adapt to new environments with less pain. In brief, a more rapid growth—say, that of the 1960s—if realized, will solve virtually all the problems that plague today's policy-makers. Many economies are in poor shape as a result of a decade-long preoccupation with inflation and growing public debts. Tight money and spending cuts have had a detrimental effect on investment on both physical and human capital. Cutting spending to reduce the debt/GNP ratio does not, however, constitute a fundamental solution: increasing the GNP does.

Another direction in which economists are seeking a solution of the unemployment problem is in the area of industrial relations. Historically, the relation between labour and capital has been one of confrontation and hostility. Despite the essential complementarity between capital and labour services in production activities, labour has remained the outsiders in business organizations. Firms view their workers as replaceable and expendable; workers, lacking a sense of belonging to their work-place and therefore the desire to contribute to it, push constantly for more benefits. The equilibrium reached by the two sides is a typical non-cooperative solution which is generally inefficient and tense. Although the historic role played by labour in the development of democratic rules and programmes such as job safety regulations, child labour laws, unemployment insurance, medicare, public pension programmes and civil rights legislation is undeniable, its militant attitude towards capital is a continued source of disturbance and welfare loss to society. There is no question that society would gain if an improvement were made in industrial relations.

One interesting and important fact about industrial relations in this context is that the degree of hostility between capital and labour apparently varies greatly across nations. Table 7.1 uses the number of days lost in labour disputes as a measure of hostility to show the extremely wide variations in the amount of work lost among the selected countries. At the one end there are Germany and Japan, which have virtually no work losses; at the other end are Canada and the UK, which lose an equivalent of 30,000–40,000 full-time jobs a

Table 7.1 Days lost in labour disputes

Country	Man-days lost (m)	Adjusted for 1984 pop. (Index: USA = 100)
Canada	7.3[a]	531
France	1.6[b]	52
Germany	0.04[c]	1
Japan	0.5[b]	7
UK	10.0[b]	323
USA	12.9[b]	100

[a] Average of 1982 and 1983.
[b] Average of 1981–4.
[c] Average of 1981–3.

Source: Bank of Japan, Comparative International Statistics, 1985.

year as a result of poor labour–management relations. The latter two countries are also plagued by highest unit labour costs among the major industrialized countries (see Table 7.2). One suspects that there is a connection between poor labour–management relations and the high labour costs.

This chapter concerns the question of industrial relations and its implications for labour productivity and macroeconomic performances. Section 2 examines the employment policies practised in

Table 7.2 Labour costs per unit in manufacturing, selected countries, 1983

	Index: USA = 100
UK	136.0
Canada	129.3
Italy	107.2
Belgium	106.3
USA	100.0
Germany	92.3
France	86.5
Sweden	73.3
Japan	61.2

Source: Report of the Royal Commission on the Economic Union and Development Prospects for Canada, Vol. 2: 189.

Western societies from the point of view of risk-sharing between capital and labour, including a reference to Weitzman's (1984) proposal that we should replace the conventional 'wage system' with a 'share system' in order to ease unemployment and inflation problems. Section 3 presents a model of a dynamic co-operative firm and summarizes the major findings. Section 4 discusses the implications of these findings for issues over wages, employment, and productivity. Section 5 concludes.

2 WAGES AND EMPLOYMENT

The allocation of produced values between labour and capital has always been a focal point of political economy. The classical economists advanced the theory of subsistence wages to explain labour's long-run share. As Malthus saw it, any increase in wages above the subsistence level would induce a population increase, which would push wages back to the subsistence level. Indeed, the subsistence wage theory could not have been far off the mark, given the generally miserable condition of labour throughout the nineteenth century. Workers were constantly abused and exploited by the owners of capital. Their sporadic resistances and uprisings were oppressed brutally by the combined forces of company thugs and the police. It was only around the turn of the century that certain basic rights of the working masses began to be recognized and grudgingly granted in a few of the more advanced economies. The end of the First World War saw the formation of the International Labor Organization, which has since contributed greatly to the improvement of labour conditions.

Perhaps reflecting this trend, a new theory called the 'marginal productivity theory of wages' emerged in the early 1900s. According to this, labour earns its marginal product as wages. While the marginal productivity theory does not necessarily contradict the subsistence wage theory, it does accommodate many other possibilities, especially since neoclassical theory has largely freed itself from the curse of the Ricardian land which dominated classical economics. The steady and substantial gains that labour has made in terms of real wages and employment over the past century certainly discredit the subsistence wage theory and lends support to a more general alternative. But this does not mean that the marginal productivity theory has withstood a rigorous test. To test the theory would require independent measurements of the marginal products of individual (groups of) workers as well as the relevant demand and supply elasticities. Gathering these data would be extremely laborious, and even impossible for many job categories. So the theory basically rests on economists' faith in the profit maximization hypothesis on the one hand and the auction hypothesis about the labour market on the other. Unfortunately, labour does not share such a faith, and continues to regard the distribution problem as a bargaining problem—a warfare—between capital and labour.

Of the two aspects of the distribution problem—the long-run trend of labour's share and the short-run fluctuations in labour's share resulting from variations in wages and employment over business cycles—the long-run question appears to have fallen off the research agenda of newer economists. One reason for this is the stable and slowly but steadily rising share of labour in the national income, observed in many advanced economies over the past century, which has produced a popular feeling among economists that it is a non-issue. Whether or not this complacency is warranted, however, is yet to be determined. Another reason for downplaying this long-run problem may be the myopia built into today's democratic system. Policy-makers know that they live or die with short-run games that produce quick results. Researchers also find short-run problems more attractive, partly because there is little demand for long-term researches and partly because 'other things' are better controlled in the short run so that short-run issues are better suited for 'scientific' research. One might say that there is a major market failure for economic research on the more important long-run matters.

At any rate, the distribution problem envisaged by researchers today is the short-run problem of how the burden of economic fluctuations falls between capital and labour and what should be done to abate the sufferings of labour. Formally, this problem comes under the category called 'risk-sharing'. A simple model may be useful to facilitate an understanding of the problem. Suppose there is a capitalist with a given wealth of Y_0. If he chooses to 'invest' this sum in a productive activity, he can expect to alter the value of his wealth to Y_1 with probability $(1-p)$ and to Y_2 with probability p. In other words, there are two possible states, 1 and 2. Assume that state 1 is a 'good' state, while state 2 is a 'bad' state; that is, $Y_1 > Y_2$. The productive activity requires a hiring of inputs. Assume that labour is the only input required, and that when the capitalist hires labour, the amount he hires is 1. Let the wages he pays in the two alternative states be W_1 and W_2, respectively, so that his net wealth in the two states becomes $Y_1 - W_1$ and $Y_2 - W_2$, respectively. Finally, this capitalist is assumed to be a risk-averter, which means that the expected wealth, $(1-p)(Y_1 - W_1) + p(Y_2 - W_2)$, must be somewhat greater than Y_0 for him to invest in this risky business. As usual, his risk-averse preferences are represented by the expected utility EU_M:

$$EU_M = (1-p)U_M(Y_1 - W_1) + pU_M(Y_2 - W_2) \qquad (1)$$

where $U_M(\ )$ is a strictly increasing and concave function of its argument. The capitalist will invest only if the EU_M in (1) is at least as large as $U_M(Y_0)$.

Next, the worker is also assumed to be a risk-averter whose preferences are represented by a similar expected utility EU_W:

$$EU_W = (1-p)U_W(W_1) + pU_W(W_2) \qquad (2)$$

where U_W is again a strictly increasing and concave function of W. The worker will take up this employment opportunity only if the EU_W in (2) is at least as large as his reservation utility, say $U_W(W_0)$. Given p, Y_0, W_0, Y_1, and Y_2, the collection $(W_1, W_2) > 0$ for which the inequalities $EU_M \geqslant U_M(Y_0)$ and $EU_W \geqslant U_W(W_0)$ hold constitutes a feasible set of wages in which a solution of this risk-sharing problem is to be found. In Figure 7.1, this feasible set is shown by the lens-shaped area bordered by the two critical indifference curves labelled $U_W(W_0)$ and $U_M(Y_0)$. The worker's indifference curves are convex to the origin and rise in value towards north-east, whereas management's indifference curves are concave to the origin and decline in value towards the north-east. Along the $W_2 = W_1$ line, the risk is borne entirely by management; along the $W_2 = W_1 - (Y_1 - Y_2)$ line, the risk is borne entirely by the worker. The area between these two lines is the area of joint risk-sharing. As shown in the first section of the appendix, the set of Pareto-optimal risk-sharings is represented by the broken line AB.

In sum, when two risk-averters engage jointly in a risky venture, the risk should be shared by both.[4] This means that wages, or the

---

[4] The theoretical literature on risk-sharing often assumes that management alone is risk-neutral, in which case the line AB coincides with the $W_2 = W_1$ line. While this assumption may be justified by the greater capacity of management to absorb risk than the workers, it does not sit well with the general theory of wealth-owners' preferences and portfolio selection.

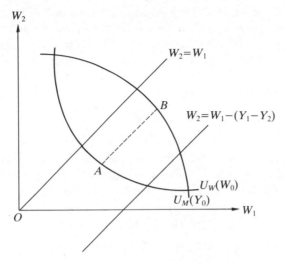

Fig. 7.1 Optimal risk-sharing.

product of the wage rate and employment in general, should be appropriately flexible: if the wage rate is rigid, the volume of employment bears the burden of adjustment; if employment is to remain stable across states, the wage rate should absorb the risk originating in Y.

It is within this framework that economists are accustomed to assessing the employment problem. Not surprisingly, they identify the conventional wage contracts as the major cause of cyclical unemployment. According to the conventional wage contracts, the wage rate is set in advance uniformly across states. Whatever the actual outcome, management is obliged to pay the same preset wage rate. This puts a great strain on management, which naturally seeks to reduce its burden of risk by adjusting the quantity, that is the volume of employment, to the actual turnout of events. Hence the economists' prescription: increase the flexibility of wage rates in wage contracts.

One concept that has evolved from this line of thought is wage indexation. Although the above analysis suggests that a partial indexation of W to Y is the thing to do in general, and although there is nothing wrong with this conclusion, the fact that Y and W above are products of prices and quantities conceals certain complexities important in applications. To illustrate these complexities, let us write $Y = Py$, where P is the price and y is the quantity of the product of the firm. There are now two distinct sources of risk for Y: the variability of P, and the variability of y. Call them a price shock and a real shock, respectively. How should W adjust to these shocks in order to stabilize employment? Consider first the real shock alone. In this case, the expected utilities are

$$EU_M = (1-p)U_M(y_1 - W_1/P) + pU_M(y_2 - W_2/P) \left.\begin{array}{r}\\ \\ \end{array}\right\} \quad (3)$$
$$EU_W = (1-p)U_W(W_1/P) + pU_W(W_2/P)$$

where $y_1 > y_2$. This model is formally identical to the one illustrated above, and so an optimal risk-sharing is a partial indexation of W to y and hence Py; that is, if $y_1 > y_2$, then $W_1 > W_2$ but $W_1 - W_2 < P(y_1 - y_2)$.

Next, consider the price shock only, in which case

$$EU_M = (1-p)U_M(y - W_1/P_1) + pU_M(y - W_2/P_2) \left.\begin{array}{r}\\ \\ \end{array}\right\} \quad (4)$$
$$EU_W = (1-p)U_W(W_1/P_1) + pU_W(W_2/P_2).$$

It is obvious that an optimal risk-sharing calls for a full indexation of W to P and hence to Py. In general, when both shocks occur simultaneously, and if they are positively correlated, W should over-adjust relative to P. When we take into account the difficulties of sorting out different types of shocks, we cannot be too optimistic about the feasibility of the notion of wage indexation as a means of stabilizing employment. Simpler alternatives are clearly in need. The 'share system' proposed recently by Weitzman (1984) is one such example.

By the share system, Weitzman means an allocation scheme whereby labour receives an agreed-upon fraction of the firm's realized total revenue. In symbols, this system may be expressed as

$$W = wL = kP(u)y(L, v) \quad (5)$$

where w is the (implied) wage rate, L is employment, u and v are the price shock and real shock, respectively, and k is the preset share coefficient. As is evident from (5), one advantage of Weitzman's scheme over a wage indexation scheme is that Weitzman's treats price and real shocks symmetrically and hence is not conditional on the specific source of shock.

Weitzman contrasts this scheme with the conventional wage system, which may be expressed as

$$w = \partial E\{Py(L)\}/\partial L \quad (6)$$

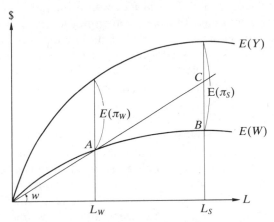

Fig. 7.2   The wage system *v*. the share system.

where E is the expectation operator. In words, the wage rate w is set
before the realization of the random variables u and v in such a way
that it is equal to the expected marginal revenue product of labour.
This system therefore leaves no room for *ex post* adjustments of the
wage rate.

Figure 7.2 illustrates the difference between the wage system and
the share system. In this figure, the curve $E(Y)$ is the expected total
revenue associated with various levels of employment.[5] Under the
wage system, each firm takes the prevailing wage rate as given and
hires a given amount of labour at this wage rate, using (6). The
resulting employment is L_W with the allocation point at A. At this
equilibrium, since the firm has precommitted to hire L_W at the
prescribed wage rate w, the entire shock coming from Y will be
absorbed by the firm, at least momentarily. If the actual Y falls below
$E(Y)$ at L_W, for example, the profit will decline by the full amount of
the shock. What the firm will do next depends very much on how its
expectations of Y are affected by the downward shock of Y. If the firm
expects lower revenues to continue, then the $E(Y)$ curve will shift
downward, and if w stays put, employment is likely to decline in the
next round. If, on the other hand, the firm's expectations are not

---

[5] The importance of expectations in this functional relationship cannot be
overstated. This function may be regarded as equivalent to Keyne's 'employment
function', which he defined as '[Y] is the proceeds the expectation of which will induce a
level of employment [L]' (Keynes 1936: 44).

affected by the drop in Y, L_W will stay put for the time being, but the dent in profits may alert the management not to repeat it. Indeed, a rational firm under the wage system will make allowance for this type of risk and will use a risk-adjusted revenue function which will lie below the straight expected revenue curve in Figure 7.2 as the basis of employment decisions. At any rate, the *ex post* rigidity of wage rates, along with the fact that labour is hired up to the point of equality between the marginal cost and marginal revenue product of labour, makes employment variations ever imminent under the wage system.

Not so under the share system, claims Weitzman. Under the share system, labour's share in the firm's total revenue is always the fraction k, *ex post*. Suppose, for the purpose of comparison, that the share coefficient is set such that the shares are the same *ex ante* at A for the volume of employment L_W. This k generates a curve denoted $E(W)$, whose height is fraction k of $E(Y)$. It is clear from Figure 7.2 that, standing at A, *if* such a share arrangement is reached between management and labour, then management has all the incentives to increase employment, because at $L = L_W$, the marginal labour cost is now below the marginal revenue product. The firm's optimum occurs at $L = L_S$ with the allocation at point B, meaning that a move from the wage system to the share system with the above k will instantly create an excess demand for labour. This fact, along with the *ex post* flexibility of (implied) wage rates, means that the condition of employment in the economy can only improve by the widespread adoption of the share system. Moreover, Weitzman claims that the share system will make the inflation problem easier to tackle. The fact that the unemployment problem is less serious will, by itself, make inflation more manageable; besides, the share system will make 'cost-push' inflation less likely.

All this sounds very good. But whether or not the share system solves the historic confrontation between capital and labour remains a moot question. First, the transition from the wage system to the share system will not be smooth. In view of the variability of its share, labour is not likely to accept a k corresponding to point A; it will demand some reward for bearing the wage risk. North Americans appear to be thinking of a bonus system as a means of securing the requisite degree of wage flexibility in this context. Realistically, however, labour will accept such a bonus only if it is an addition to the current rate of pay. But to add anything to wages in this slow-growth age is extremely difficult. Second, once k has been chosen, management would want to move to L_S, but labour would not prefer a point like B to A, for the expected per capita wages would be less. Anticipating this, labour would demand a higher k than that under the wage system.

In short, the very implementation of the share system is likely to create a major confrontation between labour and management. Given the deep mutual distrust between them in many Western countries, a share agreement, if attained, would be tentative and would fail to generate the kind of harmony and stability Weitzman expects from the system. Reading his book, one is left with a feeling that, although the mechanics are there, the spirit is not. It may very well be that the share system is superior to the wage system, because it nurtures the sense of mutual trust and co-operation between capital and labour, and because the improved atmosphere in the work-place enables management to invest in human and non-human capital more eagerly, thereby raising the efficiency of the firm.

One notable fact about industrial relations in the West is that, whereas big businesses have systematically internalized markets by horizontal and vertical integration in order to reduce their exposure to the vagaries of markets and improve inventory control, they have steadfastly refused to do the same about labour. Consequently, labour has remained the most vulnerable and expendable part of business organizations, and this in turn has intensified the conflict between capital and labour. Public unemployment insurance and other welfare programmes have made it easier for businesses to dismiss workers. But from the societal standpoint, investment in human capital is probably the most risky and irreversible type of investment. It does not seem right, therefore, to let labour absorb the burden of economic fluctuations while capital can get out of contractual (if implicit) obligations without cost. It seems only fair to make capital bear a greater share of the burden, to make it more responsible for the consequence of its own commitments. Once a fairer allocation of the burden is attained, labour–management relations will improve.

As shown in Figure 7.3, it is in Canada and the USA that employment (= the number of regular workers on the payroll) varies most readily in response to changes in production. In the other economies, employment fluctuations are significantly milder. In Japan and France employment is remarkably stable in the face of large changes in production. How can these economies stabilize

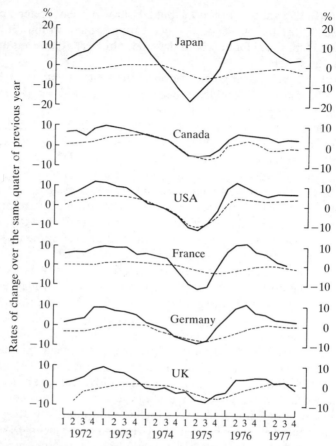

Fig. 7.3 Variations in industrial production and employment, selected OECD countries, 1972–1977. *Source: Ono* (1981: 22, *Chart* 2.2).

employment when the North American economies cannot? According to Ono (1981), one explanation is the relative inflexibility of working hours in the Canadian and US economies. For the same 1973–7 period, Ono correlates employment and working hours and shows that the correlation is much higher in the other economies than in North America. Focusing primarily on Japan, he also points out the importance of flexible *internal* labour markets for employment stabilization. In the Japanese system, workers are expected to perform a variety of different tasks. Auto assembly workers do maintenance and cleaning jobs in slack time, for example. In some cases they may even be loaned out to another firm to perform totally different kinds of machine work. In contrast, in North America, where every individual aspires to be a 'specialist' and where many jobs are filled by those specialists (see Chapter 8), this kind of flexibility is not possible. Even where jobs do not involve specialized skills, unions impose such rigidities upon themselves. The unemployment problem in North America could (and, in my opinion, should) be eased by increasing flexibility in these areas. It goes without saying that maintaining stable employment in a fluctuating environment increases the firm's cost, which must be covered by a more efficient running of the organization. A fundamental solution of the unemployment problem seems to lie in the extra efforts of tenured employees and in better planning on the part of management, which a more co-operative behaviour of capital and labour is capable of generating.

3 A CO-OPERATIVE SOLUTION

Although explicitly co-operative business organizations are a rarity in the capitalist economies of the world, some are more co-operative than others. Examples of greater co-operation between capital and labour include those jointly managed firms in Germany and the many Japanese firms which operate under the rules of lifetime employment and seniority wages. In the case of the Japanese firms, co-operation is more implicit. Nevertheless, the Japanese worker fresh out of school behaves as if he were employed on a lifetime contract, and his right to expect non-dismissal in ordinary circumstances has been upheld by the courts in a series of decisions since 1955 (Hashimoto 1979: 1088, n. 5). It seems reasonable, therefore, to model these firms as co-operative ventures between capital and labour. The fact that they have grown out of many years of hostility and bitter fights (and Japan is no exception) increases their relevance as a model of industrial relations in the future. The following analysis and discussion proceed with the Japanese firms in mind, but the implications are not limited to Japanese organizations.

Comparing the employment tenure and wage earnings profiles in Japan and the USA, Hashimoto and Raisian (1985) note the following points.

1 Long-term employment is distinctly more common in Japan than in the USA.

2 Job retention rates are considerably higher in Japan than in the USA. By age 24, the average Japanese male has held 2.06 jobs out of the 4.91 jobs he will hold in his working life; an average US male has held 4.4 jobs out of 11 or so jobs he will hold. During the next ten years, by age 34, the Japanese male will have held an additional 1.1 jobs, but the US male will have held 3.0 jobs.

3 The employer–employee attachment is stronger in Japan than in the USA. There is also a definite tendency for longer tenures to occur in larger firms.

4 For all firm-size groups, growth rates between the peak earnings year and the initial year are greater in Japan than in the USA.

5 Growth rates attributable to tenure are far greater in Japan than in the USA.

6 Both the earnings–tenure and earnings–total experience profiles are more steeply sloped in Japan than in the USA, holding firm size constant.

As the above facts indicate, one essential feature of a co-operative scheme is the longer job expectancy of the workers. A quick calculation of the average job expectancy from Table 2 of Hashimoto and Raisian yields 11.58 years for the Japanese workers as against 2.97 years for the US workers, both evaluated at age 22.[6] According to a recent newspaper article, MBAs from top US business schools are expected to stay with their first job for only 1.5 years. When the new recruits' job expectancy is this short, the employers have little incentive to 'invest' in them, let alone regard them as partners.

Lack of a sense of partnership is not limited to the employers. US workers are much less interested in job tenure than their Japanese counterparts. The old adage that a rolling stone gathers no moss

---

[6] In view of Japan's popular practice of retiring at age 55, these expectancies ignore jobs beyond that age. My own calculation from the Japanese *Wage Census* (Japanese Ministry of Labour 1986) yielded job expectancies for male university graduates employed as 'administrative, clerical and technical workers' in the manufacturing sector at age 22 as follows: 5.2 years for small firms (less than 100 employees), 10.4 years for medium-sized firms (more than 100 but less than 1000 employees), and 15.1 years for large firms (more than 1000 employees). For female university graduates, the corresponding figures were 3.5, 4.5, and 9.0 years. In general, the higher the educational level, and the larger the firm size, the longer the job expectancy for both sexes. Also, the job expectancy of females is considerably shorter than that of males up to the Middle Ages.

appears to have two totally different meanings. To the Americans it admonishes them to keep rolling so as *not* to gather moss; their ideal career consists of a constant changing of jobs for the better. To the Japanese, the adage stresses the importance of staying put and gathering moss, namely, all sorts of knowledge and skill specific to an individual work-place. As a result, US firms and workers find themselves in a kind of equilibrium similar to that of a used-car market described by Akerlof (1970). Workers desiring a long job tenure cannot persuade their employers into long-term contracts because of the high (job) mortality rates; the employers desiring long-term co-operative arrangements cannot persuade workers into them because the starting wages under co-operative arrangements would have to be less than the marginal productivity rates prevailing in the spot market, as will be shown shortly.

Now the model. In order to capture the long-term co-operative arrangement, the object of the firm is specified as a maximization of the joint utilities of the firm and the worker over his lifetime:

$$\Pi = \int_0^T [aU\{PF(S) - W - C(I)\} + (1 - a)V(W)]E(t) \, dt. \qquad (7)$$

In this equation, a is the fraction representing the present allocation coefficient, S is the worker's human capital, $F(S)$ is his output, P is the output's price, W is his wage earnings, I is the flow of investment in the worker's human capital, $C(I)$ is its cost, $E(t)$ is the worker's statistical 'survival rate' adjusted for the usual interest factor, and T is some maximum age of the worker at which his working life will end (such as age 65). Although uncertainty is not treated explicitly, the assumed concavity of the utility functions U and V builds into the co-operative solution an element of risk-sharing.

One important assumption in the formulation of (7) is that the cost of investment in human capital is borne by management. This suggests that the worker's human capital is primarily firm-specific, although it does not exclude the accumulation of general human capital with work experience. To the Japanese accustomed to long job tenures, the hypothesis that firm-specific capital is the driving force behind wage growth comes naturally, but not so to the Americans, who aspire to 'keep rolling'. They suspect that the observed significance of the duration variable (as a proxy for firm-specific human capital) in explaining wage growth may reflect not so much the growth of human capital as the conventional, irrational, seniority rule. Medoff and Abraham (1981), for example, make an interesting attempt to validate this suspicion. In the present model analysis, the importance of the assumption that the firm will bear the cost of human capital investment relates to a somewhat different question. In a joint maximization problem, the question of who bears the cost of investment is, in a sense, merely a matter of bookkeeping. The management could pay out wages equalling $W' = W + C(I)$, with the worker spending $C(I)$ out of W' to retain W as net wages. In another sense, however, the issue of who bears the cost of investment is of crucial importance. This is so because it changes the interpretation of observed wage earnings W. With management bearing the cost, W is net of investment cost; with the worker bearing the cost, W is gross of investment cost. Equation (7) chooses the former because it is more in line with reality.

The worker's initial capital at age 'zero', determined by such factors as educational achievement and work experience, is a given datum to the contracting parties, as are his survival probabilities, these being the characteristics of the group to which he belongs. Given his initial capital, the future path of that capital is determined by the rate of investment subject to depreciation and obsolescence:

$$\mathrm{d}S(t)/\mathrm{d}t = I(t) - \delta S(t), \quad \text{given } S(0), \tag{8}$$

where δ is an exponential depreciation rate. The choice variables are $W(t)$ and $I(t)$. How should W and I be selected in order to maximize Π in (7) subject to (8)? This problem is an optimal control problem, whose solution is the time paths of W and I over the entire horizon, which is what we are after.

In what follows, we study a somewhat simplified version of the above model for ease of exposition. We chop the horizon into two 'periods', the current and the future. While this simplification carries a price, the main points of the more general model will be brought out more easily. The model is now written:

$$\Pi = aU(Y_1) + (1-a)V(W_1) + E\{aU(Y_2) + (1-a)V(W_2)\} \tag{7'}$$

where $Y_1 = P_1F(S_1) - W_1 - C(I)$, and $Y_2 = P_2F(S_2) - W_2$. Also, (8) becomes

$$S_2 = (1-\delta)S_1 + I. \tag{8'}$$

Substitution of these expressions into (7') makes Π a compact function of the three choice variables, W_1, W_2, and I. Leaving the technical details to the second part of the appendix, the results of my comparative-statistics analysis are reported in Table 7.3. A positive sign in the table means that the choice variable in question moves in the same direction as the change in the parameter. Similarly, a negative sign means that the choice variable in question moves in the direction opposite to the initiating change in the parameter. A question mark indicates that the prediction of the model is ambiguous.

In this table, the most interesting and important effects are those of E (first row). We shall henceforth refer to this parameter as the 'job expectancy'. The longer the job expectancy, the *lower* the current period wage but the higher the future wages. The rate of investment in human capital is also higher, the longer the job expectancy. Comparing two groups of workers with identical initial capital, we infer from this that the one with a longer job expectancy will start with a lower wage but a faster-growing wage profile than the one with a shorter job expectancy. A worker's lifetime productivity is also expected to be higher if he has a longer job expectancy, on account of the higher rate of investment. The implications of these findings for comparative studies of the wages between Japanese and US workers or between male and female workers are obvious. The effects of the initial capital stock (second row), which may be identified with the specific human capital hypothesis of the Chicago school, is self-explanatory, as are the effects of the allocation coefficient a (last row). The effects of a change in the current-period price P_1 on W_1 (third row) reveals the fact that the present co-operative scheme embodies

Table 7.3 Optimal wages and investment

Change in:	Effect on:			
	W_1	W_2	I	$W_1 + C(I)$
E	−	+	+	+
S_1	+	+	?	?
P_1	+ *	+	+	+
P_2	?	+	?	?
a	−	−	?	−

* A positive fraction times $F(S_1)$.

the notion of revenue-sharing in the sense that W_1 does not increase by the full amount of the increase in the value of the worker's product.

4 INTERPRETATION OF RESULTS

Observed lifetime wage profiles for stayers exhibit clear growth trends. The slopes are steeper in Japan than in the USA. Why such growth trends, and why are they more pronounced in Japan? A number of hypotheses have been advanced in the literature.

The specific capital hypothesis of the Chicago school, led by Becker (1962), attributes the growth trend to the accumulation of worker's firm-specific human capital. Although eminently sensible, this hypothesis has a few flaws. It cannot explain why many US workers keep 'rolling'. It also faces the Medoff–Abraham-type criticism that the observed growth trend of wages may not be fully explained by workers' productivity. Moreover, this hypothesis is incomplete in that it is devoid of any contractual elements in wage determination. Indeed, under the assumption of a perfect capital market, the time shape of lifetime wages *per se* (apart from its present discounted value) is totally irrelevant.

The screening hypothesis of Salop and Salop (1976) views rising wage profiles as an employers' device to discourage those with high mortality rates from applying for jobs. Their conclusion is based on the observation that, because workers with different job expectancies have in effect different discount rates, an employer can manipulate the time shape of wages (of a constant present discounted value) in such a way that only those with low mortality rates will want the job. While their point is well taken, Salop and Salop's treatment of workers' productivity as exogenous and independent of job expectancy and job tenure precludes the real source of difference between long-term jobs and short ones. If the exogenous and common productivity is interpreted to mean a given present discounted value of lifetime wages at a 'pure' interest rate, even those with long job expectancies would prefer a flat wage profile to a rising profile, which means that they would not reveal their true preferences.

The agency hypothesis of Lazear (1979) views rising wage profiles as an employers' device to discourage employee-shirking. Instead of paying out straight productivity wages W_1 and W_2 over two 'periods', an employer pays $W_1' = W_1 - x$ in the first period and $W_2' = W_2 + y$ in the second, where x and y are some positive numbers. The amount y contains x, namely, that part of the first-period wage that was withheld, but its payment is nevertheless made conditional on the worker's performance in the second period. In this way the employer induces the worker to give his best over the two periods. Although this hypothesis brings out an element of reality, it is open to the same kind to criticism as those directed towards the screening hypothesis. Besides, a rising wage profile creates room for the other type of shirking, employer-shirking or malfeasance.

In short, all these hypotheses suffer from certain deficiencies. The specific capital hypothesis is too general and weak to cast much light on the question of why long-term contracts should pay and why lifetime wage profiles should keep rising. The screening hypothesis and the agency hypothesis focus on a particular effect of rising wage profiles but lack proper general equilibrium considerations. In general, it is not easy to rationalize rising wage profiles in an economy where workers believe in upward mobility and employers care little about training their workers.

The purpose of the previous section was, first, to identify an optimal wage profile under an explicitly dynamic joint maximization model, and second, to use the result of the comparative-statics analysis of the model in order to gain further insights into the questions of wages, employment, and productivity. The wage profile derived from the model has two components: capital and equity. The capital component reconfirms the specific capital hypothesis. It explains the growth of wage earnings by the accumulation of human capital and the resulting increase in labour productivity. But this component in a multi-period context will peak out at mid-career and hence will not be able to rationalize the monotonic upward trend of wage earnings over the entire working life. The concern expressed by Medoff and Abraham seems justified. The equity component constitutes an additional source of growth in wage profiles. The job expectancy variable gives rise to the worker's equity in the firm organization by tilting the wage profile in favour of the future. The equity component is the greater, the longer the job expectancy of the worker, other things being the same; it will be zero for workers hired in the spot market. As Table 7.3 shows, spot market wages are higher than the long-term contract wages paid to comparable workers. It is this shortfall of long-term contract wages that constitutes the equity of the worker under long-term contracts. It is as if he trades part of his current wages to the firm for later repayments.

In this way, the equity component offers an answer to the query raised by Medoff and Abraham. It also improves on the screening hypothesis of Salop and Salop by allowing workers' productivity to improve as a result of investment in their human capital under long-term contracts. To the extent that firms withhold part of a worker's wages under long-term contracts in the early part of his career and the actual repayment of this portion of the wages is conditional upon the worker's performance, the equity component is in agreement with Lazear's agency hypothesis. But in another sense, the present analysis brings out a difficulty with Lazear's theory: how to ensure a full repayment of workers' equities by employers. Employers naturally have an incentive to default, especially in a hostile environment as in North America. These observations point to the importance of mutual trust or a sense of co-operation between capital and labour for the successful operation of long-term contracts, which offer many significant advantages over spot market contracts, such as a sensible sharing of risks and benefits and a high productivity of workers.

On the other hand, the present joint maximization model appears to fit the Japanese system quite well. It lends support to the main features of the Japanese wage profiles, as pointed out by Hashimoto and Raisian. Moreover, it provides a consistent explanation as to why the productivity of Japanese workers is high, why female workers' wage profiles do not grow as much as those of males (because of females' higher job mortality rates), and why small-sized firms have trouble exploiting the benefits of long-term co-operative arrangements to the full (because of the relatively high job mortality rates and low educational levels of the workers they have to deal with, and the lack of credibility of small establishments' future promises).

Finally, a brief remark about the model's implications for empirical research. The conventional, specific capital, model of wages measures the capital stock variable S by the educational level, S_1; general experience by the age after entrance to the labour force, A; and job duration or tenure by the number of years the worker has been with his current job, D. That is, the current capital stock S is specified as

$$S = S(S_1, A, D).$$

The firm size and sex, and sometimes S_1 itself, are treated as dummies. Assuming that wage earnings are a function of S, we can estimate the effects of A and D separately, which allows us to examine the effect of staying (a parallel increase in A and D), of pure ageing (an increase in A only), and of pure job tenure (an increase in D only) on wage earnings.

The present model identifies another, *forward-looking*, determinant of wages, the E variable, so that W is now a function not only of S but also of E. Its crude estimates are obtainable from the conventional wage census data for each class of workers distinguished by education, sex, firm size, age, etc. The model predicts that, since the chief effect of E on W is to accelerate the latter's growth, the product variable AE should capture it with a significant positive coefficient. An experiment with the 1985 Wage Census data for the 'administrative. clerical and technical' workers in the Japanese manufacturing sector has produced estimates for the coefficients, all of them correct in sign and statistically significant, for the group of male university graduates, among others (Table 7.4).

Table 7.5 tabulates hourly wages at select ages as estimated from Table 7.4, assuming that the worker is staying with the same job. It shows the general pattern of lifetime wages as predicted by our optimizing model. It also shows the advantages of being with larger firms as opposed to smaller ones. It is safe to assume in Japan that every university graduate prefers a larger firm to a smaller firm, but

Table 7.4   Lifetime wage profiles for male university graduates

Firm size	Const. Age	Duration	Expectancy	Age × expectancy	Crossing age
Small	2.015 0.1340 (−1) (14.90)(4.71)	0.1307 (−1) (12.73)	−0.1155 (0) (−5.32)	0.3318 (−2) (7.85)	34.83
Medium	1.735 0.2405 (−1) (26.75)(15.25)	0.1203 (−1) (10.21)	−0.4122 (−1) (−7.36)	0.1187 (−2) (7.67)	34.70
Large	1.948 0.2169 (−1) (24.26)(11.39)	0.1432 (−1) (9.76)	−0.3182 (−1) (−8.33)	0.8914 (−3) (9.59)	35.70

Notes:

1. Estimating equation is of the form: $\ln W = \text{constant} + a_1 (\text{age}) + a_2 (\text{duration}) + a_3 (\text{expectancy}) + a_4 (\text{age} \times \text{expectancy})$, where W is the regular hourly wage in hundreds of yen.

2. Negative integers in parentheses following estimates denote the power of 10 by which the preceding coefficients are to be multiplied.

3. Numbers in parentheses below estimates denote t-values.

4. The 'crossing age' denotes that age at which the effects of the last two terms of the estimating equation cancel each other out, namely, that age at which workers start receiving more wages than their productivity justifies.

Labour

Table 7.5 Regular hourly wages for stayers at select ages (yen)

Firm size	Age				
	22	27	37	47	52
Small	807	979	1613	2074	2228
Medium	822	1017	1695	2456	2840
Large	930	1063	1954	2952	3388

that the university's reputation and the student's grades affect his or her chance of entering a large firm. Hence the stiff competition for entrance into a handful of 'good' universities, which works its way back to primary schools. Though not reported here, it is possible to compute the return to education by comparing the wages of workers with different educational achievements. It is also possible to compute the cost of switching jobs, the extent to which the observed differences in wages between male and female workers is due to the differences in job expectancies, and a few other figures of interest.

5 CONCLUDING REMARKS

The extent to which an economy can effectively manage its labour is perhaps the single most important key to its success. Yet, generally speaking, labour–management relations have not seen much progress over the past century, despite the dramatic improvements in wages, working hours, and other conditions of labour. The antagonism between capital and labour continues in much the nineteenth-century style. On the one hand, there are still many bush capitalists around who have little perception of democracy, let alone of their social responsibility as job providers. There are many union leaders, on the other hand, who are interested in nothing but the fight against capital. Neither side recognizes the possibility of a mutually beneficial co-operative arrangement between the two. The results of this continued conflict are constant disruptions of business activities and a high rate of unemployment, which put additional strain on the public purse. The failure of naive Keynesianism to solve the unemployment problem has much to do with this deeper problem of poor industrial relations.

Good labour–management relations are important in the context not only of short-term economic stability but also of long-term growth and development. Both capital and labour need much enlightenment on this point; for, as history shows, natural resources cannot bring about a lasting economic prosperity, but human resources, along with their organizational abilities, can.

APPENDIX: TECHNICAL DETAILS

1 The management's indifference curves have slopes

$$\mathrm{d}W_2/\mathrm{d}W_1\big|_{EU_M} = -(1-p)U_M'(Y_1-W_1)/pU_M'(Y_2-W_2).$$

Differentiation of this expression with respect to W_2 shows that $\mathrm{d}^2 W_2/\mathrm{d}W_1^2 < 0$; that is, the management's indifference curves are concave to the origin. Also, the above slope along the $W_2 = W_1 - (Y_1 - Y_2)$ line is $-(1-p)/p$.

The worker's indifference curves have slopes

$$\mathrm{d}W_2/\mathrm{d}W_1\big|_{EU_W} = -(1-p)U_W'(W_1)/pU_W'(W_2).$$

A further differentiation of this expression with respect to W_1 shows that $\mathrm{d}^2 W_2/\mathrm{d}W_1^2 > 0$; that is, the worker's indifference curves are convex to the origin. Moreover, the above slope along the $W_2 = W_1$ line is $-(1-p)/p$.

Hence, the set of Pareto-optimal risk allocations must lie somewhere between the $W_2 = W_1$ line and the $W_2 = W_1 - (Y_1 - Y_2)$ line.

2 From equations (7') and (8'), the problem is one of maximizing

$$\Pi = aU\{P_1 F(S_1) - W_1 - C(I)\} + (1-a)V(W_1)$$
$$+ E\langle aU[P_2 F\{(1-\delta)S_1 + I\}] + (1-a)V(W_2)\rangle \qquad (A1)$$

with respect to W_1, W_2, and I. The first-order conditions for a maximum are

$$-aU_1' + (1-a)V_1' = 0 \qquad (A2)$$

$$-aU_2' + (1-a)V_2' = 0 \qquad (A3)$$

$$-U_2' C' + EU_2' P_2 F_2' = 0 \qquad (A4)$$

where primes denote derivatives and subscripts denote the periods; thus, $U_1' = dU(Y_1)/dY_1$, for example. The second-order conditions are satisfied by the assumed curvatures of the functions involved, i.e. U, V, and F concave and C convex. The rate of investment I is naturally non-negative, and an optimal I can be zero, which would be the case if E were very low. We have ignored this possibility in (A4).

The system of equations for a comparative-statics analysis is obtained from (A2)–(A4) in the usual manner:

$$
\begin{bmatrix} aU_1'' + (1-a)V_1'' & 0 & aU_1''C' \\ 0 & aU_2'' + (1-a)V_2'' & -U_2''P_2F_2' \\ U_1''C' & -EU_2''P_2F_2' & U_1''C'C' + EU_2''P_2F_2'F_2' \end{bmatrix} \begin{bmatrix} dW_1 \\ dW_2 \\ dI \end{bmatrix}
$$

$$
= \begin{bmatrix} 0 \\ 0 \\ -U_2'P_2F_2' \end{bmatrix} dE + \begin{bmatrix} aU_1''F_1 \\ 0 \\ U_1'F_1C' \end{bmatrix} dP_1 + \begin{bmatrix} 0 \\ aU_2''F_2 \\ -EU_2''P_2F_2F_2' - EU_2'F_2' \end{bmatrix} dP_2
$$

$$
+ \begin{bmatrix} U_1' + V_1' \\ U_2' + V_2' \\ 0 \end{bmatrix} da + \begin{bmatrix} aU_1''P_1F_1' \\ aU_2''P_2F_2'(1-\delta) \\ U_1''P_1F_1'C' - E(1-\delta)U_2''P_2^2F_2'F_2' \end{bmatrix} dS_1. \qquad \text{(A5)}
$$

To simplify computation, the production function F is assumed linear; i.e., $F_1' = F_2' = F'$. The determinantal value D of the coefficient matrix on the left-hand side of (A5) is negative, and the results in Table 7.3 are obtained by straightforward computation.

The term $\partial W_1/\partial P_1$ has the form

$$
\frac{\partial W_1}{\partial P_1} = \frac{a(1-a)EU_1''U_2''V_2''P_2^2F'F'}{D} F_1,
$$

which is positive but less than F_1. This fact is easy to establish by noting that the numerator is a part of the expression for D.

8

Anti-Monies

> I said there was a Society of Men among us, bred up from their Youth in the Art of proving by Words multiplied for the Purpose, that *White is Black*, and *Black is White*, according as they are paid. To this Society all the rest of the People are Slaves.
>
> Jonathan Swift, *Gulliver's Travels*

1 INTRODUCTION

From the point of view of economics, democracy is an expensive system to run. Part of the expense comes from the various sources of inefficiencies known to economists, such as myopia and the failure of decentralized markets. The rest comes from ever-rising costs of transactions among the members of a democratic society. This chapter focuses on the latter.

One inevitable trend in individualistic societies is the growth of élite professionals. When unregulated, they use their specialized knowledge to gain control of society. As a result, their charges can raise overhead and transaction costs of society so much so that society may cease to function smoothly, as is indicated below.

2 DEMOCRACY AND RENT-SEEKING ACTIVITIES

The pure theory of democracy in political science has very much in common with the theory of perfect competition in economics. The theory of perfect competition assumes that all individuals are equally well informed and capable, when they in fact are not. The pure theory of democracy assumes that all men are created equal, when they are not. The theory of perfect competition asserts that, when individuals trade freely among themselves on an equal footing (as price-takers), all of them will benefit and the total gains from this trade to society will be maximal. The pure theory of democracy asserts that, by granting equal rights to all, democracy will achieve the greatest good of the greatest number.

But society has not developed as asserted by these theories. In economics, the trend has always been away from atomistic competition and into monopolistic structures. This is inevitable, given the differences in abilities and other resource endowments among individuals and the democratic environment that encourages the pursuit of self-interest. Investing in 'bigness' has proven to be a winning strategy in business.

True, every democratic nation has enacted a set of laws to discourage or punish such strategies in an effort to restore fair competition. In every case these regulations started out stiff but have been mutilated over the years. The first setback for the regulatory movement came when it conceded to the argument that being big is not a crime by itself. Behind this argument is the democratic supposition that the basic human rights should also apply to legal 'persons', large and small. Once this concession was made, the movement lost its teeth. In order to lay charges successfully on a large corporation, the accuser must now bear the burden of proof that the accused has actually committed an act of conspiratory with a view to 'unduly' restricting competition, and that this act has actually resulted in 'substantial' damages on the part of its rival firms. As a result, the regulations have been rendered ineffectual except for the occasional revelation of a badly handled scheme, allowing society to make scapegoats out of the perpetrators. In a loosely operated system like Canada's, the entire process of deliberation and of drafting the competition law is conducted by agents of the large business interests with complete disregard for the consumers, and this at the expense of the public purse. Even those who cannot invest in bigness because of a shortage of capital, the absence of economies of scale, or unfavourable market conditions have formed associations and lobbies to reduce their exposure to competition. And Canada is by no means an exception.

Similarly discriminating movements have been noticed in the political and sociological fields. The more democracy permeates, and the more legal rights are granted to the masses, the more effort and ingenuity individuals exert in order to differentiate themselves from the masses. One prime example of such movements is the high and increasing demand for university and college degrees. In the USA today, about 50 per cent of all the highschool graduates go on to colleges and universities,[1] (although many of them do not finish their courses). This democratization of higher education has altered the basic character of the universities and colleges. With students whose IQs range from 100 to 115 forming the majority in many university and college campuses, the teaching methods and course contents of higher education have had to be adapted to accommodate them. The popularization of the bachelor's degree has also increased the demand for more advanced degrees in general and for those of professional schools in particular.

In democratic societies, and especially in individualistic societies, élite jobs are well defined and tend to be occupied by advanced degree holders. Table 8.1 shows the proportion of élite jobs to the total number of jobs for selected countries, and indicates the rising trend of these élite jobs, both over time within each society and over stages of economic development. The growth of élite jobs is in part a natural

Table 8.1 The growth of élite jobs: proportion of 'élite' to total number of jobs, selected countries[a] (%)

Country	Year		Professional/ technical		Managerial/ administrative[b]	
Australia	1982	(1966)	13.53	(9.26)	5.94	(6.26)
Canada	1982	(1968)	14.65	(12.20)	7.80	(9.02)
France	1975	(1962)	15.45	(9.13)	3.25	(3.09)
Germany	1980	(1961)	13.43	(7.59)	2.86	(3.11)
India	1971	(1961)	2.74	(1.71)	0.93	(0.95)
Italy	1971	(1965)	7.29	(5.32)	0.61	(n.a.)
Japan	1982	(1968)	8.15	(5.49)	3.81	(2.55)
Korea	1981	(1967)	3.97	(2.59)	1.39	(0.80)
Mexico	1977	(1960)	6.20	(3.61)	2:60	(0.83)
Spain	1979	(1967)	5.85	(3.39)	1.37	(0.81)
Sweden	1981	(1965)	26.15	(15.28)	2.17	(2.20)
UK	1971	(1960)	11.14	(9.55)	3.69	(3.07)
USA	1981	(1967)	15.24	(12.39)	10.70	(9.36)

[a] Earlier years, and the figures relating to them, are given in parentheses.
[b] Excluding the military.

Source: ILO, *Yearbooks of Labor Statistics*.

[1] Canada is a close second with over 40%; major European countries are in the 20% range.

consequence of the general improvement in the human capital stock. But it is also the result of the open race for degrees and titles in today's societies where every mother wants her child to be a doctor, lawyer, accountant, or some other specialist, or else a business executive. The table shows that one job out of every four in the USA is such an élite job. If one assumes that every child attends high-school, and that the upper 50 per cent of all the high-school graduates go on to colleges and universities, this means that up to one-half of all the college and university graduates will be élite job holders. If one assumes the standard deviation of the IQ distribution to be 15, this means that US society must dig deep into a group whose average IQ is between 100 and 115 in order to fill its large number of élite jobs. An inflation of degrees and licences is inevitable.

A similar trend is observed outside the academic community. The rapid growth of the government sector has resulted in an overproduction of supervisory positions and senior research posts. The private sector has not been far behind. Corporations have liberally increased the number of vice-presidents and other high-profile offices.[2] All types of research firms have sprung up to serve these high-status occupants.

Last but not least, lawyers, accountants, and other types of consultants have mushroomed to look after the expanded legal rights and other personal affairs of the masses. In the USA, for example, there were 651,000 lawyers and judges in 1983. This number exceeds the total number of the police, which stood at 645,000.[3] It takes more human resources to serve law than to enforce it. At a modest estimate of annual earnings of $100,000 per head, these lawyers and judges are earning $65.1 billion annually, which compares favourably with the GNP of Denmark (population 5.12 million) or Taiwan (population 18.27 million). At an estimated annual income of $200,000, their income would far exceed the GNP of Switzerland (population 6.48 million) or Belgium (population 9.85 million), and would amount to one-half of US defence spending in a year.

---

[2] A fair-sized bank in California, for example, has 15 executive vice-presidents and 40 other vice-presidents, a situation any rational and responsible owner would lose no moment to correct.

[3] Both figures are for 1983 (cf. US Department of Commerce, *Statistical Abstract of the United States*, 1985). Lawyers are specially abundant in Anglo-Saxon countries. Lieberman (1983: x) cites a study that rates Australians and Canadians as more litigious, and Danes, English, New Zealanders, and West Germans as a little less litigious, than Americans.

Are the services of lawyers and judges really more valuable than these gross national products? While there is no precise way of answering such a question, many doubt it. A major reason for this doubt is that, in the 'market' for legal services, the principle of consumer sovereignty, namely the basic premise of free and rational consumer choice, does not apply. In this market the client is typically an ignorant, helpless, and distressed being, vulnerable to manipulation and exploitation. Without the guidance of the lawyer, he often does not know what his rights are and when they have been infringed upon, much less how to defend or claim them. In this situation, the user's 'demand curve' is not well defined, the price-setting mechanism becomes arbitrary, and the economists' favourite market test loses its ground. If the matter is left to the 'market', the providers end up setting both the quantity and the price so as to maximize their well-being. This is exactly what is happening in the US market for legal services. The result is a sky-rocketing of costs, both private and public, of one of the essential services in this democratic society. Canada faces a similar problem.

As a rent-seeking group, the legal profession in North America runs its business exceedingly well, even better than the medical profession. First, they keep the law completely out of reach of the public. Throughout the North American school cirriculum, including university bachelor's degree programmes, students are kept from even the most rudimentary introduciton to law. Guidebooks and commentaries about law, including those on such basic acts as the constitution and the civil and criminal code, are non-existent.[4] The result is the widespread false belief among the populace that the law is beyond their comprehension, and consequently their total dependency on the legal profession. This is an utterly absurd phenomenon. The law is *not* beyond the comprehension of an average citizen. If taught the highlights of the constitution in an elementary school and the elements of social philosophy behind the legal system of society in high-school, and given a few courses in selected areas of law as undergraduates, most people will have acquired a degree of familiarity with the law sufficient to dispel their blind fear, plus a basic

---

[4] In 1982 the government of Canada published a special volume to commemorate the repatriation of its Constitution. This several-hundred-page volume is full of colourful photographs of the ritual, celebrating events, and a description of the history leading to the repatriation. But nowhere in the volume can one find the text of the Constitution Act!

skill of reading and interpreting legal documents. They will then discover that they can write up their conveyances themselves and save the $300 fee they would otherwise pay a lawyer for 30 minutes of service. North Americans are basically self-reliant and creative people. Many of them are respectable carpenters, electricians, and mechanics. Yet when it comes to legal matters, they are probably the poorest of all the peoples in the world, owing to their complete lack of opportunities to learn about the law.

Second, the legal profession has managed to control its members well so as to protect its monopoly. Not only has it succeeded in making the practice of law by non-members illegal, but it has restricted the power of the para-legals. In addition, it has forbidden its members to publicize their fees. The result is a fee structure, if there is one, that simply mystifies the public. Third, the legal profession has not confined itself to its proper business of litigation, but has been expanding its scope into the general area of mediation where the issues involved have little to do with law. Many labour disputes and wage negotiations, for example, are arbitrated or mediated by lawyers whose expertise on the matter is very much in doubt. Malpractice suits in medicine are another area where the issues are not legal but exclusively technical and economic, and where the arbitrariness of results is inevitable. Consider the following example:

During the surgery her doctor damaged some of her nerves; despite subsequent repairs, her left arm and hand are disfigured and atrophied. If she had been a 25-year-old watchmaker, say, her complete disability would have been worth about $340,000 over 40 years. The surgeon's insurer refused to offer even $225,000 to settle, as his lawyer suggested. So they went to trial and the jury awarded nearly $800,000. During the appeal, both sides agreed to settle for $734,000. After paying her lawyer one-third, she's left with $482,000 in the bank . . . (*Newsweek*, 17 February, 1986: 74)

Apart from the arbitrariness of the awards, the magnitude of the lawyer's fee cannot fail to impress ordinary citizens. This type of formula, known as the contingency fee formula, is very popular in North America. Under this, the lawyer gets a preset fraction (one-third in the above example) if he wins and nothing if he loses. It is a rational solution for cases involving clients unable to pay the $200-an-hour-plus expenses fee. But it clearly has the tendency to inflate the awards. The award money must come from somewhere. In the above example, it came from the surgeon's insurer, who collected it from client-surgeons in the form of malpractice insurance premia, which, *Newsweek* reports, are running at $30,000–$80,000 per surgeon per annum, and are fast rising. This means that the surgical fees are also fast rising. *Newsweek* goes on to report that these premia are forcing some surgeons to abandon high-risk operations. Whether or not the actual amount of medical services performed declines, the public ends up bearing the cost of expensive transactions. The point is that the victims individually have no incentive to turn down lawyers' offers. The victim in the above example would not otherwise have won as large an award as she did. Once a damage has occurred, the victim and the lawyer are a team pursuing a maximum joint 'profit', at the expense of society. Unless the medical profession devises an effective means of quality control of its members, or unless the contingency fee formula is made illegal, the market will keep generating large settlements and lucrative earnings to the mediating lawyers.

Lately the legal profession in North America has been showing signs of moving into academia, a field the profession thus far shied away from. The new business concerns student–professor (–university) conflicts. In Quebec, a student recently took his professor and university to court on the grounds that the content of a course he enrolled in was not in conformity with the course description and that, because of this, his effort and money were wasted. The student won the case, which, according to the spokesman of the legal profession, set a very important precedent. While this particular case concerned a fairly standardized course content and hence a relatively clear case, university professors' teaching and guidance are often in much more nebulous, judgemental, and even controversial areas such as the supervision of doctoral dissertations. These are potentially very lucrative areas for the legal profession, and its intrusion into them seems just a matter of time. But again, apart from providing the legal profession with new jobs, the net social benefits of opening up academia to litigation is by no means obvious.

In addition to lawyers and doctors, there are no less than 400,000 accountants in the USA thriving on their ever-growing business. Some 250,000 of these are in the currently fashionable business of financial planning, in which they offer professional advice to rich clients for handsome fees. Others cater to the demands of the more ordinary citizens concerning income taxes and other financial problems. Many income tax pros use a scheme whereby they 'buy out' people's income tax forms at a discount, prepare the forms, and claim the refunds. The rate of discount is said to be as high as 15 per cent. The difference between this business and loan-sharking is slight.

While the cases mentioned above are quite alarming, government nevertheless has been the single greatest victim of these rent-seeking activities. Government today is dominated by all types of 'professionals', so much so that it cannot make one decision without first consulting the relevant outside experts. It is as though the big bureaucratic machine stopped thinking altogether. The US government was said to be spending $1 million a day for contract research works a number of years ago. It is not that the bureaucrats are incapable of doing research and policy formulation for themselves, or that the outside professionals are so much superior to the bureaucrats as a matter of fact. But such a feeling seems to be widespread. Moreover, the principle of 'procedural rationality' governing the conduct of the bureaucrats encourages them to establish alibis by hiring professionals (see Chapter 3 above).

A common feature of all these rent-seeking activities is that the commodity involved is specialized knowledge of one type or another. The source of rent is the differential access to such knowledge between the provider and the client. Economists are fond of saying that knowledge is, and should be, a public good available to everyone at little or not cost. But this is not what one finds in reality. Professionals, namely those who possess specialized knowledge, have formed themselves into a variety of organizations and have more or less successfully preserved their monopoly of knowledge to earn the high rent.

This constitutes a blind spot in democracy. Contrary to the basic premiss of the theory of democracy, people are not created equal, and no amount of legislation can make them equal. Some individuals are more talented than others, and the talented can and do prey on the untalented, the charter of rights notwithstanding. If the monopoly problem in ordinary industries has proven to be difficult to crack, this monopoly by professionals will prove to be several times more difficult to dissolve, for a number of reasons. First, the professionals are the victors of individualistic competition, and North Americans obviously approve of their high rewards. The public may envy the professionals, but they do not seem to hate them. Second, the monopoly power of the professionals is based to a large extent on their innate abilities and therefore is inalienable. And no one can take away these advantages as such, whereas the monopoly by business organizations, in theory at least, could be removed by dissolving the organizations themselves. Third, the interests of the professional and the client tend to coincide. No matter how objectionable from the society's standpoint, an expensive but competent professional promises a maximum return for his client. The client therefore has no incentive to avoid him. This is in sharp contrast to the usual corporate monopoly, where the alternative is an increase in competition among the producers and a lower price of the product, a situation definitely preferred by the consumers. Fourth, in societies where a majority of politicians are themselves lawyers on leave from their law firms, as in North America, the chance of their taking a resolute stand on this problem is slim.

At the present time, no effective solution to this new type of monopoly and its suffocating effects on the economy is in sight. And the situation is getting worse by the day. Another recent magazine article on the liability insurance crisis highlights the devastating consequences of a free, litigious society: the five doctors in Molokai, Hawaii, have stopped delivering babies because of the high malpractice insurance cost; Chicago and other municipalities are dismantling playground equipment because of the soaring costs of damage suits and insurance premia; an aircraft company is forced to pay $80,000 of liability insurance premium on each plane it sells; one of the only two US makers of lacrosse equipment has gone uninsured in the face of a $200,000 premium for just $1 million coverage, meaning that one large judgement against him would put an end to his business (*Time*, 24 March 1986). If the present trend is to continue, every high-school or university graduate who cannot find a job will soon be suing his or her school for failing to deliver adequate education and training.

A latest addition to this already alarming situation has been the campaign against mandatory retirement. Canada's justice minister has recently revealed his intention to abolish mandatory retirement in the federal civil service as a starter, and the campaign is spreading into universities and other public sector jobs. The significant features of this campaign are, first, that it has been organized as a class action on the part of the senior group in the labour force against age discrimination, and second, that it has been aimed primarily at the government, the most vulnerable institution to the plea of discrimination. The puzzle is whose interest this campaign represents. The wide majority of the workers, including élite job holders, are barely making it to age 65 and are looking forward to the few years of green old age in retirement to which the mandatory retirement rule has entitled them. They cannot therefore be the driving force behind such a political campaign. These senior workers now stand to suffer once the mandatory retirement is removed, for they will not be able to enjoy leisurely retirement life without suffering an inferiority complex and a sense of guilt to their family members. If my assessment is correct, this is another case in which the aggressive few take the quiet and reluctant majority to their side and resort to litigation to achieve their goals, when a more equitable and socially less costly market solution is clearly available. Life in today's affluent societies is becoming increasingly nasty, mean, brutish and short, as Hobbes predicted more than 300 years ago.

3   A WAY OUT?

This phenomenon of the professionals using their specialized knowledge and intervening in people's affairs for profits poses a social problem more malign than that of ordinary monopoly. For one thing, monopoly of knowledge goes counter to the spirit of democracy. For another, a large portion of the professionals' services is expended in essentially zero-sum games, and, worse still, their exorbitant fees have increased transaction costs for all. The situation surrounding legal services is especially serious because the universal availability of a legal service, like that of a health service, is one of the basic conditions of a democratic society. But is there a way to contain, within reason, the economic inefficiencies and wastes arising from this problem?

Basically, the problem with the services of professionals is that the usual market concept based on the principle of consumer sovereignty is not applicable. Because of a lack of knowledge of the services on the part of the users, and because of the unequal relation between the users and the providers of the services, the market cannot be relied upon to do its job. In the absence of any other constraints, the providers' professional judgements become absolute and the users become completely subordinate to the providers, who control both the price and the quantity of their services. This is where we stand. So the question is how to moderate the tyranny of the professionals within the accepted framework of democracy.

It may be useful at this point to review briefly what has been happening to the medical profession and national health care in view of the similarity between the two. In the USA, the provision of medical services has, in principle, been left to the private sector. Like legal services, the consequence has been the overall market failure and the emergence of a provider dictatorship. The national medical cost as a fraction of GNP has been steadily rising and now stands around 15 per cent. Canada, in the meantime, broke away from the US path, opting for a public scheme. In 1971 the Canadian federal government instituted a universal hospitals and medical services insurance programme. The programme is financed by the federal government out of its general revenues and nominal user premia and is administered by the provinces. The programme assures access to hospital accommodation and physicians' services to every citizen to the extent deemed necessary by doctors. The fees for hospital accommodation and physicians' services are negotiated every year between the federal government and the profession.

How has Canada's 'political' solution worked in comparison with the US private solution? According to Robert Evans, North America's leading expert on health economics, the trends of health cost in the USA and Canada had been very similar up to 1971, when the health cost–GNP ratio was about 7 per cent in both countries. Since 1971, Canada has been able to maintain this ratio, while the health cost in the USA has risen to nearly 15 per cent of the GNP, as mentioned earlier. Evans attributes the relative cost increase in the USA mainly to increases in physicians' fees. In a recent article he summarizes his argument thus:

Discretionary power is commonly defended by denial of its existence, the allegation of inevitability. Objective external conditions and forces are claimed to dictate policy decisions with tangible distributional effects. In health policy, such forces include the aging of the population, the extension of technology, and the demands of ethical standards. Taken together, these forces create relentless upward pressure on costs, to levels which society 'cannot afford', necessitating sacrifice of the interests of the 'less eligible'. Yet quantitative analysis of these forces does not sustain the argument; in each case the source of cost escalation is not external pressure but the way in which the health care system itself reacts. Less costly and equally effective options are demonstrably available, but would threaten provider interests and broader ideologies. A spurious cloak of inevitability serves to promote and justify political choices. (Evans 1985: 437)

Carl Schramm, another health economist, echoes Evans and concludes that 'only through government can we assert our collective best interest over our individual self interest' (Schramm 1984: 731).

These authors propose an eye-for-an-eye solution, the use of government as a monopolist to represent the collective interest of the public. This is not an economic solution but a political one, and a sensible one where markets have failed. If Canada's health care system has been a 'success', then credit should go to the government for judicious use of its political power; and, by analogy, government's role in establishing an orderly provision of 'Judicare' seems important and promising. The banning of the contingent fee scheme may dampen the current suitmania and inflated awards. The government hiring of lawyers (on fixed salary) in social work and other civic areas to provide legal services more efficiently and cheaply is also advisable. As a more basic solution, governments should make an effort to ensure that the law is more accessible to the public by incorporating it into school curricula and promoting the publication of law and related guidebooks and commentaries and the sale of frequently used legal forms.

More generally, governments should learn ways to protect themselves from predators on the public purse. One strategy commonly used by lawyers and other professionals is the pretence to objectivity. The prevailing theory is that governments must seek the 'objective opinions' of lawyers, doctors, accountants, and economists before they take any action. This is ironical, because the governmental bureaucracy was originally conceived as a team of professionals to offer these very objective opinions to the policy-making legislators. Over the years, however, the bureaucrats in North America have given up doing this important task for themselves and instead become mere buyers of the services from the outside talents. The anti-governmental sentiment, deep-rooted in the minds of North Americans, no doubt has been a contributing factor to this shift of duties. While the overall quality of the purchased opinions and advice remains uncertain, current practice has definitely added to the costs of public administration.

Private corporations too have been affected by this intrusion by the professionals. Today's corporations are owned by the public but have gained virtual independence from their owners. Hired managers have helped themselves to an ever-increasing number of managerial positions on the one hand and have become avid buyers of the services of outside experts on the other, all at the expense, directly or indirectly, of the owning and non-owning public. The larger managerial staff and the more intense use of outside advisers have not apparently resulted in better and more efficient firms (see Table 7.2). A recent study on managerial salaries by the Conference Board of Canada is indicative of the general behavioural pattern of the contemporary corporate executives. The study, based on a survey of 928 major corporations of Canada, reveals that the median annual pay increase for directors from 1985 to 1986 was 15 per cent for financial institutions and 11 per cent for manufacturing firms. It also reports that executive salary increases, though somewhat below those of directors, outpaced those for all others employee groups, and also outpaced inflation, for a third straight year. And this in a troubled economy with a 10 per cent unemployment rate and where union wage increases averaged only 3.5 per cent over the three years 1984–6.

If the additional managers and professional advisers are not helping the corporations to improve their performances, it seems reasonable to conclude that these professionals are pure rent-seekers. Unfortunately, this is not a problem that can be solved by a piece of legislation. Yet the need to secure a good performance out of the highly bureaucratized businesses remains the key for further economic progress.

4 CONCLUSION

The ideal state of democracy is akin to the state of perfect competition in economic theory. It is beautiful, but not viable. The reason is that the two basic premises of democracy—equality and the free pursuit of self-interest—conflict, in that the latter tends to work to destroy the former. This chapter has focused on the growth of élite jobs in democratic societies as a result of the efforts by the more talented individuals to differentiate themselves from the rest. Professionals, who are defined in this context as those who use their specialized knowledge to advantage, have emerged as the new ruling class. Their rent-seeking activities have raised transaction costs to the point where the economic efficiency of our society is seriously impaired.

The problems are not limited to economic ones. Democracy is a political system, aimed at stability on the strength of people's common sense. But once the professionals take possession of power, common sense loses its force, to be replaced by their technical arguments. The legal profession in North America has been challenging a variety of conventional social rules for reasons of discrimination. The conventional mandatory retirement rule is a discrimination by age and therefore unconstitutional; the law restricting the political activities of civil servants is similarly discriminating; the tax law favouring the married over the unmarried violates the charter of rights; and so on.

The fact is that all social rules are inherently discriminating. But they have been justified by the common sense of the people for the collective good of society. The rule prohibiting minors from drinking or driving *intends* to discriminate against minors, on the judgement that the benefit from the discrimination outweighs the cost. Smilarly, many tax laws favour married couples because society attaches a value to the institution called marriage. Challenging these social rules by indiscriminant applications of the principle of equality will most certainly do more harm than good, paving the way for a mobocracy, a system which the ancient historian Polybius predicted would follow democracy. Democratic societies must learn ways to confine the power of the professionals and restore the power of common sense.

9

Economic Policy-Making: Japanese and Canadian Styles

> When you have a wide range of people who contribute without looking carefully at it, you don't improve your knowledge of the situation by averaging.
>
> Richard P. Feynman
>
> If you want a corporation to take your advice, buy its shares and give it.
>
> Soichiro Honda, former president of the Honda Motor Company

1 INTRODUCTION

This chapter is somewhat personal in tone. I have had the good fortune to live in two totally different economies, the Japanese and the Canadian. The contrast between them is fascinating, and I have long wanted to put my own feelings about them in writing, preferably in a form acceptable to economists. However, the nature of the problem is essentially historical, cultural, and institutional, and so what I have to offer has, I am afraid, rather little in common with conventional economic theory. I feel uneasy about this, but Japan has 'succeeded' by violating practically every tenet of neoclassical theory, while all the development policies based on neoclassical theory and tried out over the past thirty years have failed. This not only relieves my uneasiness somewhat, but suggests that certain factors normally omitted from economic theory are indeed very important.

Upon graduation from a Japanese university in 1959, I joined the civil service with the Japanese Ministry of Finance and, fortunately for me, was assigned to a post at the very heart of the organization. The Japanese Ministry of Finance has power unparalleled by Western governmental departments. Its jurisdiction includes the formulation and administration of the national budget, governmental investments, taxation, customs and duties, foreign exchange and international finance, management of the Treasury and government properties, and supervision of the Bank of Japan, banks, trust companies, insurance companies, and other financial institutions. To be able to watch and hear the minister, vice-minister, and other high-ranking members of the Ministry discuss important policy matters on a daily basis was a truly revealing experience.

My specific areas of duty concerned first the Bank of Japan, banks, and other financial institutions, and later, governmental investments and security companies. It was a time when the Japanese economy was shifting from postwar reconstruction to growth, a time that required a new vision and new strategies in economic management. During my six years with the civil service, the groundwork for the phenomenal postwar growth of the economy was completed. I was lucky to have witnessed Japan's economic policy-making during this memorable period.

My experience in government, however, was as shocking as it was revealing. When I graduated from university, I was a neoclassical economist. That is not to say that I believed in neoclassical economics, but rather that I recognized it as the only orderly body of theorems about the performance of an economic system. These theorems included how competition enhances economic welfare, how free trade yields maximum benefits to trading nations, and how an underdeveloped economy can hope to be, in 50 years' time, where developed ones are today by copying what the latter did 100 years ago (with the aid of foreign capital and technology). In the Japanese government, it was as if these theorems did not exist.

My first assignment was a survey of the current interest rates. This kept me busy for two months. To begin with, I had to familiarize myself with the institutional complexities of the Japanese financial system, which was enough to drive a naive neoclassical economist to despair. There was a system of financial institutions in the agricultural sector for the purpose of keeping and utilizing for itself the savings generated in that sector. Similarly structured institutions existed for small businesses. Apart from these enclaves, the government ran several special banks which channelled the funds obtained through postal savings and a public life insurance programme into a number of strategic areas of the economy on terms largely independent of market forces. The discount rate of the Bank of Japan in those days was in the order of 7–8 per cent, as compared with the 2–3 per cent range for the major Western countries, but the governmental special banks loaned long-term funds at 4.5–6.5 per cent. To further complicate the matter, the Japanese economy in the postwar years (at least up to 1965) depended on central bank (Bank of

Japan) credit for monetary growth. With the government abstaining from deficit finance (and the enormous wartime national debt voided by decree) and the nation's foreign exchange reserves chronically running low, there was only one way by which the Bank of Japan could increase high-powered money: by buying up or lending against private notes. In extending its credit, the Bank was therefore able to exercise an enormous discretionary power in setting rates and other conditions. In short, interest rates were anything but market-determined.

Japanese industries were still in a transition phase from recovery to postwar growth. Toyota was producing 20,000 cars a year; Mazda was producing only three-wheeled mini-trucks and small coupés. One of my less lucky classmates took a job with an obscure company called Sony, for want of a better opportunity. The only Japanese products I saw in US supermarkets in the early 1960s were give-away lighters attached to cartons of cigarettes (ten packets to a carton). The industries' total demand for investment funds was very high and constantly exceeded private savings. The Bank of Japan did everything it could to meet this demand, but the higher the rate of investment was, the more intense was the pressure on the nation's foreign exchange reserves. As a result, Japan's economic policy in this period was characterized by jerky, alternating acceleration and braking, which made Japan a perennial winner of the annual IMF award for the most audacious economic management.

Credit had to be rationed in this situation, and it was. With the government at the chair, major borrowers and lenders met regularly, and loans were secured for industries of high national priority. This government-led, semi-military strategy paid off handsomely in later years.

I still remember the great excitement I experienced when I first witnessed investment (I) being equated to savings (S), literally in front of my eyes. In a modest conference room in the Ministry of Finance, a large table occupied the middle. On one side of the table were the representatives of the dozen major industries under the supervision of the Ministry of International Trade and Industry. On the other side were the representatives of the major lending institutions. In addition, there were representatives from the Bank of Japan, academia, and consumer groups. The Minister of Finance was in the chair. The Minister first asked the borrowers to reveal their desired amounts of investment funds, and then he asked the lenders what they were willing to supply. After a few rounds of 'tâtonnement', the aggregate planned I was brought into equality with the aggregate planned S at a level deemed optimal by policy-makers, at which point the meeting adjourned. This meeting was not a mere ritual: the amount of information the government obtained from it was vital for an effective policy formulation.

In 1965 I resigned my job with the government and came to the USA to earn my doctorate. Although the Ministry kindly assured me of a position if I wanted to return in a few years, I knew I could not accept such an offer, given the way Japanese organizations operated. In the Japanese labour market, where lifetime employment is prevalent (at least in the top layers of the market), second-hand markets are almost non-existent, and individuals participating in them are suspect. If one chooses to quit a job voluntarily in such a system, one must be prepared to earn a living elsewhere or pay a substantial cost of re-entry. The Ministry's offer to reinstate me without penalty (that is, on the same terms as if I kept working for them without interruption) was a most generous one, given the circumstances, and I was moved. But an odd-ball would disturb the peace and harmony in the work-place, and either the organization or the individual would be sorry. I held no grudges against the fact that my Ph.D. degree would count for nothing in Japan, for, after all, earning a Ph.D. degree was a pursuit of personal interest; moreover, the value of such a degree in public administration was questionable. (I still believe that top undergraduates are more teachable and make better organization members than advanced degree-holders.) At any rate, the reason I quit was simply that I did not want to make a precommitment.

Once in a US university, I was back in the neoclassical world. Indeed, neoclassicism was at its peak at that time. There was still an ample afterglow of the great American era; the great success of the 1964 tax cut convinced many people of the validity of the Samuelsonian neoclassical synthesis; and, having mastered the art of short-term stabilization, economists were busy applying neoclassical tools to long-term questions of economic growth and development. Again, I had to go through a period of shock, this time in the opposite direction. I discovered that the theory of the firm, which I had thought of as an artificial construct to generate supply curves, was believed to be describing real-world firms. The life-cycle theory of saving as a vehicle to explain people's saving behaviour was equally shocking to a person from a society where lifetime wage profiles were much lower and steeper, and where bank loans to consumers were unheard of.[1] The entire body of price theory, which I had regarded as little more than an IQ test to economics students' suddenly became an all-important apparatus in terms of which a wide variety of real-world phenomena were to be made comprehensible.

In the area of macroeconomics, the cultural gap was much smaller, but it nevertheless existed. To the Japanese, economic growth and development were a national project to be designed and executed by the will of the nation; to the Americans, they were more an objective phenomenon fit for scientific studies. This difference in perception led to some fundamental differences in the style of policy-making. The Japanese placed emphasis on long-term growth strategies, while the Americans stressed short-run stabilization policies. The Japanese regarded the choice of policies as essentially nation-specific and time-specific, while the Americans believed in the universal applicability of optimal policy controls established by scientific research. Whereas Japanese academics took the back seat in policy-making, Ph.D. economists ran the US economy.

Since I moved to Canada in 1968, I have become increasingly aware of Canada's unique style of policy-making, which is different from both the US and the Japanese styles. The Canadian style is similar to that of the USA in its scientific approach, but Canadians do not have as much faith in it as Americans. On the other hand, Canadians seem to be more aware of the nation-specific nature of optimal strategies.

While sharing some features with both the US and Japanese styles,

---

[1] I once compared my starting salary with that of my vice-minister, the highest-ranked civil servant in the bureaucracy: the ratio was 1 to 11. (Incidentally, our salaries were stipulated in a schedule attached to the Civil Servants' Salaries Act, and therefore a matter of public knowledge.) This steep salary and wage profile has a few interesting implications for the aggregate saving and the labour markets. First, combined with the lack of opportunities for borrowing against one's future earnings, it forces down the consumption of the young. I strongly suspect that this has had the effect of increasing the aggregate saving. Second, it affects the workers' mobility and work incentives in a subtle but significant way (see ch. 7 above). I used to feel that I was being exploited in the sense that I was paid less than my marginal product, and although the relation between my salary and my marginal product was certain to reverse at a later stage, I knew that I would have to stay with my job for a long time to come out even and that by how much I would come ahead over my entire career would depend on how well I continued to perform. In this environment, there is a strong incentive for workers not to quit early and to give more to the organization to which they belong.

the Canadian style is distinct in its democratic character. In both the USA and Japan, one notices the clear intent of the policy-makers behind each policy, but this is not so in Canada. In Canadian politics one does not sense the strong will of the national policy-makers. Policy debates are ever popular and many ideas are actually tried, but these attempts are tentative and often ineffectual. One fails to see any degree of intertemporal consistency in Canada's national economic policies. New ideas constantly make news headlines; royal commissions are set up one after another on issues of any significance in order to crystalize public opinions into policy guidelines; and yet a master policy plan is never drawn up. Canadians' small-open-economy mentality and their affluence may explain this lack of determination.

This chapter is concerned with the broad differences in the style of policy-making between Japan and Canada. For ease of reference, I shall refer to the Japanese style as 'paramilitary' and to the Canadian style as 'democratic'. These terms already suggest a difference in efficiency, and I do not deny that. My purpose is not to pass a judgement as to which style is 'better', but to examine factors contributing to the shaping of particular styles of policy-making with a view to explaining policy choices themselves as endogenous variables of individual nations.

2   THE JAPANESE PARAMILITARISM

In the mid-1850s, when Japan was forced to pen its economy to the world, its future as a nation, not to mention its economy, looked bleak. For a start, Japan had lost practically all of its monetary gold to the westerners in a matter of two decades. At that time, Japan was under a system of bimetallism, with both gold and silver coin in circulation. The gold coin had such a large denomination that it was practically out of daily use, at least as far as the public was concerned, and large-scale transactions were settled by transferring gold bullion. The Tokugawa government had been in the habit of debasing silver coins to cope with the chronic shortfall of revenues, with the result that the silver content of the silver coin in circulation at that time had been reduced to a mere one-third of its face value. The international exchange rate between gold and silver was 1 to 16, whereas the effective rate within Japan was 1 to 5. The western powers forced Japan to exchange their silver coins for Japanese ones at par values (as against face values), which enabled them to acquire 1 part gold for every 5 parts of silver, thus causing a massive drain of gold from the island economy. The loss of gold was unquestionably a major economic factor leading to the downfall of the 250-year-old Tokugawa government. Moreover, the price structure of this closed economy was very much out of line with that prevailing abroad. This, along with highly unequal commercial treaties, resulted in a heavy outflow of the few exportable goods (such as raw silk and tea), with little gain to Japan. In addition to these economic woes, during the turbulent years up to the Restoration in 1868, the very existence of Japan as a nation was in danger from western powers competing fiercely for a foothold in what they saw as another potential colony.

Although the price was high, the Japanese learned a precious lesson in this brief period, which was to become the basic philosophy of their economic management. The main points of this lesson were as follows. First, a late starter must do something different from its forerunners in order to protect itself from their invasion. In this sense, economic development was inseparable from national defence. Second, time was a scarce resource, and unless an adequate level of economic development was attained quickly, there was no future for the nation. Third, in doing so, it was important to keep foreign dependency, and dependency on foreign capital in particular, to a minimum for the sake of national autonomy. The result was a unique form of 'state capitalism'.

The most striking general feature of Japan's state capitalism was its anti-neoclassical character. Virtually everything Japan did defied neoclassical welfare theory.

First and foremost, the visible hand of the state replaced the invisible hand of decentralized markets. Resources were allocated not by the price mechanism but by the will of the state. Achieving a desired pattern of resource allocation through price incentives is a very time-consuming process. Klaus Knorr (1956), for example, states that, during the Second World War, it took the USA three years to fully mobilize her resources for war purposes through price incentives. That kind of delay was not acceptable to the Japanese.

Similarly, the importing of western industrial and financial technologies could not be left in the hands of private entrepreneurs, to whom the entrepreneurial risk was often too high, so the state took this task upon itself. It built the first steel mill, the first copper refinery, the first cotton-spinning factory, etc., test-ran them, and later sold them to private interests on very general terms (see Table 9.1 below). The state financed these industrial projects with tax revenues, which were very heavy in the agricultural sector. It also collected the small savings of the public through postal savings and the public life insurance programme, and used these funds to carry out its ambitious development projects.

Second, Japanese policy-makers have consistently placed a greater emphasis on long-term planning than on short-term stabilization. This choice is due partly to the usually insurmountable technical difficulties of coping with sporadic shocks, and partly to the Japanese belief that, so long as long-term matters are going well, short-run troubles will take care of themselves. To ensure effective long-term planning, they established a tradition by which government and business leaders met regularly to review the performances of the various industries and to decide which industries deserved support and which did not. The Ministry of International Trade and Industry chaired these review sessions, while the Ministry of Finance took care of the financial aspect of the industrial policy. The Japanese economy, on the other hand, never did particularly well in dealing with short-run shocks, which the Japanese have traditionally regarded as acts of god. In terms of the distinction I drew earlier, short-run stabilization is an act of 'passive rationality', whereas long-term planning is an act of 'active rationality'. Whether one believes that economic management requires any degree of active rationality is a matter of one's *Weltanschauung*. Neoclassicism denies such a need in principle.

Third, the Japanese made special efforts to minimize conflicts, both within and between organizations, again for the purpose of achieving a maximum aggregate performance. Whether it be a private firm or a governmental department, the governing principle is horizontal equity and fair promotion rules.

Individuals of the same cohort are given comparable jobs and paid equally until enough observations of individual differences have been made. Cadets start their jobs at the bottom as union members, while blue-collar workers can be awarded managerial positions. There was even a case in which the chauffeur of a corporate president was eventually promoted to the presidency of an affiliate firm. Promotion decisions are made with utmost care so as not to disturb the peace of the work-place. The now world-famous lifetime employment and seniority wages have contributed significantly to a high retention rate and a low unemployment rate, although these rules were established only during the interwar years after a half-century of experiments.

As for inter-organizational relations, the several large capital groups called *zaibatsus* and government–business relations deserve special mention. While the origins of the individual *zaibatsus* vary somewhat, they have all grown with the nation's economy. A typical *zaibatsu* has a major bank and a general trading company at its centre, plus a number of family firms in a variety of areas including steel, machinery and equipment, mining, textiles, electronics, and, more recently, petrochemicals and motor cars. The fact that, in a *zaibatsu* organization, a single capital owns a portfolio of firms covering a wide variety of industries has a number of interesting and important implications for macroeconomics. First, it enables capital to bear more risks than a one-firm capital. Second, it enables capital to adapt to a changing environment with less pain; to cut one firm in a declining industry and set up another in a new promising field is far easier. Third, it enables the capital to make more efficient use of its financial resources and labour force. Fourth, it enables capital (or its management headquarters) to gain a better global view of its economic environment and to plan more wisely for the long-term future.

Japan's perennial low unemployment rate in comparison with other economies must be due at least in part to the manner in which capital is organized and the ability of capital to absorb shocks better. A neoclassicist would argue that the same degree of risk-spreading can be attained by wealth-owning individuals through financial markets, *à la* Modigliani and Miller; but not all the workers are significant wealth-owners capable of exploiting such market opportunities, especially in developing economies.

Fourth and lastly, the Japanese made efforts to produce a wide range of goods from the start, even if their quality was poor. The neoclassical principle of specialization was never in their manual. This choice, to first produce what the domestic public could afford to pay, was responsible for the reputation abroad of 'cheap Japanese products', but it contributed significantly to the fostering of a common desire for economic development in business and the public, and to a smoother collaboration between capital and labour. To do otherwise would most certainly have created a rift between these groups and the kind of serious political instability that plagues many developing nations today.

While these policy choices may be interesting in themselves as a case study in development economics, the more significant aspect of the Japanese system is its organization. I have already alluded to the fact that the Meiji government took the entrepreneurial risk upon itself in starting a variety of key industries and subsequently sold these outfits to private interests. Many of these sales were carried out during the 1870s and 1880s. Two things about them are worth noting. First, the buyers were all merchants closely affiliated with the new government. Second, the terms of sales were extremely generous. Some of the conspicuous examples are cited in Table 9.1. Many of these buyers later became prominent industrialists and founders of the large business concerns known as *zaibatsus* which still thrive today.

Apart from the big boost given to the private recipients, these sales of government properties were a big gamble for the new government because the worst that could have happened was an indefensible sell-out, enriching the handful of already rich merchants with little or no societal gains. But fortunately, both government leaders and merchants were united in their support of the national cause and were able to work in close co-operation with each other.[2] This relationship, which has become a tradition, has never been one in which government issues orders and business takes them, nor one in which businesses lobby and government accommodates them; it has always been more genuinely a relationship of equals, in which both share

Table 9.1   Sales of government enterprises during the 1880s

Asset	Date of Sale	Amount of govt. investment	Sale price	Buyer
Fukagawa Cement	1884	101,559	61,742	S. Asano
Kosaka Silver Mine	1884	542,426	273,660	S. Kuhara
Innai Silver Mine	1884	703,093	108,977	I. Furukawa
Ani Copper Mine	1885	1,673,211	337,766	I. Furukawa
Nagasaki Shipyard	1887	1,130,949	527,000	Mitsubishi
Hyogo Shipyard	1887	816,139	188,029	S. Kawasaki
Kamaishi Iron Mine	1887	2,376,625	12,600	C. Tanaka
Miike Coal Mine	1888	757,060	4,555,000	Mitsui
Horonai Coal Mine and Railways	1889	2,291,500	352,318	Hokkaido Coal Mine and Shipping
Tomioka Cotton Spinning	1893	310,000	121,460	Mitsui

Source: Irokawa (1971: 350).

[2] Morikawa (1973), for example, cites the writings of Yukichi Fukuzawa, Eiichi Shibusawa, and other leading entrepreneurs of Meiji Japan to show that 'national interest' was the overriding concern of the Meiji businessmen.

information, both have inputs to policy-making, and, most importantly, both share public responsibilities for the consequences of policy.

To facilitate communications with the government, business has long had a centralized economic research and policy-making organ of its own (now known as *Keidanren*). The most important function of this organ, from the standpoint of national economic policy-making, is its centralization and co-ordination of diverse business interests of the member-firms and the rational selection of policy priorities. Keidanren is widely subscribed, and its costs are paid for by the member-firms. It is, in a sense, an industrial version of the Federal Reserve System in banking. It assumes a public character by virtue of its large membership, although it has no legal status.

Once a course of policy action has been agreed upon between the government and this central organ of business, an (implicit) contract comes into force such that, if an honest effort by business along the set path should fail owing to unforeseen factors, the government will help the business out; but, at the same time, misconduct on either side is punishable in a variety of forms. Although this kind of business insurance is run by every government in one form or another, the Japanese contract has an advantage over others in that the insurer (the government) can monitor the behaviour of the insured (business) closely, and consequently moral hazard inherent in insurance contracts (negligence, sloth, and other misconduct of the insured) is minimized. What makes the Japanese government an effective, tough insurer is the great amount of information about business that it can gather through constant consultation with business and the existence of a self-regulating organ like the Keidanren. The big favour it did to business at the start by assuming entrepreneurial risks (mentioned above) also helped maintain its authority.

Turning to the relations between business and labour, one must concede that Japan had to go through the same gloomy historical process as western forerunners did, and in a hurry. As western notions of democracy were introduced in the early years of Meiji government, civil liberty movements sprang up all over the country and contributed to the formation of groups critical of the rather autocratic and sometimes inhuman development policies of the new government. Marxism was imported, and the great labour movement was on the horizon. The general condition of labour in the newly industrialized state was very poor. The conflict between labour and capital was intense and often violent throughout the Meiji era (1868–1912), with government taking the side of capital. It is definitely not true that the generally friendly labour–management relations observed today existed from the beginning as part of Japanese culture. Through experience, however, management and labour have managed to build a co-operative and productive partnership. The cultural factor may have been a major reason for this happy resolution, as many scholars have pointed out; but the necessity, or need, to survive as a nation in a hostile environment must also have been an important factor.

In any event, the new partnership has been based on another insurance contract,[3] under which business assures workers' jobs and security of income in exchange for their total commitment to the organization. The contract is highly paternalistic in character. It covers the worker's entire career, and extends to the worker's family in the sense that the employer usually keeps complete family data on each worker and that wages traditionally contain family and travel allowances (see e.g. Nikkeiren 1962). Career wage profiles and promotion prospects are set in such a way that most workers are convinced that it pays to stay rather than move. In a word, the employment insurance contract makes workers feel secure, wanted, and motivated.

But what is the order of magnitude of the 'insurance premium' that Japanese workers have been made to pay for all this? First, Japanese employers have controlled wages, employment, and general working conditions very tightly and successfully through another central organ called *Nikkeiren* (Japanese Managers' Association). With the member-firms acting under the guidance of the Nikkeiren, competitive wage escalations are minimized, labour mobility is severely limited, and workers are made more dependent on their employers than in free markets. The Nikkeiren also sets guidelines for managers about annual wage increments and working hours. The result is a group of contented workers who have forgotten to calculate their opportunity costs.

Second, Japanese firms operating under the job insurance contract are naturally more eager to maintain ample contingency reserves than typical Western firms. They accomplish this goal chiefly by not rendering the benefit of productivity increases and speculative gains to the public to the full. For example, the Japanese yen appreciated

---

[3] The aforementioned governmental insurance may be thought of as re-insurance of this one.

approximately 27 per cent against SDR (a cocktail currency made up of the five key currencies) and 50 per cent against the US dollar from June 1985 to June 1986. But none of the great cost savings brought about by the big appreciation of the currency have found their way into consumer prices. Ther reason? Presumably because Keidanren deems it necessary for its member-firms to add to their reserves in the light of the dismal outlook of the world economy. In general, Japanese prices are harder to understand than those in Western economies because of their high administered content, and the Japanese are trained to accept them without suspicion. The Japanese are not price-rational to the extent that Westerners are. This general attitude of the public makes price administration by government and business easier. In short, the Japanese system manages to collect large enough premia to keep its comprehensive insurance scheme running.

3 THE CANADIAN DEMOCRACY

There are two aspects to Canada's democratic style of economic policy-making. One is the diffusion of power from the federal government to the provincial governments. The other is the Canadians' bent for amateurism. I shall discuss them in order.

Of the several federal states extant in the world, Canada is the weakest, or the most decentralized, in terms of the distribution of legislative power between the federal and provincial governments. From the outset, the Ontarians' attempt to give the new Parliament of Canada the type of monopoly of legislative power that the British Parliament had was blocked by Quebec and the two maritime provinces. The British Parliament, the sponsor of the Canadian federation, took an easy route of compromise, distributing the legislative powers between the two levels of governments in a manner not based on any principle, but politically acceptable to all the parties concerned. Formally, Section 92 of the British North America Act (now called the Constitution Act) defines the scope of exclusive powers of provincial legislatures, which reads:

92. In each province the legislature may exclusively make laws in relation to matters coming within the classes of subject next herein-after enumerated: that is to say,—

1. Repealed 1982.

2. Direct taxation within the province in order to raising of a revenue for provincial purposes.
3. The borrowing of money on the sole credit of the province.
4. The establishment and tenure of provincial office and the appointment and payment of provincial officers.
5. The management and sale of the public lands belonging to the province and of the timber and wood thereon.
6. The establishment, maintenance, and management of hospitals, asylums, charities, and eleemosynary institutions in and for the province, other than marine hospitals.
8. Municipal institutions in the province.
9. Shop, saloon, tavern, auctioneer, and other licences in order to the raising of a revenue for provincial, local, or municipal purposes.
10. Local works and undertakings other than [those of interprovincial character].
11. The incorporation of companies with provincial objects.
12. The solemnization of marriage in the province.
13. Property and civil rights in the province.
14. The administration of justice in the province, . . .
15. The imposition of punishment by fine, penalty, or imprisonment for enforcing any law of the province in relation to any matter coming within any of the classes of subjects enumerated in this section.
16. Generally all matters of a merely local or private nature in the province.

In addition, Section 93 grants the provincial legislature the power to make laws regarding education; and Section 109 stipulates that all lands, mines, minerals, and royalties belong to the province in which they are situated. Moreover, Section 92A, added by the 1982 Amendment, grants the provincial legislature broad powers over exploration, development, conservation, and the management of non-renewable natural resource, forestry resources, and electrical energy, including the taxation of these resources and the export of their products to other parts of Canada.

These stipulations provide the provinces with a substantial amount of legislative power. Their real power, however, derives from the actual manner in which the two levels of government interact in the formulation and execution of national and regional economic policies. Take, for example, the annual first ministers' conferences, where the federal ministers and provincial premiers meet. This type of conference exists in every country, whether federal or unitary. In a unitary state like Japan, the conference is a place where the national ministers educate the provincial ministers about their national policies in order to secure compliance and co-operation from the lower-level governments. In a federal state, one would expect a more equal participation of the two levels of participants; in Canada it goes a good way towards decentralization.

In the Canadian conference, the federal ministers and the provincial premiers discuss *national* policy issues as absolute equals. If the federal government wants to carry out a policy of its own, it must consult the provincial premiers and solicit their support. Conversely, if the provincial premiers all want the federal government to adopt a particular policy, it has little choice but to comply. The first ministers' conferences thus ensure that the federal government will *not* have the authority to act as a higher and superior government. As a matter of fact, it is difficult to find an area, outside of social security (old age and retirement pensions, hospitals and medical services insurance, and unemployment insurance), in which Canada's federal government has virtual control, and this despite a lengthy list of subjects over which it has been granted exclusive legislative powers by Section 91 of the Constitution Act.

The other aspect of Canada's democratic style of policy-making is the broad participation of the public in national policy debates. Again, an example will best illustrate the point.

In 1982, the then prime minister Trudeau suggested (in the course of a lunchtime conversation) that a serious study concerning the future prospect of Canada's economy might be in order. The suggested task was subsequently delegated to a royal commission headed by Donald Macdonald, a former Liberal MP. When the formation of the commission was announced, thousands of individuals and organizations volunteered their opinions and advice. For months, Macdonald toured all over the country to hear these voluntary discussants out. The actual number of such submissions is reported to have been 1500. Having thus heard the opinions of the public, the commission organized a team of political economists to carry out the background research for the commission report. The report was completed three years and $20 million later, in the late summer of 1985. The central theme of the report was a support of free trade as a means of revitalizing the Canadian economy.

To a relatively new Canadian like myself, this whole democratic procedure is both revealing and puzzling. First, it is incredibly expensive and inefficient. Why didn't Mr Macdonald tell these self-appointed advisers to send their opinions to him within a set period of time, instead of flying all over the country to hear them? Second, what do you do with 1500 submissions? So many, collectively, must cover amost every possible policy idea. What then? Do you average them, or pick out those you like? And why are these submissions never revealed to the public, even in a summary form? Third, the nature and the status of a royal commission report are very vague. It certainly binds no one; it is not even an official document. After all this effort to take public opinion into account, the end product is, once again, background material for another round of public debate. If it were a discussion paper, after all, a group of Ottawa bureaucrats could have written and circulated it to the public. Fourth, how credible is a royal commission report when used as a guide for policy-makers? Given the fact that the participants are drawn largely from outside the government (and hence are essentially 'kibitzers'), the content of the report must be lacking in concrete details useful to policy-makers. Especially disturbing is the fact that the report lacks any policy itinerary.

Fifth, I have trouble understanding the very idea that the government leaders should ask the public what to do; it is the same as a baseball manager asking the fans which relief pitcher should be brought in to save the game. The leaders are supposed to know what the public wants, or, rather, what is best for the nation: they, together with the bureaucracy under them, are supposed to be the pro-fessionals. It is irresonsible and amateurish of them to rely on 'outside experts' on every issue of any significance. Broad participation of the masses in the public decision-making process does not necessarily improve the quality of the final decisions reached. The majority of the masses do not have a good knowledge of the issues involved. Nor can they organize themselves into an effective political voice. An open invitation to them to participate in the public policy-making process therefore has a tendency to encourage lobbies by special interest groups. It is of vital importance for the leaders to stand above these pressure groups and pursue policies in the interest of the whole nation. But such statesmen are a scarce resource in Canadian politics. I have a feeling that the Canadian tradition—the diffused legislative power, political bargaining behind closed doors, the effective shutting-out of the bureaucratic machine and media influence from the policy-making process, the lenient public, and the consequent lack of accountability of policy-makers—has turned public policy-making into something less than a serious national endeavour.

4   THE STYLE OF POLICY-MAKING IS ITSELF A PEOPLE'S CHOICE

From the standpoint of aggregative economic efficiency, the Canadian democratic style of policy-making is incomparably inferior to the paramilitary style of the Japanese. This is not at all surprising, because democracy is an inherently inefficient system, whereas militarism is a system designed for efficiency and nothing else. One gains nothing, therefore, by comparing the two systems by a criterion of efficiency. A more interesting and useful way of understanding the two systems is to view them as outcomes of the choices derived from people's preferences.

From this angle, the Japanese style is relatively easy to comprehend. As late starters in the modern capitalist development race, the Japanese faced a serious danger of foreign invasion. This external pressure induced them to adopt a highly centralized system. Japan had a few advantages at the start over today's developing economies. The country had had 250 years of peace, which enabled it to accumulate a sizeable amount of commercial, if not industrial, capital. Second, this long peace played a vital role in shaping a national mentality suited for a major national endeavour.

The ruling Tokugawa government placed the prosperity of the family first and foremost, and enforced law and order with such austerity and to such an extent that citizens' lives were severely constrained. A form of occupational caste was rigidly enforced and loyalty was promoted as the virtue of highest order.[4] The result was a people dwarfed by suffocating rules but by and large obedient to authority and loyal to the organizations to which they belonged. These preconditions were certainly helpful to the nation's modernization.

It is wrong, however, to think that the Japanese at that time were a homogeneous people. Owing to the general poverty and the government's restrictive policy on people's movements, most Japanese spent their lives within their own provinces without ever seeing other parts of the country. Each clan's land had its own dialect, commercial policy, and even money. People's loyalties were to their

---

[4] Morishima (1981) has stressed the importance of 'loyalty' in Japan's economic development. He claims that it originated in Confucianism but that its central concept of benevolence was changed into loyalty when the doctrine was imported into Japan.

own feudal lords. In a word, provincialism was the mode of the time. It took a while (and a few local rebellions) before the people came to accept the new national government and unite under it. Regional differences exert centrifugal forces towards decentralization. In the case of Japan, it was the external pressure that created a strong enough centripetal force to overcome the forces towards decentralization.

Turning to Canada, I have long been impressed by the apparent consensus among Canadians that a decentralized system is better than a centralized system with a strong federal government. The chief reason for decentralization of power is the regional differences in people's needs and tastes, and the desirability (cost conditions permitting) of serving different groups differently. The Canadians are in fact made up of many groups with different racial, cultural, religious, and political backgrounds. Their tastes as consumers differ too.[5] Given this diversity, Canadians believe that the federal government should confine its power to matters of common interest to all Canadians, which are not many.

It would be wrong to say that Canada has greater regional differences than other nations. Many others, such as the Soviet Union, India, China, Brazil, the USA, and the UK, have racial and cultural differences similar to or greater than Canada's and yet have adopted much more centralized systems. This suggests that the Canadians' taste for decentralization may have been largely the product of the fortunate history of the nation. Since the mid-eighteenth century, the only 'national crises' in Canada have been the wars between the British and the Americans (1775–6 and 1812). In both cases, however, Canada was spared the tough decisions.

Apart from these occasions, Canadians have not faced a situation that called for a genuine national choice, thanks to the country's stable and friendly relations with Britain and the USA. In the absence of the 'principal contradiction'[6] arising in international affairs, the domestic contradiction of secondary magnitude has naturally occupied a prominent place in Canada's politics. This same reasoning also explains why the other nations mentioned above have chosen

---

[5] According to the Canadian Distillers Association, Quebecers' favourite spirit is gin and Nova Scotians' and Prince Edward Islanders' choice is rum, while other Canadians prefer to drink rye whiskey.

[6] In the words of Mao Tse-Tung (1956).

more centralized systems, despite regional differences: to cope with major international conflicts.

Although Canadians appear to believe that they are born provincialists and that nothing can change that, history abounds with examples of rulers who have controlled such sentiments in their subjects quite effectively. Mao Tse-Tung observed that the best way to solve a contradiction is to find another, bigger, contradiction. If there is a domestic feud or unrest, you look for (or create, if necessary) a bigger, international, conflict. Judging from the wide fluctuations in Sino-Russian relations during his reign, Mao Tse-Tung must have practised his own teaching very well. All the eminent rulers in history have been great masters of this manipulative technique. It is remarkable that Canada's federal leaders have not resorted to this expedient as a means of enhancing the people's sense of national unity. Again, the absence of a need to do so and the nation's affluence, which permit democratic inefficiencies, explain this fact.

Although I have labelled the Canadian style of policy-making 'democratic', and although the Canadians do participate more widely and eagerly in policy debates than most other peoples, there is something very undemocratic about the manner in which the Canadian political leaders make final policy decisions. It is, in a word, secretive. Policy meetings take place behind closed doors as a rule, and information is controlled very tightly. Bureaucrats are kept out of the game, and even politicians are tight-lipped. The result is that the mass media are left in the dark and the public has no way of knowing how policies are shaping up. This is true of even the most basic items, such as the annual budget and occasional tax reforms. Such secretism was quite a shock to me, because I had been so accustomed to the Japanese system where newspapers compete with one another in publishing a series of analyses and criticisms of the upcoming budget several months before the budget is tabled in the Diet, and where the bureaucrats publish explanatory articles on the budget for months after its dietary sanction.

What is true of the budget is true of other policy decisions as well. In Canada, final decisions are merely announced, without explanation as to what the choice set was, or how the final choice was made. The awarding of public contracts and appointments of high offices are regularly made according to ministers' personal preferences and with complete disregard for the feelings of the public.

How does one explain this sharp contrast between the open

invitation to the public to participate in policy debates and the deliberate exclusion of the public from the final stage of the policy-making process? I have no good answer, but it seems fair to say that Canadian democracy is more apparent than real. The resulting lack of 'procedural rationality' (see Chapter 3) is probably a more serious source of inefficiency than the cost of democracy itself (such as the $20 million spent by the Macdonald Commission). A cynic might say that all the apparent democracy is a cover for the politicians to do as they please. Indeed, if you consult the public, who you know can never agree on anything, you cannot seriously be seeking their advice. As a Canadian politician, you also know that, with such a diverse populace, your popularity is stable in the middle range no matter what you do. You don't live or die with the GNP, as your Japanese counterpart does. With the diverse and relatively laid-back public, you too can relax. The small-open-economy mentality of the Canadians makes your task even easier, because a small open economy can always find enough causes abroad for the economic troubles at home.

Many Candians have told me that they are not too happy about the way the Canadian leaders handle policy matters. They all agree that it can be improved upon. When pressed, however, they say they prefer their style to a more disciplined, centralized, style of the Japanese, even if it means a few billion dollars' extra GNP. It may be that the Canadians' affluence has made them rather scornful of the stifling notion of efficiency. Or it may be that they like the loose system because it leaves open a chance for anyone to take advantage of it with a little ingenuity, or to seize ministerial power and enjoy it some day.

Needless to say, personal life-styles are affected by a country's style of economic policy-making. Under the Japanese paramilitary style, an individual's life tends to revolve around his work. To him, his work-place is much more than the place where he trades his labour services for wages. It is a place where he learns about life, makes lifelong friends, and forms his outlook on life. It is an institution which provides him with shelter and recreational facilities for his entire family. In return, he works for it and even buys some of its shares with his savings.

An individual's involvement with his firm becomes total. A young employee rushes to the rescue of his company in the midst of a big earthquake, ignoring his own home. A groom cancels his honeymoon upon a phone call from his office. These are the kind of stories

Japanese business leaders fondly relate to their employees. Most Japanese business organizations (including governmental departments) keep updated lists of all the employees and alumni, and issue personal news about them. If you die twenty years after retirement, chances are that there will be an official representative from your former company at your funeral.

On the basis of my own experience, I may say that being part of the Japanese system makes you feel secure and carefree, because the people around you look after you. If you are good at school work, your teacher will tell you which university to try and what field to major in. In your senior year at the university, your professor will choose a list of jobs for you. Once in a company, the firm will arrange your room and board at a nominal price, and in a few years the chief of the personnel section will visit you with a head-and-shoulder photo and vital statistics of your potential wife.

Japanese lifetime wage profiles largely reflect the varying needs of the workers over life-cycles, and this, along with seasonal bonuses, reduces individuals' need for financial planning to a minimum. When you reach mandatory retirement, at 55, your company will, as a rule, find you another job. If you are willing to rub along with the others, you will have very few things to worry about in your life, and because you have few worries of your own, you will tend to spend your surplus energy worrying about others. So goes the whole system.

The Japanese system does have some problems, though. One is how to deal with individuals with independent minds. A society based on the principle of conformism applies all sorts of pressure on individuals to be like the others. A mother tells her child to imitate the star child in his or her class. Many teachers use the same technique to control their classes. When I was a member of a secondary school baseball team, I devised a unique batting style which resembled the Charlie Lau style, which is now very popular among the major league players in the USA. As a result of this new technique, my hitting improved significantly. But my coach told me that how well I could hit was of no significance, 'because my form was bad'. So that was the end of my ingenuity. In general, the only chance that self-willed Japanese have to do things their way and be accepted as individuals is by demonstrating some extraordinary talent.

Another and more serious problem with the Japanese system is that it discourages individuals from thinking for themselves. The Japanese, who have been brought up under the protective wings of the organizations they belong to and of people around them, often have trouble imagining a life without guardians, let alone carving out a new way by themselves. If the Japanese were to be subjected to the mass unemployment currently experienced by the Canadians, many would take their own lives out of shame and despair. Even if they did not go that far, a grave social unrest would certainly ensue. It is only natural that the Japanese economy has developed a social compact whereby business, labour, and the government collaborate to minimize the chance of such a catastrophe. It is a socioeconomic cooperative equilibrium in which every side does its part. The government's style of policy-making is a part of the package.

My image of Canadians is rather different. The single most remarkable feature of Canadians is the toughness with which they cope with their economic difficulties—the calmness with which they accept, say, the loss of a job. After 20 years in Canada, I still have trouble understanding the absence of anger and despair in people's faces when they are served with a redundancy notice. Whatever the explanation, Canadians must have a conviction that no such setback can endanger their survival. Could it be that they all have large personal savings to tide them over the sudden loss of income? Or that the government's unemployment insurance benefits are so generous that they won't feel a dent in their income? The answer to these questions is an emphatic no. What, then, is the source of their optimism? I can only point to their history. Less than a hundred years ago the Canadians, and especially the Westerners, were carving their modest lives out of the harsh wilderness (see e.g. Broadfoot 1976). Nature demanded hard work but ensured survival for most of those who put in sufficient time and effort. It may very well be that Canadians today retain the survival instinct and technique of their grandparents and feel secure in their ability to use it if the need arises. In short, their basic characteristic is self-reliance, which forms the backbone of the nation.

While this individual toughness is unquestionably a great national asset, it does not necessarily contribute to a high aggregative efficiency. Independent minds do not accept rules or take orders easily. They are reluctant to accept authority and are difficult to organize for a common societal cause. While government to the Japanese is something to obey, to Canadians it is something to challenge, to exploit. Canadian individuals do not expect much from their government and are unwilling to do their part to make it work, and so the government lacks the sense of responsibility and mission that its Japanese counterpart has. The result is an often tenuous, non-cooperative equilibrium that resembles a troubled marriage in which each partner seeks happiness behind the other's back.

All this does not mean that Canada is less of a welfare state than Japan. The fact is just the reverse. In 1979/80, for example, Canada's cost of social security was 17.9 per cent of GNP or $1246 per person as against Japan's 13.9 per cent and $814. Moreover, governmental share in the cost of social security was 71.2 per cent in Canada as against 31.3 per cent in Japan (ILO 1980). Does this mean that Canadians enjoy a greater economic security than the Japanese? Not necessarily. The number of arrests made by the police is not an accurate measure of the efficiency of the police force or of the safety on downtown streets. (The most efficient police force should make no arrests.) In my judgement, the Canadian government is doing a poor job of providing economic security to its citizens, despite its huge spending; and the chief reason for its poor performance is that the tri-party insurance contract alluded to above has been drawn up so naively that adverse selection, moral hazard, and other problems inherent in the insurance business have all but defeated the government's good intentions. It runs a basically free, no-fault insurance; the result is liberal shirking and malfeasance on the part of the insured and a constant excess demand for the insurance. A more successful operation of a governmental insurance programme like this would require a closer monitoring of the behaviour of the insured or a more serious co-insurance scheme in which the insured remains the main bearer of the loses caused by his own actions.

5   IS DECENTRALIZED ECONOMIC POLICY-MAKING VIABLE?

My argument so far has been that the different histories of the two countries have led their inhabitants to develop differnt 'tastes', and that the different styles of economic policy-making adopted by the two governments are largely a reflection of these differences in taste. Ordinarily, when the economist has traced the difference in question to one of taste, his job is done. Here I take a more evolutionary view of people's tastes, and ask whether the current styles of policy-making are indeed the best choice for the two countries.

What we call tastes, preferences, utilities, or value systems is not an immutably given datum but is, itself, a constantly changing endogenous variable. Individuals are frequently seen to change their tastes with changes in environment, usually in the direction of rationalizing what they have done or complying with the mode of the time. In my own experience, the most conspicuous example of changes in taste was demonstrated by some of the Japanese academics, who intellectually led Japan's expansionist movement during the 1930s and turned back to democracy after 1945. Politicians routinely adapt their opinions to new environments. We call a person with rigid tastes stubborn, or even crazy. An old saying admonishes us to learn to appreciate what we have, which may be interpreted to mean that we should change the shape of our utility function so as to derive a greater satisfaction from a given basket of goods. These examples indicate that tastes are endogenous variables determined relative to the owner's experience. (They also suggest that explaining man's behaviour in terms of his tastes may not be all that valid.)

Returning to the subject of policy styles, the particular policy style adopted by a nation, even if it matches the tastes of the populace, may be short-lived, because a major change in the international environment is likely to induce a new style of policy-making. The world-wide structural changes since the 1970s are particularly relevant in this context. Starting with the breakdown of the Bretton Woods system in 1971 and the world's transition to a floating exchange regime, followed by the two oil shocks and the emergence of conservationist tastes and technologies, a massive redistribution of wealth among nations, a rapid growth of global financial markets, and a major change in the pattern of world trade have occurred. The postwar American era has given way to a new era of uncertainty and tougher economic competition. Faced with these earth-shaking changes in the economic environment, every nation has been reassessing its situation and reformulating its economic policies.

Canadian policy-makers have been very slow to react to this new environment. The only major national economic policy launched during the 1970s was the poorly researched, ill-fated National Energy Policy of the Liberal government (which was virtually scrapped when the Conservatives came into power in 1984). The long inaction on the part of the Canadian policy-makers was due partly to the great uncertainty concerning the direction of the US economy and policy, which still plagues Canadians, but in the main it was due to the lack of leadership of the federal government operating in a highly decentralized political system. The Canadian economy, in the meantime, has performed more poorly than the US economy since 1973, with higher unemployment and inflation rates. The inaction of the federal government has prompted the provincial governments to take an even larger role in economic policy-making.

The major problem with this decentralized approach, however, has been that provincial efforts are uncoordinated and the provinces as units are too small to deal with foreign states. The international economic race has much in common with warfare. Just as an efficient execution of a master strategy is essential for a victory in war, so a well prepared, well co-ordinated policy plan is necessary for success in the international economic game. This well prepared and well co-ordinated plan is precisely what is lacking in the Canadian economic policy.

Canadians are fighting the economic war without a supreme commander, which results in much wasted effort. For example, in the summer of 1985 the US Congress was deliberating a possible quota or tariff against British Columbian lumber exports, in order to protect foresters in the states of Washington and Oregon. The premier of British Columbia flew to Washington, DC to persuade Congress not to vote for it, but his pleas were virtually ignored, and understandably so. A provincial premier simply lacks the political clout needed to influence policy-makers of a sovereign state. The premier and other cabinet members of the province of British Columbia have been making frequent trips to Japan to promote provincial exports, but I would be surprised if they have had any greater impact on the Japanese government or Japan's largest corporations than on the US Congress. When Toyota announced (also in the summer of 1985) its plan to build an assembly factory 'somewhere in Canada', the ten provincial trade ministers rushed to Japan in competition with one another—not a wise move from the national standpoint.

The Canadians' favourite argument in favour of decentralization is that, while a single federal mistake may destroy the whole nation, a provincial mistake will not only leave the nation intact, but will also teach the nine other provinces a valuable lesson. But of course, you cannot fight a war on the principle of risk minimization.

It is obvious that, in order to bargain effectively with foreign states and multinationals, the Canadians have little choice but to have the federal government take over from the provinces. It must stop being a push-over and rise to the occasion. Recently the federal (Conservative) government signed a free trade agreement with the US government (which took effect in January 1989). This may be taken as an encouraging sign that it *has* risen to the occasion. What is puzzling about this action, however, is that the concept was extremely vague, that no details of the plan had apparently been worked out, and the government had made little information available to the public. Even though I have learned from experience that deliberate obscuration is the norm in Canadian politics, and probably is the only way to get anything done, given the diverse populace, this excessive secrecy in handling a matter as important as free trade will certainly invite many more rounds of criticism and dissension.

My prediction is that the new economic realities facing Canadians will sooner or later induce them to alter their tastes towards an increased centralization of power, at least in areas in which it counts. The highest goal of macroeconomic policy is job and income security for the working masses. Experience shows that government alone cannot achieve it; with business and labour playing their selfish game, no amount of wisdom and resources on the part of government is good enough. It is equally plain that the task cannot be simply imposed on business. For business to provide job and income security for labour it must win labour's co-operation, because the provision of job and income security for the work-force adds to firms' costs, which must be made up for by increased efficiency of the work-force. Once this co-operation is secured, government's macroeconomic policy will be greatly simplified and more effective. Much of the so-called failure of Keynesianism seems to stem from these organizational defects in many democratic economies. Specifically in Canada, every political leader talks about job and income security and the need to 'diversify' its industrial structure, but so far no agreement has been reached between the government and business on this important long-term question. The government in the meantime is trying to cut down on its social programmes in order to reduce budgetary deficits. This is a wrong move. For one thing, it shifts the burden of economic hardships back on to individuals. For another, the problem lies not in the governmental insurance coverage being too broad but in the free shirkings on the part of the insured.

It is interesting to note in this context that the Japanese are also changing their style of economic policy-making—in, if anything, the opposite direction. There are indications that the government is losing its control over business under the external pressure towards liberalization. The officials of the Ministry of Finance and the Ministry of International Trade and Industry are increasingly concerned that the industries they have supervised are more defiant than ever, and that this liberalization may deprive them of most of their traditional tools of control. The era of slow economic growth is forcing a serious review of their traditional lifetime employment and seniority wages as more firms find these difficult to maintain financially. The current indication is that the wage structure, rather than lifetime employment, is going to be altered. But because the two are related, a flatter lifetime wage profile is bound to affect the nature of employment contracts as well. The people are changing too. Having now achieved a decent standard of living, the Japanese appear to be seeking more diversified and individualistic life-styles.

All these signs of change may bring Japan closer to the Western nations. It may be that, as the people become richer, their demand for the traditional comprehensive insurance at a high premium is weakening. This possibility is undeniable. On the other hand, there are a number of factors that contribute to the preservation of their traditional ways of life. One of these is the fact that the Japanese have yet to learn how to enjoy life. Despite the substantial increase in their income levels in recent years, their life still revolves around their work. Their traditional habit of viewing work as a virtue and play as a sin remains strong. This means there is a strong inertia against Western life-styles. It also means that a vast investment opportunity still exists in the economy in the area of building social and private capital for recreational purposes. Filling their long shorelines with yacht harbours, for example, is definitely a major national undertaking. Another factor contributing to the inertia is Japan's unique geographic setting and linguistic and cultural 'barriers'. It is unthinkable that the Japanese will make a mass exodus in pursuit of better lives elsewhere, as other people have done. It will be some time, if ever, before Japan adopts a Canadian style of democratic economic policy-making.

6 CONCLUSION

In his classic work, Downs (1957) severely criticized the economists' modelling of the government as a faceless and egoless entity that simply carries out the task of maximizing social welfare as defined by the 'will of the people'. What if government is an organization run by hired agents who are also selfish utility-maximizers?

As soon as this potential conflict of interest in policy-makers is recognized, society faces some tough political decisions: how much power and discretion should the policy-makers be given, and how can their behaviour be monitored? Generally speaking, the more clearly defined is the mandate, and the closer is the people's monitoring, the smaller is the danger of malfeasance on the part of the policy-makers, but the smaller also is the chance of benefiting from their wisdom. Different societies arrive at different solutions to the problem.

This chapter has been an attempt to humanize government, in the spirit of Downs. It has used the different styles of policy-making in Japan and Canada as examples, and illustrated the general proposition that a country's style of economic policy-making is determined largely by its history, the international environment it faces, and, finally, by the nature of the game played by the policy-makers and the public.

APPENDIX: LOOKING INTO THE 1990S

Since I wrote this chapter, some relevant new developments have occurred. In Canada the prime minister and the provincial premiers reached a 'Meech Lake Accord' on constitutional issues in April 1987. Specifically, this gave the provincial premiers a veto power on future constitutional amendments. 'Agreeing to disagree' has long been the Canadians' way of describing their system. The accord has made this self-description official. It is safe to predict that the federal government's power will be further curtailed, and well co-ordinated national economic policy-making will become even less feasible in future, once the accord becomes law.

In contrast, the Japanese have been making a concerted nation-wide effort, under the joint sponsorship of the government and business community, to establish a vision of the twenty-first century and an optimal industrial strategy to facilitate the transition from the conventional 'heavy, thick, long, and big' products to the 'light, thin, short, and small' products of the future. More concretely, a central organ called the National Institute for Research Advancement (NIRA) was founded to co-ordinate the research activities of the many think-tanks, both private and public, and to collect and store the information centrally. As a whole, this national project covers themes ranging from science and technology to human affairs such as marriage and crime. In the meantime, the business sector has worked hard to pare down costs in order to survive in the US$1 = ¥130 environment. Larger firms are said to have completed the requisite adjustments without defaulting on the existing lifetime employment contracts. Indeed, an overwhelming majority of large firms have already extended the retirement age from the conventional 55 to 60. Apparently, Japanese managers believe that the rigidities arising from the long-term commitment to the workers will be more than offset by the higher morale and greater productivity of workers in the long run, a typical non-neoclassical thinking.

So, once again, the two economies are resorting to their respective favourite styles of policy-making in an effort to restore prosperity. The Canadians entertain all sorts of ideas such as free trade, international financial centres, and venture capital in a democratic fashion, while the Japanese embark on grand long-range planning quietly but systematically. How the two differnt policy styles will work out remains to be seen.

10
Summing Up

The central question for macroeconomics is how a national economy can attain and sustain prosperity. The role of academic economists is to provide a framework which enables the country's decision-makers to identify the pattern of behaviour of the economy and prescribe for policy. Economists have been doing this task consciously for the past fifty years with, I would say, a modest success. But the last fifteen years or so have been very difficult for both economists and policy-makers. This has been a period of transition and uncertainty. The economic order of the postwar world collapsed, and people's faith in their economies was shaken.

The drastic change in the economic environment and the resulting pessimism left economists and policy-makers in a state of frustration and self-doubt. The economists overreacted. They threw away much of the conventional wisdom and replaced it with a novel paradigm in order to demonstrate why conventional policy tools should not work. The policy-makers have resorted to the same old conservatist measures of the 1930s. Both economists and policy-makers have lost sight of the above-mentioned central question for macroeconomics. They have failed to restore people's faith. In the meantime, the world has suffered from a prolonged and deep recession. Ugly neo-mercantilist strategies have surfaced, and life in general has become meaner and more brutish.

The present state of the world economy is at a very unsatisfactory equilibrium, well below the potential level prescribed by the available resources and technology. Many resources remain idle or are being used up in political zero-sum games. Nevertheless, it *is* an equilibrium in the sense that no 'individuals', including national governments, have the incentive to break away from it, given the way others are behaving. It is a type of equilibrium known as a non-cooperative game solution, which suggests that co-operation among individual members holds the key to prosperity. As a matter of principle, co-operation is the direction to take, but it is easier said than done. Diverse national interests tend to reduce a mutually agreeable pact to an abstract statement of broad guidelines, as evidenced by the results of the several summit conferences in recent years. Subject to these guidelines, the pursuit of economic prosperity remains the task of each nation. It is my belief that individual countries can do many things in order to bring their economies closer to prosperity without beggaring their neighbours.

This book has stressed the human and organizational aspects of macroeconomic management. This is because the total product of a group of individuals can vary greatly depending on how they are organized. The observed wide differences in labour productivity across economies using similar technologies lend support to this view. From this perspective, macroeconomies as currently practised has certain systematic deficiencies.

First, macroeconomic theory lacks proper macro foundations; it has no theory of group behaviour; it is blind to the many possible ways in which individuals interact with one another; more importantly, it cannot accommodate large economic organization and the *power* they wield in our society over important social choices including macroeconomic policies. Second, macroeconomic theory is too abstract to be useful for policy prescriptions for individual economies; it is devoid of historical and institutional details; it fails to recognize the fact that a national economy is much like an individual, with a life-cycle of its own. Different economies are at different stages of life-cycle; some are young and others are old, some are poor and others are rich; the problems they face and the solutions called for to solve them differ from one economy to another. Each economy must find strategies right for it. General prescriptions derived from abstract theory are nice to have, but they cannot be a cure for all. Third, macroeconomics has a strong bias in favour of 'short-run' questions. This is a reflection of the neoclassical philosophy, which denies the need for human interferences in the long run. The procedural rationality of researchers and the myopia of political leaders reinforce the bias. However, given the immense informational and technical difficulties associated with short-run stabilization policies and the importance of the institutional or organization aspects of macroeconomic management, more emphasis in research should be placed on long-run matters.

The actual policy measures adopted since the early 1970s have been equally ineffectual as far as their contribution to economic prosperity is concerned. The breakdown of the Bretton Woods system and the first oil shock infused a panic psychology into people's minds and caused a disruption in economic activities and a speculative mania. The unemployment rate shot up, but so also did the pace of inflation. After a few years of confusion, governments all over the world began to fight a long battle with inflation which was brought under control by the continued monetary squeeze of the early 1980s. Encouraged by this 'success', the conservative governments world-wide have since been busy fighting growing government debts and budget deficits. This new battle is expected to last well into the 1990s.

This sequence of monomanic policies, though understandable in the short-run context of the time, has already caused a great many losses in jobs and output around the world and will continue to do so in the foreseeable future. Its benefits, on the other hand, are highly questionable even to the USA, the instigator of the current recession and chief architect of the conservative policies. The big question here is what these policies have done to the future prosperity of the US economy. Although a careful assessment of this matter may have to be left for future economic historians, it seems safe to say that the policies have done a considerable damage to the economy by discouraging investment in human and non-human capital. They may have secured the world's faith in the dollar for the time being, but in the long run a currency is only as good as the economy that supports it. We all should learn a lesson from the British experience of the 1920s.

Another and more serious damage that the prolonged policies of restraint have produced is the decline in general morale. People have already suffered enough since the mid-1970s from diminished opportunities and prospects; more of the same for another ten years is simply depressing. The worsening of the economic environment has encouraged rent-seeking and other deviant activities in which the enterprising minority of individuals seek gains at the expense of others. The resulting sense of frustration and injustice on the part of the masses has caused a further demoralization. Once the morale of the public deteriorates, it becomes harder for political leaders to win their compliance and co-operation. This leads to policy failures, which in turn destroys the credibility of policy actions. History shows that the morale of the public largely reflects the status of the nation and the performance of the economy. This is why keeping the economy on a healthy long-run path is so important.

When the economy is on a healthy long-run path, optimism

prevails and people's economic horizons expand. These forces in turn help support the strength of the economy. Such was the global atmosphere in the 1950s and 1960s. But it would be wrong to attribute the good performance of the world economy in those decades to deliberately wise policy choices aimed at growth and development: rather, the generally supportive policies were the by-product of the good times. Readers who retain their faith in the wisdom of policy-makers may wish to argue this point; they are referred to what policy-makers the world over have done in the past fifteen years and asked to rationalize their choices. The fact of the matter is that the bad times have *caused* defensive, negative policies. Policy-makers are human too. If the rest of the citizens revise their economic prospects downward, the same set of information tends to induce a similar adjustment on the part of government, in perfect agreement with the tenet of the rational expectations theory. The economic policies over the past fifteen years have been ineffective not because the smart citizens have frustrated the good intention of the government (as rational expectationists make one believe), but because the policies themselves have been misdirected. One can even say that they have been quite *effective*: that they were never meant to restore growth and development, and that they achieved their goal raher convincingly by producing a long recession. (See Eisner 1986 for a similar verdict.)

Whether one likes it or not, today's global democratic community is best served by policies aimed at stimulating growth and development. Indeed, there is no alternative. For this purpose the major economies must first free themselves from the spell of pessimism, and lead others. A policy co-ordination among the major industrial economies is a natural thing to seek, and has actually been tried in the past decade. It may be too soon to tell how effective these attempts have been, but there are indications that they have been rather ineffectual, at least as judged by short-term impacts. International co-ordination in the area of monetary policy has so far been ineffective, as the USA has refused to ease money in the way the rest of the world wanted. Similar co-ordination attempts in the area of fiscal policy have had at best very modest effects. (See, for example, Oudiz and Sachs 1984 for a quantitative analysis of the effects of policy co-ordination.) But again, these judgements may be premature, for two reasons. First, given the goal of restoring the pace of growth and development on a global scale, the real effects of policy co-ordination should be assessed in the long-term context. Second, in order for international co-operation to be really effective, the participating governments must have a clear mandate and authority to stick to their commitments, which presupposes a similar co-ordination within individual economies.

Without this precondition, political leaders may agree on free trade, for example, while domestic political pressure forces them to take steps in the opposite direction. In general, international co-operation is more difficult than domestic. As I indicated in Chapter 9, there are substantial costs, economic and social, to domestic co-operation which some economies would not be willing to pay. This suggests that the content of any international co-operation will be rather vague. Even so, if the Big Ten can agree, in principle, on the primary importance of economic growth and development, and can direct their policy efforts towards this goal in unison, we can look forward to a brighter future.

A serious pursuit of economic prosperity cannot, however, be left in the hands of the government alone. It requires the co-operation of all the other major economic groups, and notably business and labour. A common feature of poorly performing economies is that these other groups are not doing their part and that governments consequently are overburdened with tasks and rendered ineffective. A domestic 'trilateral commission' made up of government, business, and labour may be a promising organ for future economic management.

References

Acheson, K. and Chant, J. F. (1973), 'Bureaucratic Theory and the Choice of Central Bank Goals', *Journal of Money, Credit and Banking* 5: 637–55.

Akerlof, G. A. (1970), 'The Market for "Lemmons": Qualitative Uncertainty and the Market Mechanism', *Quarterly Journal of Economics* 84: 488–500.

Aliber, R. Z. (1983), *The International Money Game*. New York: Basic Books.

Allen, G. (1976), *The Rockefeller Files*. Seal Beach, Cal.: '76 Press.

Angly, E. (1931), *Oh, Yeah?* New York: Viking Press.

Arnold, T. W. (1937), *The Folklore of Capitalism*. New Haven, Conn.: Yale University Press.

Aufricht, H. (1965), *Comparative Survey of Central Bank Laws*. London: Stevens & Sons.

Bach, G. L. (1950), *Federal Reserve Policy Making*. New York: Alfred Knopf.

Bagehot, W. (1873), *Lombard Street*. New York: Charles Scribner's Sons.

Barro, R. J. and Grossman, H. I. (1971), 'A General Disequilibrium Model of Income and Employment', *American Economic Review* 61: 82–93.

Becker, G. S. (1962), 'Investment in Human Capital: A Theoretical Anaysis', *Journal of Political Economy* 70: 9–49.

—— (1983), 'A Theory of Competition among Pressure Groups for Political Influence', *Quarterly Journal of Economics* 98: 371–400.

Beckhart, B. H. (1972), *Federal Reserve System*. New York: American Institute of Banking.

Bellamy, E. (1887), *Looking Backward, 20000–1887*. Aberdeen University Press.

Broadfoot, B. (1976), *The Pioneer Years, 1895–1914*. Toronto: Doubleday.

Buchanan, J. M. and Wagner, R. E. (1977), *Democracy in Deficit*. New York: Academic Press.

Buchanan, J. M. *et al.* (1980), *Toward a Theory of the Rent-Seeking Society*. College Station, Texas: Texas A & M University Press.

Cantillon, R. (1755), *Essai sur la nature du commerce en generale*, published posthumously. Paris.

Clower, R. W. (1967), 'A Reconsideration of the Microfoundations of Monetary Theory', *Western Economic Journal* 6: 1–9.

Coase, R. H. (1960), 'The Problem of Social Cost', *Journal of Law and Economics* 3: 1–44.

Coddington, A. (1976), 'Keynesian Economics: The Search for First Principles', *Journal of Economic Literature* 14: 1258–73.

Chandler, A. D. (1977), *The Visible Hand*. Cambridge, Mass.: Harvard University Press.

Crawford, A. C. (1985), *Credit Rationing with an Individual Short-side Rule: Estimation for Business Loans in Canada*. Doctoral dissertation, University of British Columbia.

Downs, A. (1957), *An Economic Theory of Democracy*. New York: Harper and Row.

Easton, D. (1953), *The Political System*. New York: Alfred Knopf.

Edgeworth, F. Y. (1888), 'The Mathematical Theory of Banking', *Royal Statistical Society Journal* 51: 113–27.

Einzig, P. (1932), *Montagu Norman*. London: Kegan Paul.

—— (1970), *The History of Foreign Exchange*. London: Macmillan.

Eisner, R. (1986), *How Real Is the Federal Deficit?* New York: Free Press.

Elias, C. (1973), *The Dollar Barons*. London: Macmillan.

Eswaren, M., and Kotwal, A. (1985), 'Risk-bearing Capacity and Entrepreneurship as Privileges of Wealth', University of British Columbia Discussion Paper no. 85-28.

Evans, R. G. (1985), 'Illusions of Necessity: Evading Responsibility for Choice in Health Care', *Journal of Health Politics, Policy and Law* 10: 439–67.

Fisher, I. (1930), *The Theory of Interest*. New York: Macmillan.

Friedman, M. (1969), 'The Optimum Quantity of Money', in his *The Optimum Quantity of Money and Other Essays*. Chicago: Aldine.

Frisch, R. (1956), Opening Address to the 1955 Econometric Society Meetings, *Econometrica* 24: 300–2.

Gilder, G. (1981), *Wealth and Poverty*. Toronto/New York/London: Bantam Books.

Gordon, R. J. (1981), 'Output Fluctuations and Gradual Price Adjustment', *Journal of Economic Literature* 19: 493–530.

Gordon, W. (1977), *A Political Memoir*. Halifax: Formac.

Goschen, G. J. (1861), *The Theory of the Foreign Exchanges*. London: E. Wilson.

Groves, T. (1973), 'Incentives in Teams', *Econometrica* 41: 617–31.

—— and Ledyard, J. O. (1977), 'Optimal Allocation of Public Goods: A Solution to the "Free Rider" Problem', *Econometrica* 45: 783–809.

Hacker, A. (1970), *The End of the American Era*. New York: Atheneum.

Hahn, R. (1967), *Laplace as a Newtonian Scientist*. Los Angeles: UCLA Press.

Haines, W. W. (1981), 'The Myth of Continuous Inflation: United States Experience, 1700–1980', in N. Schmukler and E. Marcus (eds.), *Inflation Through Ages: Economic, Social, Psychological and Historical Aspects*. New York: Columbia University Press.

Hamada, K. (1985), *The Political Economy of International Monetary Interdependence*, Cambridge, Mass.: MIT Press.

Hartle, D. G. (1978), *The Expenditure Budget Process in the Government of Canada*. Toronto: Canadian Tax Foundation.

Hashimoto, M. (1979), 'Bonus Payments, On-the-Job Training, and Lifetime Employment in Japan', *Journal of Political Economy* 87: 1086–1104.

—— and Raisian, J. (1985), 'Employment Tenure and Earnings Profiles in Japan and the United States', *American Economic Review* 75: 721–35.

Hawtrey, R. G. (1932), *The Art of Central Banking*. London: Longmans, Green.

—— (1938), *A Century of Bank Rate*. London: Longmans, Green.

Hayek, F. A. (1964), *Monetary Nationalism and International Stability*, first published 1937. New York: A. M. Kelley.

International Labour Organization (ILO) (1980), *Costs of Social Security*. Geneva: ILO.

Irokawa, D. (1971), *History of Japan*, Vol. 21. Tokyo: Chuokoron-Sha.

Jaffé, W. (1935), 'Unpublished Papers and Letters of Leon Walras', *Journal of Political Economy* 43: 187–207.

—— (1965), *Correspondence of Leon Walras and Related Papers*. Amsterdam: North-Holland.

Japanese Ministry of Labour (1986), *Wage Census*. Tokyo: Rodo Horei Kyokai.

Jevons, W. S. (1886), *Letters and Journals of W. Stanley Jevons*, ed. Harriet Jevons. London: Macmillan.

—— (1957), *The Theory of Political Economy*, first published 1871. New York: Kelly & Millman.

Jones, S. R. G. (1984), *The Economics of Conformism*. Oxford and New York: Basil Blackwell.

Keynes, J. M. (1923), *A Tract on Monetary Reform*. London: Macmillan.

—— (1930), *A Treeatise on Money*. London: Macmillan.

—— (1936), *The General Theory of Employment, Interest and Money*. London: Macmillan.

Klein, L. R. (1947), *The Keynesian Revolution*. London: Macmillan.

Knorr, K. (1956), *The War Potential of Nations*. Princeton University Press.

Lange, O. (1944), *Price Flexibility and Employment*. Bloomington, Ind.: Principia Press.

Laplace, P. S. (1809). *The System of the World*, first published 1796. Trans. J. Pond (2 vols.).

Lazear, E. P. (1979), 'Why Is There Mandatory Retirement?' *Journal of Political Economy* 87: 1261–84.

Leibenstein, H. (1966), 'Allocative Efficiency vs. "X-Efficiency"', *American Economic Review* 56: 392–415.

Leijonhufvud, A. (1968), *On Keynesian Economics and the Economics of Keynes*. Oxford University Press.

Lerner, A. P. (1944), *The Economics of Control*. London: Macmillan.

Letourneau, R. S. (1980), *Inflation: The Canadian Experience*. Ottawa: Conference Board of Canada.

Lieberman, J. K. (1983), *The Litigious Society*. New York: Basic Books.

Lundberg, F. (1975), *Rockefeller Syndrome*. Syracuse, NY: Lyle Stuart.

Mackay, C. (1980), *Memoirs of Extraordinary Popular Delusions and the Madness of Crowds*, first published 1852. Toronto: Coles Publishing Company.

MacLeod, H. D. (1866), *Theory and Practice of Banking*. London: Longmans, Green, Reader & Dyer.

—— (1979), *The United Kingdom* Vol. II of W. G. Sumner *et al.*, *A History of Banking in All the Leading Nations*, first published 1896. New York: A. M. Kelley.

Maisel, F. W. (1983), *Great American Ripoff*, San Diego, Cal.: Condido Press.

Malthus, T. R. (1836), *Principles of Political Economy*. London: William Pickering.

Mao, Tse-Tung (1956), *On Contradiction*. Peking: Foreign Language Press.

Marx, K. (1906), *Capital*, first published 1867. New York: Random House.

McNees, S. K. and Ries, J. (1983), 'The Track Record of Macroeconomic Forecasts', *New England Economic Review* (Federal Reserve Bank of Boston), 15: 5–18.

Medoff, J. L. and Abrham, K. G. (1981), 'Are Those Paid More Really More Productive?' *Journal of Human Resources* 16: 186–216.

Menger, C. (1950), *Principles of Economics*, first published 1871. Trans. J. Dingwall and B. F. Hoselitz. Glencoe, Ill.: Free Press.

—— (1963), *Problems of Economics and Sociology*, first published 1882. Ed. L. Schneider and trans. F. J. Nock. University of Illinois Press.

Moggridge, D. E. (1972), *British Monetary Policy 1924–31: The Norman Conquest of $4.86*. Cambridge University Press.

Morikawa, H. (1973), *The Origins of the Japanese-Style Management: The Concept of Managerial Nationalism* (in Japanese). Tokyo: Toyo Keizai Shimposha.

Morishima, M. (1981), *Why Has Japan 'Succeeded'?* Cambridge University Press.

Nagatani, K. (1983), 'Macroeconomic Foundations of Macroeconomics', in R. Sato and M. J. Beckmann (eds.), *Technology, Organization and Economic Structure*. Berlin: Springer-Verlag.

Negishi, T. (1979), *Microeconomic Foundations of Keynesian Macroeconomics*. Amsterdam: North-Holland.

Nikkeiren (Japanese Managers' Association) (1962), *Survey of Wage Formulae*. Tokyo: Nikkeiren.

Nisbet, R. (1982), 'Boredom', *Commentary*, September: 48–50.

Olson, M. (1982), *The Rise and Decline of Nations*. New Haven and London: Yale University Press.

Ono, A. (1981), *Nippon no Rodoshijo* (Japanese Labor Market). Tokyo: Toyo Keizai Shimposha.

Oudiz, G. and Sachs, J. (1984), 'Macroeconomic Policy Coordination Among the Industrial Economies', *Brookings Papers on Economic Activity* 1: 1–75.

Patinkin, D. (1965), *Money, Interest and Prices*, first published 1956. New York: Harper and Row.

Radner, R. (1975), 'Satisficing', *Journal of Mathematical Economics* 2: 253–62.

Riker, W. H. (1963), *The Theory of Political Coalitions*. New Haven and London: Yale University Press.

Salop, J., and Salop, S. (1976), 'Self-Selection and Turnover in the Labor Market', *Quarterly Journal of Economics* 90: 619–27.

Sampson, A. (1981), *The Money Lenders*. Harmondsworth: Penguin.

Samuelson, P. A. (1965), 'A Catenary Turnpike Theorem involving Consumption and the Golden Rule, *American Economic Review* 55: 486–96.

Sato, R. (1987), *The Economics of M & A* (in Japanese). Tokyo: TBS Britannica.

Sayers, R. S. (1957), *Central Banking After Bagehot*. Oxford: Clarendon Press.

Schramm, C. L. (1984), 'Can We Solve the Hospital-Cost Problem in Our Democracy?' *New England Journal of Medicine* 311: 729–32.

Schumpeter, J. A. (1950), *Capitalism, Socialism and Democracy*. New York: Harper & Row.

—— (1954), *History of Economic Analysis*. Oxford University Press.

Sidrauski, M. (1967), 'Rational Choice and the Pattern of Growth in a Monetary Economy', *American Economic Review* 57 (Papers and Proceedings): 534–44.

Simon, H. A. (1972), 'Theories of Bounded Rationality', in C. B. McGuire and R. Radner (eds.), *Decision and Organization*. Amsterdam: North-Holland.

—— (1978), 'Rationality as Process and as Product of Thought', *American Economic Review* 68 (Proceedings): 1–16.

Sklar, H. (ed.) (1980), *Trilateralism*. Boston: South End Press.

Smith, A. (1910), *The Wealth of Nations*, first published 1776. London: J. M. Dent & Sons.

Smith, V. C. (1936), *The Rationale of Central Banking*. London: P. S. King & Sons.

Solow, R. M. (1981), review of E. Malinvaud's *Profitability and Unemployment, Journal of Economic Literature* 19: 582–3.

Stackelberg, H. Von. (1952), *The Theory of the Market Economy*, first published 1934. Trans. A. T. Peacock. London/Edinburgh/Glasgow: William Hodge and Co.

Stanley, D. T. and Girth, M. (1971), *Bankruptcy*. Washington DC: Brookings Institution.

Stiglitz, J. E. and Weiss, A. (1981), 'Credit Rationing in Markets with Imperfect Information', *American Economic Review* 71: 393–410.

Tobin, J. (1965), 'Money and Economic Growth', *Econometrica* 33: 671–84.

Toda, T. (1984), *Preventive Measures against Corporate Bankruptcies* (in Japanese). Tokyo: Dobunkan.

Tooke, T. (1838), *History of Prices*. London: P. S. King.

Trevelyan, G. M. (1937), *British History in the Nineteenth Century and After* (1782–1919), first published 1922. London/New York/Toronto: Longmans, Green.

Van Dillen (ed.), *History of the Principal Public Banks*. New York: A. M. Kelley.

Veblen, T. (1898), 'Why Is Economics Not an Evolutionary Science?', *Quarterly Journal of Economics* 12: 373–97.

Walras, L. (1954), *Elements of Pure Economics*, first published 1874; in English 1954. Trans. W. Jaffe. Homewood, Ill.: Richard D. Irwin.

Weber, M. (1947), *The Theory of Social and Economic Organizations*, first published 1922. New York/London: Free Press of Macmillan.

Weitzman, M. L. (1984), *The Share Economy*. Cambridge, Mass.: Harvard University Press.

Wicksell, K. (1934), *Lectures on Political Economy*. London: Routledge & Kegan Paul.

Index